Our Governors' Mansions

Our Governors' Mansions

CATHY KEATING
First Lady of the State of Oklahoma

with

MIKE BRAKE AND PATTI ROSENFELD

Foreword by

CHARLES KURALT

Harry N. Abrams, Inc., Publishers

Editor: James Leggio

Designer: Carol Robson with Gilda Hannah

Photo Editor: John K. Crowley

Library of Congress Cataloging-in-Publication Data

Keating, Cathy.
  Our governors' mansions / Cathy Keating ; with Mike Brake and Patti Rosenfeld ;
foreword by Charles Kuralt.
    p.   cm.
  Includes index.
  ISBN 0-8109-3688-7
  1. Historic buildings—United States.   2. Mansions—United States.   3. Governors —
Dwellings—United States.   4. Governors—United States—History.   I. Brake, Mike
(Charles Michael).   II. Rosenfeld, Patti.   III. Title.
  E159.K43   1997
  973—dc 21   97–3677

Published in 1997 by Harry N. Abrams, Incorporated, New York
All rights reserved. No part of the contents of this book may be reproduced without
the written permission of the publisher

Printed and bound in the United States of America

Harry N. Abrams, Inc.
100 Fifth Avenue
New York, N.Y. 10011
www.abramsbooks.com

Photograph Credits
The following list is keyed to page numbers. ©
D. J. C. Arnold: 289–95. © Randy Barger:
273–80. © Robert Benson: 49–56, 89–96. ©
Damon Bullock: 217–19. © 1988 Dick Bush-
er: 313–20. © Richard C. Collier: 321–28. ©
Robert M. Coleman: 129–35. © Dennis Craft:
196–97, 199. © Shane Culpepper: 337–44. ©
Jed Dekalb, State of Tennessee Photographic
Services: 113–20. © Matt Ferguson and Matt
Craig: 153–60. © Gib Ford, Jr.: 145–52. ©
Robert Fouts: 161–68. © Thomas Gennara:
193–95, 198. © Doug Gilmore, Office of the
Governor: 65–72. © Bill Hagstotz: 364–68.
© Nathan Ham: 249–56. © 1996 Ken
Hawkins: 41–48. © Allan Holm: 25–32. ©
Charlie Jones: 97–104. © Greg Kinder: 372.
© Ronald Klein: 353–59. © Scott Klette:
265–71. © J. K. Lawrence: 305–11. © Dan
Lee: 121–28. © Richard Lippenholz: 57,
60–64. © Ronald Klein: 353–59. © J. K.
Lawrence: 305–11. © Dan Lee: 121–28. ©
Richard Lippenholz: 57, 60–64. © Scott Lit-
tle: 220–24. Maryland State Archives: 58–59.
© Frank Mikacevich and Patrick O'Leary:
233–40. © Melabee M. Miller: 33–40. © Rich
Miller: 137–43. © 1996 Vic Moss/Moss Pho-
tography: 281–88. © James T. O'Brien:
17–24. © Robert Overton: 201–7. Pho-
tographs property Missouri Mansion Preserva-
tion, Inc.: photo Robert Berg, 177 (sculpture
©1994 Jamie G. Anderson, All Rights
Reserved); photos Hugo W. Harper and Neil
W. Sauer, 178–79, 181, 182 above; photos
Alise C. O'Brien, 182–83 below, 183 above. ©
Jerry Rabinowitz: 345–51. © Bill Records
Photography, courtesy Friends of the Gover-
nor's Mansion, Austin: 210–11. © Hickey
Robertson Photographers, Houston, courtesy
Friends of the Governor's Mansion, Austin:
209, 212–16. © Gary Robinson, Photography
Supervisor, Division of Creative Services:
105–12. © Steven Wayne Rotsch, Governor's
Photographer: 257–64. © Gary Sampson:
73–79. © Evan G. Schneider: 241–48. © Stan
Sinclair: 373. © Stanley Solheim: 228–32. ©
Mike Tibbit: 185–91. © Brian Van den Brink:
169–78. © Katherine Wetzel: 81–88. © Craig
Wilson: 225–27. © Thomas H. Woolsey:
361–63. © Scott Zimmerman: 329–36.

Contents

FOREWORD BY CHARLES KURALT 6

INTRODUCTION BY CATHY KEATING 8

ACKNOWLEDGMENTS 11

☆ ☆ ☆

DELAWARE 17

PENNSYLVANIA 25

NEW JERSEY 33

GEORGIA 41

CONNECTICUT 49

MARYLAND 57

SOUTH CAROLINA 65

NEW HAMPSHIRE 73

VIRGINIA 81

NEW YORK 89

NORTH CAROLINA 97

KENTUCKY 105

TENNESSEE 113

OHIO 121

LOUISIANA 129

INDIANA 137

MISSISSIPPI 145

ILLINOIS 153

ALABAMA 161

MAINE 169

MISSOURI 177

ARKANSAS 185

MICHIGAN 193

FLORIDA 201

TEXAS 209

IOWA 217

WISCONSIN 225

MINNESOTA 233

OREGON 241

KANSAS 249

WEST VIRGINIA 257

NEVADA 265

NEBRASKA 273

COLORADO 281

NORTH DAKOTA 289

SOUTH DAKOTA 297

MONTANA 305

WASHINGTON 313

WYOMING 321

UTAH 329

OKLAHOMA 337

NEW MEXICO 345

ALASKA 353

HAWAII 361

☆ ☆ ☆

MASSACHUSETTS 369

RHODE ISLAND 370

VERMONT 371

CALIFORNIA 371

IDAHO 372

ARIZONA 374

☆ ☆ ☆

FOR FURTHER INFORMATION 375

FOREWORD

BY CHARLES KURALT

*C*athy Keating, First Lady of the State of Oklahoma, gives a fine gift to the nation in this collection of words and pictures evoking the dwelling places of our state governors. Why hasn't somebody thought of this before? It's always fun to poke around in other people's houses, especially important people's houses, which are bound to be rich in legends, lies and fables, and real memories, too.

Here is one memory:

We piled off the bus, schoolboys in awkwardly fitting coats and ties and schoolgirls in their best dresses. We walked through an iron gate and down a long curving driveway to the red brick house with the big porch and tall gables. We were seventh-graders in Raleigh, our state capital, for an oratorical contest. (By the way, what ever happened to oratorical contests? What ever happened to oratory?) As part of the program, we were paying a self-conscious visit to the governor's mansion. The governor wasn't there that afternoon, but the governor's wife showed us around and offered us punch and cookies. When we got home, the one important-sounding thing we had to tell our families and friends was that we had been to the governor's mansion.

This is the real purpose of governors' mansions, probably—not to give the governors a place to lay their heads at night, but to give the schoolchildren a place to visit. There is precious little ceremony in the lives of schoolchildren today, and not much sense of historical continuity. A trip to the governor's mansion automatically provides them some of each. It is a felicitous experience for them; also, for that matter, for the garden-club ladies, the small-town mayors, the visiting Elks and Rotarians and county clerks and out-of-town families on vacation who keep the public rooms of our governors' houses constantly abuzz. Most of the states try to keep at least the governors' bedrooms off-limits, but when the governor of Mississippi hauled me into his bedroom one time so that we could complete a television interview in peace, the door kept opening anyway—another old friend who "just wanted to stick in my head and say hello." Few governors can afford to tell such acquaintances to get out of their bedrooms and leave them alone. Consequently, the governor's mansion is usually a nice house but not much of a home.

There is an added poignancy to occupying an executive mansion, of course: governors carry around with them the certain knowledge that, sooner or later, they will have to find another place to live. They can rearrange the furniture on a whim and change the wallpaper to their hearts' content, but always with the gloomy intimation that their tasteful refurbishing may not outlast the next election. They can't leave the house to their children the way the rest of us can. They must leave it to a successor, perhaps even an enemy, who will soon be busy rearranging the furniture and changing the wallpaper.

Governors have been known to get around this problem by moving out of the official house and seeking digs of their own. California, that rich and populous adornment of the Union, owns a drafty old relic in downtown Sacramento with creaky floorboards and (so it is said) bats in the attic. This is pointed out to visitors as the governor's mansion, but Governor Ronald Reagan fled the place in the late 1960s, and in the decades since, California has been unable to find another governor willing to live there. It appears that to the list of states like Rhode Island, Massachusetts, and Vermont, which are officially indifferent as to whether their governors live in a rented house, a condo, or a tent, we may now add California.

Arizona doesn't have a governor's mansion either, and to tell you the truth, many of the states that do provide a home for their governors have been careful not to build showplaces that outshine all the other houses in town. You can see from Cathy Keating's marvelous compilation that while these are comfortable dwellings steeped in history, many a corporate C.E.O. or Hollywood mogul lives more lavishly than the typical governor.

I have a theory about this: I think Americans carry in their bones a disdainful memory of their bewigged, high-and-mighty overseers of Colonial days, and want to be sure that modern governors don't get too uppity. North Carolinians show off the elegant Tryon Palace, where a lordly British governor lived amid much pomp and splendor, but when the time came to build a house for their present-day governors—the Victorian house I visited as a boy—they cut corners by having state prison inmates do the work.

There are many examples in this volume of such savings to the taxpayers—mansions donated to the states by rich benefactors and then supported by private contributions. Most of us want to see a roof over our governors' heads, but if the roof leaks, we don't want to pay much to fix it.

Not having a governor's mansion at all may be carrying egalitarianism too far, however. I am aware that this comes under the category of states' rights: if a commonwealth of the people chooses not to supply a house for its governor, it's no business of the rest of us.

But it cheats the schoolchildren. They have no place to visit.

INTRODUCTION

By Cathy Keating
First Lady of the State of Oklahoma

What is it like to live in a governor's mansion?

On Wednesday afternoons if I skip downstairs to the kitchen for a snack, I might bump into a tour group. ("Look! She eats our brand of pretzels!") Eight or ten times a week there's a banquet, a reception, or some other public function under way in the ballroom or the dining room. If I pause to brush a bit of dust from a vase, I know I'm touching history. And on Sunday afternoons, when my husband and son are watching a football game on the TV in the basement family room, they're likely to be joined by a visiting celebrity—not exactly your typical suburban scene.

Like the people who live in it, a state executive residence is always on display. The governors and first families who come to stay for two, four, or eight years are the temporary guests. These homes really belong to the people of the states they symbolize, and they are as unique and distinctive as the plains, mountains, seashores, and deltas of our broad and varied land. Some truly merit the name of mansion; they are spacious and palatial. Others are simply nice homes. A few, like Drumthwacket in New Jersey or Terrace Hill in Iowa, had fabled lives as private estates before they became governors' mansions. Others were built especially for state service. While most states call their executive residence a "mansion," that doesn't require that those who live there "put on airs." The stairway banisters in many of our executive residences have often served as playtime slides for children, and in one mansion, the first family's youngsters kept pet alligators in the upstairs bathtub. First families are people, too.

This book would not have been possible without the help and guidance of the first families of our states. They arranged photography and unearthed tantalizing nuggets of history from their archives. Every first family we contacted gave its support to our project. They weren't interested in seeing their names or photographs in the book; rather, they understood and supported our desire to create a timeless pictorial and textual record of our "little White Houses"—the executive residences of the states.

Every state and community has its share of historic mansions, the homes of famed industrialists or eccentric legends. Local lore usually calls them by the names of their original residents: the Vanderbilt mansion, the Getty mansion. Many are priceless architectural showpieces, and many are listed on state or national historic registries.

But in the forty-four states with official executive residences, there is only one such mansion. These executive homes are surrounded by a special mystique: one part history, one part the power we traditionally associate with the office of governor—and perhaps a dash of legend. Several of our governors' mansions have been home to men who became president. They have sheltered colorful characters who are enshrined in books, great leaders who shaped the course of history, and even an occasional scoundrel.

As we researched the stories of each state's executive residence, we found some common themes—and some startling differences. Five states have no mansion; a sixth has purchased the home owned by its incumbent governor and designated it as the official residence, but, as we prepared the manuscript, there were indications that this solution would be only temporary. In the other forty-four states, the mansions reflect local tastes or accidents of history—sometimes, lucky coincidence.

Some mansions were built specifically as executive residences. Others were bequeathed to states or purchased after having been originally constructed as private homes. A number of states have had two, three, or more official residences, while others continue to use an original mansion, grown venerable with age. There are mansions with grand ballrooms and wide, open staircases, ideal for entertaining and for large public events. There are smaller mansions that serve only as residences, and some have pedigrees dating to the Colonial period. Some mansions have sweeping, columned porticoes and rolling, manicured grounds; there is no mistaking their roles as public buildings. Others sit side by side on suburban streets with similar private homes. There are mansions of one, two, and three stories; mansions in a broad variety of architectural styles; mansions you approach with reverence for the history and tradition they represent; and mansions as comfortable and inviting as your next-door neighbor's house.

Three common threads soon emerged from our research.

First, the period surrounding the American Civil War, from the 1850s to the 1870s, touched a great many of our executive residences in a profound way. The war was a defining event in our national history. So, too, with our state governors' mansions. Many were built during or immediately after that tumultuous era, and others, especially those in the South, were forever changed. This was also true, to a lesser degree, of the era that Mark Twain called the Gilded Age, the closing years of the nineteenth century and the first decade of the twentieth. Many of our mansions were built or dramatically modified between 1850 and 1910.

A second theme concerns more recent events, the explosion of restoration and historic preservation efforts during the last quarter of the twentieth century. Beginning in the 1960s and extending through the 1990s, virtually every state has launched at least one ambitious effort to restore and protect its executive residence. Many of these national treasures were reaching their centennial years in this period, and quite a few have been added to national and local historic registries. Even those that were aging gracefully have undergone dramatic renovation. America's governors' mansions are probably in better shape today than at any time in our history.

Our final discovery was the development of private mansion foundations. One after another, first families and historic preservationists have founded privately funded groups dedicated to maintaining and improving their executive residences. They have added immensely to mansion collections of furnishings, artworks, and artifacts. In state after state, our executive residences are truly becoming "the people's houses," as businesses, preservationists, and individuals come together, at no cost to taxpayers, to ensure that these historic treasures will live on and thrive in the new century. All royalties from this book will benefit one such group, Oklahoma's Friends of the Mansion, Inc.

In the pages that follow, you can visit each of our executive residences and marvel at how each reflects the character of its home state. In Alaska, there's a Tlingit totem pole beside the front door. Florida's mansion has a glorious multihued decor that reminds visitors of the Everglades. The walls in the New Mexico residence are adobe. George Washington really did sleep in some of our Eastern mansions, and in Montana the huge living-room picture windows give a majestic mountain view. All the homes are unique, and they all speak of state pride and long tradition.

I remember the first time I walked through the front door of the Oklahoma governor's mansion. I thought to myself as we moved in: this is where the governors I'd read about in the history books lived and worked. In that corner office, famous men and women decided matters of state. Here is the dining room that hosted the presidents of nations and of great corporations, film stars, and famous authors. That antique bed was once owned by the emperor of Mexico. Down this staircase came first ladies in fashions that ranged from the flapper era of the Roaring Twenties to the 1960s and beyond. And Oklahoma is one of our youngest states. Imagine the history and decor of governors' mansions twice as old.

It took some time for the truth to sink in: this is our home, but we hold it in trust for its real owners, the people of Oklahoma. One of my proudest achievements is our ongoing effort to restore and refurbish the Oklahoma governor's mansion, an effort that has been mirrored in many other states as Americans take a renewed interest in their historic public and private buildings.

They say that the ghost of William H. Murray inhabits our mansion. Murray was known affectionately as "Alfalfa Bill" when he served as governor from 1931 until 1935. He had been a country editor, a lawyer, president of Oklahoma's Constitutional Convention, and a member of Congress. Murray once moved to Bolivia to start a ranch; he also ran for president, without much luck, in 1932. Alfalfa Bill was a wild and colorful character who settled a dispute with Texas over Red River water rights by calling out the National Guard, taking possession of the bridge that linked our two states, and challenging the Texans to fight (they didn't). In the ballroom of the mansion is a framed photograph of Alfalfa Bill and his family; his son Johnston Murray lived here as a boy and returned twenty years later as Oklahoma's fourteenth governor.

I've never seen or heard Alfalfa Bill's spirit, but I'm sure he's here, along with many others. Oklahoma's mansion is far from unique in that respect; each state's executive residence has its own set of legends, its own historic treasures and artifacts, and its own character. Some are old, some relatively new. Each is special in its own way. Our book explores the art and architecture, the heritage and traditions, of all of America's governors' mansions. It presents the residences in the same order that the states joined the Union, to give a sense of the nation's own history.

Come along as we begin our tour.

ACKNOWLEDGMENTS

This book had its beginnings in the 1995 restoration of the Oklahoma Governor's Mansion. As we worked to restore this architectural and historical treasure, we asked other states and first ladies for advice. We found that many of them had undertaken similar efforts in recent years as part of a national movement to preserve and restore a priceless part of our heritage. There are thousands of public and private buildings in danger of being lost or irretrievably neglected as we near the new century, and in community after community, private and public groups are forming partnerships to save them. In many cases, efforts to restore a state executive residence have had a ripple effect, like a pebble in a pond, prompting similar projects that have preserved and restored thousands of historic private homes and commercial buildings. Americans have an enduring love of the national past, and nowhere is that past more permanently inscribed than in the places we call home. Our experience in Oklahoma, when people came by the thousands to our first post-restoration Mansion open house, indicated a broad and growing public interest in historic preservation efforts. Why not, we asked, expand this story to encompass all fifty states?

Patti Rosenfeld, dear friend and loyal partner in this project, undertook the imposing task of managing the fifty-state logistics as we contacted each first family and asked for their involvement in the project. She was always there, always efficient and always optimistic. Her mark is on every page of this book. May all of us be blessed with such a friend.

Mallory Van Horn of my office staff served with equal dedication, tackling the ever-growing logistical challenge of collecting material, mailing proofs, answering calls, and providing daily answers to questions that seemed insoluble. It is no easy job to manage the countless details of a project of this scope. A superb crisis manager and juggler of multiple tasks, Mallory held things together. Barbara Jobe, my chief of staff, balanced book time and First Lady time with incredible skill and patience, somehow finding extra hours beyond the standard twenty-four. Deby Snodgrass co-chaired our Oklahoma Mansion renovation and restoration effort, the inspiration for this book. Katie

Gumerson spent a busy summer internship in my office gathering information and resources from every state. Duchess Bartmess scanned the many contracts and releases with a lawyer's precise eye, as did Jack Sargent, a member of the board of Friends of the Mansion, Inc., and a skilled attorney. Finally, Dan Mahoney, communications director in the Office of the Governor, offered creative advice in our efforts to publicize and promote the book.

In the executive residences of the states, forty-eight first ladies and two first spouses gave the project their enthusiastic backing, and opened doors for us everywhere. Their staff members and the officials of their state historical societies were unfailingly helpful. The local photographers who recorded the visual images in this book have amassed what amounts to a historic, and unprecedented, national snapshot of our executive residences. May these photos always be a treasured part of their portfolios.

A special thank-you to the Gilcrease Museum in Tulsa for lending us the services of the photographer Shane Culpepper. Shane did more than photograph Oklahoma's Mansion; he helped devise a uniform format to best depict all the executive residences displayed here.

At Harry N. Abrams, Inc., those who know so much about producing a book like this were always kind and encouraging to those who were still learning. Their skills are evident on every page. Paul Gottlieb, President and Publisher, made this ambitious project a reality. John Crowley, our photography editor, is a great hand-holder. John insisted that each photo tell a special story, and he was unwavering in his commitment to the book. James Leggio, our project editor, shared his brilliant editorial ability while attending to every request to "change this, move that." Carol Robson wins my Oscar as the best and most creative book designer in the business, weaving what began as a huge pile of seemingly unrelated transparencies into a seamless visual presentation. The Abrams marketing and sales staff listened to my sometimes wild ideas with tolerance and, occasionally, an affirmative nod of the head.

Charles Kuralt was a national treasure. Charles had retired as longtime host and commentator on CBS's "Sunday Morning" when he agreed to contribute to our project by writing the foreword to this volume. He died just as the book was going to press. Like all of his viewers and readers, we will always cherish his wisdom and clarity of vision.

Leslie Davey collected the background material on each state as it arrived in the office, researching masses of material to extract the most salient and intriguing facts. An upholsterer who specializes in antiques, Leslie brought a keen professional eye to the many unique treasures that decorate our executive residences.

Mike Brake of the Office of Public Affairs wrote the texts devoted to the individual states in this book. Years ago he majored in journalism and history, and he applied the training of both disciplines to a daunting writing task, asking and answering two basic questions about each mansion: What is it like, and how did it come to be that way?

Finally, I will be eternally grateful to my wonderful and supportive family; my mother, my children and, of course, my loving husband, Frank. Frank has encouraged me and been my mentor—my sounding board, helper, and best friend. He was my partner in the restoration and development of a permanent collection at the Oklahoma Governor's Mansion, and when I proposed the idea for this book he said, "Go for it!" Thank you, Frank, for your patience, support, and love.

Every penny of the royalties from the book will benefit Oklahoma's Friends of the Mansion, a non-profit foundation dedicated to the preservation of our Mansion into the next century. With pride we offer this volume to all who love our country's history, art, and architecture, and who cherish the America that these historic homes represent—America the Beautiful.

CATHY KEATING

☆ ☆ ☆

The generous cooperation and support of the following individuals and organizations were essential to the preparation of this volume.

Alabama
Bobbie James, *First Lady*
Ebby Sechriest, *Personal Secretary to the First Lady*
Jeannie Winford, *Winmill Flowers, Birmingham*
Kathy Miller, *Winmill Flowers, Birmingham*

Alaska
Susan M. Knowles, *First Lady*
Karen M. Newton, *Executive Residence Manager*
Patience Frederiksen, *Librarian, Alaska State Library*

Arizona
Ann Symington, *First Lady*
Tricia Reynolds, *Assistant to the First Lady*
Arlissa Reynolds, *Governor's Office*
David Hoober, *State Archivist*
Melanie Sturgeon, *Assistant State Archivist*

Arkansas
Janet McCain Huckabee, *First Lady*
Kamala R. Williams, *Mansion Administrator and First Lady's Assistant*
John L. Ferguson, *State Historian, Arkansas History Commission*
Kelly Tibbit, *Photographer's Assistant*

California
Gayle Wilson, *First Lady*
The California Department of Parks and Recreation
Gold Rush Historic Sites District
Governor's Mansion State Historic Park

Colorado
Bea Romer, *First Lady*
Helen Williams, *Executive Residence Director*
Judith Whitaker, *Executive Residence Chef*
Susan Westling, *Executive Residence Events Captain*
Colorado Historical Society
Denver Public Library

Connecticut
Patricia Rowland, *First Lady*
Jo McKenzie, *Assistant to the First Lady and Director of the Governor's Residence*
Gabrielle Davis Barrett, *Gabrielle Davis Barrett Interiors*
John LaFalce, *LaFalce, Campbell, Robbins, Inc.*
The Wadsworth Atheneum
The Mattatuck Museum
Lyman Allyn Art Museum
The Nelson White Family Collection
The Connecticut Historical Society
The Mark Twain House
John Canning and Co., Ltd.
The Connecticut Governor's Residence Conservancy

Delaware

Martha Carper, *First Lady*
Sande Warren Price, *General Administrator, Woodburn*
Cynthia Lindenlauf, *Traveler Information Services Coordinator,*
Delaware Tourism Office

Florida

Rhea Chiles, *First Lady*
Kimbel Orr, *Governor's Mansion Foundation President*
Catherine Reed, *Governor's Mansion Commission Chair*
Jerome Cummings, *Mansion Manager*
Dennis Gephardt, *Mansion Curator*
Jill Alford, *Mansion Horticulturist*

Georgia

Shirley Miller, *First Lady*
Caroline Leake
Beverly Messer

Hawaii

Benjamin J. Cayetano, *Governor*
Mary Matayoshi, *Governor's Volunteer Services Office*
Mary M. Peters, *Chairperson, and all the Docents*
of Washington Place
Jo-Lynn Igarta-Pieters, *Historian*
Jim Bartels, *Curator, Iolani Palace*
Alohalani Pang, *Governor's Volunteer Services Office*
Peter Rosegg, *Executive Assistant, Office of the Governor*

Idaho

Jacque Batt, *First Lady*
Claudia Simplot, *Assistant to the First Lady*
Idaho Historical Society
Idaho Division of Tourism

Illinois

Brenda Edgar, *First Lady*
Tom Faulkner, *Assistant to the First Lady*
Maynard Crossland, *Illinois Historic Preservation Agency*
Illinois Executive Mansion Association

Indiana

Judy O'Bannon, *First Lady, 1997–*
Susan Bayh, *First Lady, 1993–96*
Kimberly Placek, *Director of Public Affairs in the Office*
of the First Lady
E. Lyle Hardin, *Governor's Residence Director*
Gerald F. Handfield, *Director and State Archivist of the*
Indiana Commission on Public Records
Indiana State Museum
Indiana Governor's Residence Commission

Tiffany and Company

Carol Ward
Marilyn Price
Carol Clemons
Mary Kay Horn
Jill Perelman
Beryl Poland
Janet Robertson

Iowa

Christine Branstad, *First Lady*
Barbara Filer, *Governor's Residence Administrator*
Melinda Prince, *Administrative Assistant*
Terrace Hill Commission, Society and Foundation

Kansas

Linda K. Graves, *First Lady*
Jennie Adams Rose, *Chief of Staff, Office of the First Lady*
Kenneth H. B. Smith, *Grounds Administrator,*
Governor's Residence
Cathy Walton, *Administrative Assistant*
David Porterfield, *Porterfield's Flowers*
Dr. Ramon Powers, *Executive Director,*
Kansas State Historical Society
Friends of Cedar Crest Association

Kentucky

Judi Patton, *First Lady*
Dr. Thomas D. Clark, *State Historian Laureate*
Rex Lyons, *Executive Mansion Director*
Lou Karibo, *State Curator*
Margaret Lane, *Coauthor of "History and Hospitality:*
The Story of Kentucky's Executive Mansions"
Marie Gardner, *Division of Historic Properties*
Kay Harrod, *Office of the First Lady*
Gary Robinson, *Photography Supervisor,*
Division of Creative Services

Louisiana

Alice Foster, *First Lady*
Debbie Broussard, *Executive Assistant to the First Lady*
Susan Afeman, *Governor's Mansion Coordinator*
The Louisiana Governor's Mansion Foundation
Roger Ogden, *The Ogden Museum of Southern Art*
Nell Fetzer, *Fetzer Interior and Antiques*
Lee Michael Berg, *Lee Michaels Fine Jewelry*
Karen Davis, *Lee Michaels Fine Jewelry*
Melissa Riser, *Assistant Mansion Coordinator*
Dennis Hargroder, *Cole's Flower and Coffee Market*

Maine

Mary J. Herman, *First Lady*

Susan E. Dowe, *Assistant to the First Lady*

Sue Plummer, *Residence Manager*

Earle G. Shettleworth, *Director, Maine Historic Preservation Commission*

J. R. Phillips, *Director, Maine State Museum*

Maine State Museum

Blaine House Restoration Committee

The Friends of the Blaine House

Maryland

Frances Hughes Glendening, *First Lady*

Maryland Historical Society

Edward C. Papenfuse, *State Archivist, Maryland State Archives*

Elaine M. Rice, *Curator, Maryland State Archives*

Government House Foundation, Inc.

Sandra L. Rose, *Government House Manager*

Massachusetts

Susan Roosevelt Weld, *First Lady*

Thomas Lyman, *State House Tours Division*

Michigan

Michelle Engler, *First Lady*

Denise Yee, *Director, Office of the First Lady*

Marianne McClain, *Governor's Executive Office Manager*

Dan Crow, *Governor's Residence Assistant Manager*

Kerry Chartkoff, *Director, State Capitol Tour and Information Service*

Minnesota

Susan Carlson, *First Lady*

Barbara Hoffmann, *Residence Director*

Aimee Kane, *Communications Assistant*

3M Corporation

Holiday decorations by:

Dayton's, *Minneapolis*

Bachman's Nursery and Landscape, *Minneapolis*

Tweed Museum of Art, *University of Minnesota–Duluth*

Minnesota Historical Society

Mississippi

Pat Fordice, *First Lady*

Cora Gee, *Assistant to the First Lady*

Sara Stankewitz, *Administrative Assistant to the First Lady*

Henri Burnham, *Mansion Administrator*

Deborah Knott De Arechaga, *Governor's Mansion Curator*

Jan Rasch, *Governor's Office*

Janie Asher, *Mississippi Department of Economic and Community Development*

Mississippi Department of Archives and History

Missouri

Jean Carnahan, *First Lady*

Theodore J. Wofford, *A.I.A., Restoration Architect*

Mary Pat Abele, *Executive Director Missouri Mansion Preservation, Inc.*

Missouri Mansion Preservation, Inc.

Montana

Theresa Racicot, *First Lady*

Kris MacIntyre, *Executive Assistant to the First Lady*

Dave Walter, *Historical Society*

Bonnie Finstad, *Finstad's Carpet One*

Jane Kartevold, *Knox Flowers*

Darrel Gustin, *Owner, Holiday Inn Express*

Nebraska

Diane Nelson, *First Lady*

Shirley Hart Arthur, *Governor's Residence Director*

Nebraska State Historical Society

Nevada

Sandy Miller, *First Lady*

Nevada State Museum:

Bob Nylen, *Curator of History*

Guy Rocha, *Administrator, Archives and Records*

Jeff Kintop, *Archives Manager*

Gloria Harjes, *Acquisition Registrar*

Helen Wiemer, *Mansion Coordinator*

Joan Turner, *Assistant to the First Lady*

Pat Wilson, *Office of the First Lady*

New Hampshire

Bill Shaheen, *First Spouse, 1997–*

Heather Maclean Walker Merrill, *First Lady, 1993–96*

Jean A. Barnes, *Assistant to the First Lady*

Van McLeod, *Commissioner of Cultural Affairs*

Nancy Muller, *Director, Division of Historical Resources*

Diana Degen, *Reference Librarian, State Library*

Paul Pelletier, *Utility Person, Bridges House*

New Jersey

John Whitman, *First Spouse*

Drumthwacket Foundation

Daphne A. Pontius

Donald C. Deluca, Jr.

Office of the Governor

Christabel K. Vartanian

Rachel E. Donington

Elizabeth R. Hance

Joseph Moore

New Mexico
Dee Johnson, *First Lady*
Elizabeth Lynch, *Assistant to the First Lady*
Cristi Sala, *Governor's Residence Director*
Robert Torrez, *State Historian*
The Allan Houser Family, *Allan Houser Inc.*
Museum of New Mexico:
Museum of Fine Art
Museum of Indian Arts and Culture
Museum of International Folk Art
Palace of the Governors
New Mexico Governor's Mansion Foundation

New York
Libby Pataki, *First Lady*
Felicia Allard, *Director of Special Projects and Protocol*
Marty Eagan, *Executive Mansion Director*
Dennis Anderson, *Art Curator*
New York's Executive Mansion Preservation Society

North Carolina
Carolyn Hunt, *First Lady*
Janice Shearin, *Executive Assistant to the First Lady*
May M. Bensen, *Residence Manager/Social Director*
Marie Ham, *Mansion Curator*

North Carolina Executive Mansion Fine Arts Committee:
Charlie E. Jones, *Photographer, Department of Transportation*
Rick Alexander, *Photographer*
Tim Buchman, *Photographer*
Leslie Wright Dow, *Photographer*
Scott Huckabee, *Photographer*
Eric N. Blevins, *Photographer*

North Dakota
Nancy Jones Schafer, *First Lady*
Steve Sharkey, *Residence Manager*
Merl Paaverud, *Director of Historic Sites,*
North Dakota Historical Society
Marilee Toman, *Dutch Mill Florist, Inc.*
Jane Feist, *Dutch Mill Florist, Inc.*

Ohio
Janet Voinovich, *First Lady*
Steve George, *Historian*
Bobbie Wiard, *Ohio Governor's Residence Administrator*
Ohio Historical Society
Ohio Governor's Residence Foundation

Oklahoma
Mallory Van Horn, *Special Projects Coordinator,*
Office of the Governor
Dan Mahoney, *Director of Communications,*
Office of the Governor
Barbara Jobe, *Chief of Staff, Office of the First Lady*
Jennifer Loeffler, *Administrative Assistant,*
Office of the First Lady
Ralph Knighton, *Mansion Manager*
David Payne, *Mansion Grounds Manager*
Leslie Mount Davey
Duchess Bartmess, *General Counsel, Office of the Governor*
Jack Sargent, *Legal Counsel, Friends of the Mansion*
Katie Gumerson, *Intern, Office of the First Lady*
Laura Rosenfeld Barnes
Gilcrease Museum
National Cowboy Hall of Fame
Oklahoma Historical Society
Oklahoma Friends of the Mansion, Inc.
Deby Snodgrass
Erica Stoller
Frankfurt Short Bruza
Mary Duffe
Paul Meyer
Kay Duffy
Fanny Bolen
Charles Faudree
Ann Henry
Vicki Hicks
Don and Brenda Philips
Stephen Edwards
Mike Mahaffey

Oregon
Sharon Kitzhaber, *First Lady*
Chet Orloff, *Executive Director, Oregon Historical Society*
Elaine Anderson, *Assistant to the First Lady*
Sharon Wong, *Governor's Office Manager*

Pennsylvania
Michele M. Ridge, *First Lady*
Lucy Gnazzo, *Chief of Staff/Press Secretary to the First Lady*
Autumn Gemberling, *Deputy Press Secretary to the First Lady*
Lucinda Smyser, *Governor's Residence Manager*
The Pennsylvania Historical and Museum Commission
The State Museum of Pennsylvania
The Pennsylvania State Library
Mr. and Mrs. Meyer Potamkin, *Philadelphia*
Allan Holm Photography, *Lancaster*
Lori Wagner, *Designer*

Rhode Island

Marilyn Almond, *First Lady*
Cynthia Wardwell, *Assistant to the First Lady*
Albert Klyberg, *Director, Rhode Island Historical Society*
Museum of Rhode Island History at Aldrich House

South Carolina

Mary Wood Beasley, *First Lady*
Ann Edwards, *Former First Lady*
South Carolina Governor's Mansion Commission
Nancy Bunch, *Curator/Tour Director*
Sue Kirsh, *Docent/Palmetto Cabinet*

South Dakota

Mary Dean Janklow, *First Lady*
Chad Coppess, *South Dakota Tourism*
Kristi Hansen, *South Dakota Tourism*
John Moisan, *Bureau of Administration*
South Dakota Art Museum, *Brookings*
Harold and Leona Schuler, *Pierre*
Godfrey and Henrietta Roberts, *Pierre*
Carla Sahr, *Pierre*
Charles H. Burke, *Pierre*
Dr. John Day, *Vermillion*
Marshall Damgaard, *Britton*

Tennessee

Martha Sundquist, *First Lady*
Anne M. Locke, *Executive Assistant to the First Lady*
Murray Lee, *Photographer*
Executive Residence Preservation Foundation

Texas

Laura Bush, *First Lady*
Friends of the Governor's Mansion
Ron Tyler, *Director, Texas State Historical Association*
Hickey Robertson Photographers
Robert Anschutz, *Photographer*
Terry Duff, *Photographer*

Utah

Jacalyn S. Leavitt, *First Lady*
Judith George, *Assistant to the First Lady*
Allison Norton, *Residence Manager*
Shawna Corral, *Housekeeper*
Division of State History
Administrative Services
Utah Heritage Foundation
Ellie Sonntag, *Interior Decorator*
Culp Construction

Max J. Smith & Associates, *Architects*
Executive Residence Commissions
Utah Governor's Mansion Foundation
Division of Facilities Construction and Management
Utah State Building Board
Utah Arts Council

Vermont

Judy Dean, *First Lady*

Virginia

Susan Allen, *First Lady*

Washington

Mona Lee Locke, *First Lady, 1997–*
Mary Lowry, *First Lady, 1993–96*
The Governor's Mansion Foundation
The Washington State Library

West Virginia

Hovah Underwood, *First Lady, 1997–*
Rachel Worby, *First Lady, 1993–96*
Martha Barnitt, *Assistant to the First Lady*
Sharon Mullins, *Director of Administration,
West Virginia Division of Culture and History*
James R. Mitchell, *Curator, West Virginia State Museum*
Otis K. Rice, *Professor Emeritus of History, West Virginia
University Institute of Technology*
West Virginia Governor's Mansion Preservation Foundation

Wisconsin

Sue Ann Thompson, *First Lady*
Carol Muller, *Director, Executive Residence*
Joy Newman, *Assistant Director, Executive Residence*
Harry Miller, *Archives, Wisconsin State Historical Society*
Peter Cannon, *Wisconsin Legislative Reference Bureau*
Mary Idso, *Assistant Director, Wisconsin Film Office,
Department of Tourism*

Wyoming

Sherri Geringer, *First Lady*
Nancy Flynn, *Personal Assistant to
Sherri Geringer, Wyoming's First Lady*
Tim White, *Curator of the Historic Governor's Mansion*
Richard Collier
Michael Jensen
Richard K. Hansen, *Horse Creek Studio*
Greg Singer, *Singer's Photography Studio*
Wyoming Governor's Residence Foundation
Wyoming State Museum

DELAWARE

WOODBURN
DOVER

PHOTOGRAPHS BY JAMES T. O'BRIEN

A view from formal boxwood gardens.

Through a secret door . . .

In the decade before the Civil War, as passions rose on both sides of the Mason-Dixon Line over the seemingly insoluble dilemma posed by slavery, the state of Delaware became a crossroads in one of the great secret dramas of American history. Countless escaped slaves, headed north to hopeful freedom, traversed the hidden passages of what came to be known as the Underground Railroad. As they journeyed through the fields of Maryland and into the coastal plains of Delaware, furtively and by night, they sensed the nearness of the free states of Pennsylvania and New Jersey. Delaware was officially a slave state, but there was much abolitionist sentiment there, and in certain homes, known to the guides who helped runaway slaves, were hiding compartments and secret sympathizers. One of those homes was called Woodburn, and according to legend, there was a hidden room in its basement, connected by a tunnel to the bank of the nearby St. Jones River, where boats would put in at night at a signal from color-coded lanterns to load and unload passengers on the final leg of the Underground Railroad.

No one knows if the tale is true. The old tunnel was filled with dirt and debris long ago, and its oak doorway in Woodburn's basement has yet to yield its secrets. It may all have been the invention of a novelist who included historic Woodburn in one of his books. But most of Delaware's governors who have lived in this revitalized and historic mansion since 1965 believe the stories and take a special pride in the role their state played in American history. Delaware was, after all, the very first state to ratify the United States Constitution in 1787.

The land north of where Woodburn stands was originally part of the only significant Swedish colony in early America. By 1655 the stronger Dutch, led by Peter Stuyvesant, held sway in the area, which alternated between being part of Pennsylvania and part of New York until 1776. In that year of independence, Delaware Bay was the scene of the first major naval battle of the Revolutionary War, and the fledgling state seated its first legislature.

The Woodburn land was part of a 1684 grant to one David Morgan. A century later, Charles Hillyard III bought the site for a hundred and ten dollars at a sheriff's sale. Not until 1790 did Hillyard erect the two-story Middle Georgian home that would later be called Woodburn and on two occasions be the official residence of Delaware's chief executives. (The name Woodburn did not appear in official records until 1845; most likely it derived from the practice of felling trees and burning them in vast piles to clear land for agriculture.)

Charles and Mary Hillyard had ten children. After the couple's death, a son-in-law, Martin Bates, owned Woodburn. Bates was a remarkable man—a doctor, a merchant, a lawyer, and ultimately a U.S. senator from Delaware. In 1820, he apparently leased or loaned his home to Judge Jacob

Stout during Stout's service as governor, making him the first of Delaware's chief executives to reside there. In 1825, Bates sold Woodburn to Mary and Daniel Cowgill, and the home was to remain in that family for nearly a hundred years.

The Cowgills were Quakers and devoted abolitionists, and Daniel Cowgill, Sr., practiced what his religion preached. He freed his slaves and allowed them to meet regularly in the great hall at Woodburn, a practice that may have also been the origin of the many myths and stories concerning the house's role in the Underground Railroad. A later owner of Woodburn, Dr. Clayton Cowgill, was often absent, being a doctor in the Army Medical Corps during the Civil War years, and he apparently rented the home to a tenant. Between 1877 and 1885 there are several deed transfers pertaining to Woodburn that involve various members of the related Cowgill, Loffland, and Wilson families, and in 1912 the home—now more than a century old—was sold to Senator Daniel Hastings. During the six years he owned Woodburn, Senator Hastings added its brick porch, pillars on the south side, and a reflecting pool, and made a number of interior modifications. In 1918, he sold Woodburn to Dr. and Mrs. Frank S. Hall. Hall was a retired Philadelphia dentist with inherited wealth. He spent lavishly on interior work at Woodburn while his wife, Frances, collected rare antiques and dolls. Among their frequent guests was a young woman who would eventually become the first lady of Delaware, and whose childhood recollections of Woodburn would help lead to its acquisition by the state.

In 1953, after Mrs. Hall died and Woodburn was again placed on the market, there was a brief effort to secure it as the Delaware governor's mansion, but the legislature killed the proposal. The property was then divided, with the house and an acre and a half of land being purchased by Thomas W. Murray, an aviation executive, and the remainder of the original Woodburn grounds going to a school. Murray was delighted with the home, now well into its second century. He said Woodburn was "put together the way Stradivari made a violin."

Prior to 1965, Delaware's first families had lacked an official residence, but under the administration of Governor Charles L. Terry, Jr. (served 1965–69), that changed. Mrs. Jessica Terry was the same woman who, as a child, had often visited Woodburn, and she oversaw the redecoration efforts after state officials bought the house from the Murray family. Her goal was to furnish the house with items from the period of its construction, with a special emphasis on furniture from the Delaware and southeastern Pennsylvania

Opposite:
The dining room.

Below:
The drawing room. The portrait over the fireplace is of Commodore Thomas Macdonough, a Delaware native who led the American fleet to victory over the British in the Battle of Lake Champlain in the War of 1812.

regions. In February 1966, Woodburn was ready for its first open house as the Delaware governor's mansion.

Although the Woodburn collection has grown over the years and subsequent first families have added small touches, the house remains very much as it was after the renovations by Senator Hastings and Dr. Hall in the early years of the twentieth century. In 1983, the state acquired a second home north of Woodburn for use as a guest residence, but every effort has been made to preserve the house and grounds as they were. After an early photograph of Woodburn revealed that a peach tree had once grown in the center of the driveway circle, the departing family of Governor Pete du Pont planted an identical tree on the same spot.

Of all the old governors' mansions in America, Woodburn may be the most pristine. Its multipaned windows are surmounted by keystone pediments. The Flemish-bond brickwork has withstood more than two hundred years of weather. Inside, the wood floors and woodwork are evidence of the skill of master craftsmen and joiners.

Visitors approaching the compact two-story brick home first encounter, at the front entrance, a paneled Dutch door with its original wrought-iron strap hinges and handmade iron lock box; the key still exists and weighs one pound. The rear veranda with its fluted columns was an addition from the Hastings era, but it matches the original Woodburn design so well that most visitors must be told of its much later origin.

Inside, the home is all tidy simplicity, endowed with a Colonial elegance. A wide hall at the west end flanks a roomy parlor and the equally spacious dining room; on the east end is the kitchen, while upstairs are bedrooms and a spacious attic level.

The downstairs great hall, measuring fifteen by forty feet, is really a living room, with the central staircase leading up to a landing and then to the left, beneath an antique brass Dutch chandelier. The heart-pine staircase makes yet another landing turn at the attic level. More than one past resident of Woodburn has claimed a ghostly encounter on this staircase. In 1815, a Methodist minister visiting the Bates family said he met a man in a Colonial-period powdered wig, knee breeches, and ruffled shirt. When pressed for details he appeared to describe Charles Hillyard III, the builder of Woodburn. Later, Mrs. Frank Hall said she often passed the ghost of Mr. Hillyard on the stairs. There have also been fanciful reports of a young female ghost who allegedly haunts the grounds, and some guests have reported the sounds of chains from the cellar.

There are no known ghosts in the great hall, but it does boast a 1765 Philadelphia walnut case clock, a Chippendale mahogany armchair, and other eighteenth-century furnishings and objects. A breakfront dates from 1800 and contains the state's official china, and there are two late nineteenth-century Queen Anne chairs. There are portraits here of Mr. and Mrs. Kensey Johns II; George Washington attended their wedding at Woodburn.

In the dining room, guests sit on ten Chippendale chairs around a Sheraton Empire mahogany table beneath a nineteenth-century Baccarat chandelier. There is a cozy fireplace, and above it hangs a portrait of Caesar A. Rodney, nephew and namesake of a signer of the Declaration of Independence.

The wood-paneled parlor, now called the drawing room, contains other Woodburn treasures, which include antique furnishings by Chippendale, Hepplewhite, and Sheraton. The room also has a fireplace, and its double exterior doors open into the garden, with a view of the St. Jones River. Among the objects in the drawing room are two antique French vases and a nineteenth-century doll collected by Mrs. Frank Hall.

In the upstairs bedrooms are an antique Chippendale mahogany desk once owned by Governor Cornelius P. Comegys (served 1837–41) and other period pieces.

The main entrance to Woodburn features the original 1790 Dutch door.

The drawing room. The secretary is from the mid-1800s, the display case from the early 1800s, and the chandelier and wall sconces are Baccarat.

The canopy on this early twentieth-century Sheraton bed is hand-tied. Volunteers created the quilt that adorns this third-floor guest bedroom.

Woodburn's grounds combine elements of the original Hillyard design and extensive work undertaken by Senator Hastings between 1912 and 1918. The brick-bordered reflecting pool with fountain is east of the main house. Also on the grounds is the 1870s frame home to the north purchased by the state as a guest residence. An older garden feature is the pattern of boxwoods and flowers planted in the French parterre mosaic manner. The gardens also contain a giant sequoia redwood tree planted in 1974 as part of Delaware's bicentennial celebration and the "bride and groom" American holly trees planted in 1992 at the wedding of Governor Michael N. Castle.

But with ghosts in the house and legends of deep tunnels connected to the Underground Railroad, the gardens can't escape Woodburn's history. On the south lawn stands an ancient tulip poplar dating from the 1680s. Its trunk is hollow—perhaps from age, or maybe by design: one Woodburn legend says that a runaway slave hid there on a long-ago October night.

PENNSYLVANIA

THE GOVERNOR'S RESIDENCE
HARRISBURG

PHOTOGRAPHS BY ALLAN HOLM

The drawing room. The wallpaper depicts Pizarro's conquest of Peru and was hand-painted in Paris around 1826.

*E*very schoolchild knows the story of William Penn, the upper-class Londoner who sided with the persecuted Quakers, convinced King Charles II to give him a land grant in the New World, and founded what was to become a cradle of American liberties. Pennsylvania was one of the success tales of the Colonial period. By the time of the Revolution, Philadelphia was the second-largest English-speaking city on earth. For a time it was our national capital, and around it swirled titanic events—the signing of the Declaration of Independence, key battles fought by the Continental Army, and the convening of the Constitutional Convention. But as the nation's capital shifted south in 1800 to the new federal city on the Potomac, Pennsylvania changed as well. Its state capital moved first to Lancaster and then to Harrisburg. The governors followed, and until the eve of the Civil War, they rented temporary lodgings or bought their own homes.

In 1858, the Pennsylvania legislature voted to acquire an official state residence on South Second Street in Harrisburg. Governor Andrew Curtin, the stalwart Civil War governor whose support was crucial to Abraham Lincoln, was the first to live there, but he soon found it too small for the many wartime crisis meetings he convened in the dark days that led up to the South's invasion of the state and the battle at Gettysburg. In 1864, the state traded the original mansion (it later became a hardware store) for a larger home overlooking the Susquehanna River. Dubbed Keystone Hall, the new mansion was expanded and modified several times over the years. It was originally a pair of adjacent four-story brick residences, later joined to double the available space. In the 1880s, the state added a delicate brownstone facade. But by the 1950s, first families were spending most of their time at the state's official summer residence at Fort Indiantown Gap, thirty miles from Harrisburg. Keystone Hall had been relegated to ceremonial use.

In 1966, the state broke ground several blocks north of Keystone Hall for what would become Pennsylvania's third governor's mansion. Keystone Hall was sold at auction (it has since been razed), and in 1968 the family of Governor Raymond Shafer became the first to live in the new residence.

The architect George Ewing chose the eighteenth-century English Georgian style for the mansion. He wanted it to reflect Pennsylvania's Colonial roots and traditions, but his design was utilitarian as well, with open, spacious rooms for entertaining and public functions.

The twenty-two-room brick Governor's Residence has a two-and-a-half-story central living section flanked by two single-story wings and a garage. From the outside, it is an imposing structure, with its three wide chimneys and four bay windows. Inside, the charm of the public room reflects a careful search for eighteenth- and nineteenth-century period furnishings.

Opposite:
The entrance hall. During the holiday season the hall can accommodate a twenty-foot Christmas tree.

Above:
The state dining room, seen from the reception room. The dining room is an expansive area capable of seating one hundred fifty guests.

Pennsylvania recruited a seventeen-member committee to oversee the decoration and furnishing of the Residence. Its efforts are apparent in every room, but the results of this work were almost lost within a decade: In 1972 Hurricane Agnes flooded Harrisburg, and state workers scrambled to salvage valuable furnishings, carpets, and draperies as muddy water rose steadily in the mansion's first floor. The extensive damage was repaired within two years, and today the Governor's Residence blends modern utility and Colonial elegance.

Guests are immediately impressed with the soaring entrance hall on the first floor; the hall can accommodate a twenty-foot Christmas tree during the holiday season. The first-floor entrance hall is dominated by a graceful staircase. The antiques-filled entrance hall and the grand hall are connected by an arched opening. The hand-painted Oriental wallpaper in the grand hall is a copy of an eighteenth-century design from an early Philadelphia home. On the floor is an antique Persian rug, and overhead hangs an 1890 Regency chandelier from England. Visitors can view multiple self-images in the unique Chippendale mirrors installed here; they date to 1760.

The governor's library is paneled in Pennsylvania walnut, with a Regency walnut pedestal desk from 1835. The fireplace andirons are of brass and date from the nineteenth century. The grand hall's Oriental wallpaper motif is reflected in the library's 1820 Chinese garden seat.

In the formal dining room, the reproduction of an eighteenth-century mahogany table accommodates twenty. Guests are seated on replicas of Philadelphia Chippendale chairs made by the Gulden Gallery of Aspers, Pennsylvania. The fireplace mantel dates from 1815–25, with classical plaster ornamentation by Robert Wellford of Philadelphia. The mantel also features a mahogany shelf and ornamented columns. Against the wall is a mahogany Sheraton bowfront sideboard, supported by unique square tapered legs with spade feet. A matching pair of bowfront commodes was once in the collection at Cannon Hall in York, England.

A mahogany wall carving of the Pennsylvania coat of arms dominates the much larger state dining room, which seats up to one hundred fifty guests. The state coat of arms can also be seen on the Lenox Springfield china and the International 1810 silver. Overhead, lead crystal chandeliers and matching sconces light the broad room; they are of Czechoslovakian origin.

The Erie room, also known as the family living room, is a showcase of Federal-period antiques. The room derives its name from the Robert Wellford antique mantel, with a central carved panel depicting the 1813 Battle of Lake Erie. The Hepplewhite tall case clock dates from around 1800. A unique secretary desk, dating from 1810, is the room's most impressive piece. Carefully crafted of mahogany in a Sheraton design, the desk has a Gothic-paned bookcase section and a number of concealed compartments. The Erie room is also a showplace for Paris porcelain lamps, vases, and

The governor's library.
The Regency walnut pedestal
desk dates from 1835.

Above:

The Erie room. The antique mantel displays a carved rendering of the 1813 Battle of Lake Erie. Furnishings in this family living area are Federal-period antiques.

Right:

The screened sun porch overlooks the perennial gardens.

pierced baskets; a 1780 miniature English chest; an 1810 mahogany card table; and a cherry Hepplewhite chest with the signature "Amos Titus, 1802." It was donated by the people of Erie.

The drawing room is also a showplace for antiques. The 1780 Hepplewhite settee matches the Hepplewhite wheelback armchairs. The room also features mahogany Chippendale armchairs and Hepplewhite window benches with carved mahogany cabriole legs. A black lacquered panel table and several stands, garden seats, and porcelain items echo the Oriental theme. So does the hand-woven Chinese rug. The wide variety of drawing-room tables includes two in the Pembroke style and a Queen Anne drop-leaf table with cabriole legs and trifid feet. The room centers on a walnut Federal-style piano made in Philadelphia between 1800 and 1825. The drawing-room chandelier is the oldest in the Residence; of antique crystal

from the Regency period, it dates from 1810 and has been wired for electricity. The wallpaper was created from antique French hand-blocked panels and depicts Francisco Pizarro's conquest of Peru. It was hand-painted by the Joseph DuFours Company of Paris around 1826.

The central portion of the Residence also includes the governor's private living quarters, and the wings house offices, staff-support areas, and the state rooms. A screened porch with wrought-iron furnishings overlooks the main lawn and provides a view of the Susquehanna River. The grounds include a formal rose garden, a vegetable garden, an herb garden, and a large sycamore tree with a tree house. There is a small fish pond, and the grounds are dotted with outstanding specimens of Pennsylvania's state flower, the mountain laurel, and the hemlock, the state tree.

A small herb garden yields a wide selection of culinary herbs.

New Jersey

Drumthwacket
Princeton

Photographs by Melabee M. Miller

Drumthwacket.

"Here Freedom stood . . ."

On January 3, 1777, in one of the decisive engagements of the American Revolution, Continental troops under the command of General George Washington surprised the British near Princeton, New Jersey, and kept alive the waning hopes of the rebellious colonists. Before the battle, the British commander, General Cornwallis, seized a nearby home named Morven and made it his headquarters. Just down the road, Washington stood and watched his troops march to victory across land that would one day give rise to a palatial home known as Drumthwacket. Both residences would eventually serve, in turn, as New Jersey's official governor's mansion, and on the land that surrounds them there is a plaque inscribed with a poem paying tribute to those who died in the cause of liberty: "Here Freedom stood . . ." the poem begins. Freedom still stands there today. Drumthwacket is one of the most fabled and elegant of America's executive residences, and in its history lie the stories of three unique families and of three centuries of American history.

The story of Drumthwacket is inextricably linked to that of Morven, as both are rooted in the rich Colonial traditions of New Jersey. The two residences share land once owned by William Penn, the Quaker who founded the colony of Pennsylvania, which originally included much of modern New Jersey. In 1696, William Olden acquired the future site of Drumthwacket from his brother, who had purchased a larger tract from Penn, and five years later Richard Stockton purchased what would become known as Morven. The home remained in the Stockton family for two centuries. In 1945, the then governor, Walter Edge, purchased Morven with the intention of making it New Jersey's official state residence. Edge and his wife deeded the home and its five-acre elm-spotted grounds to the state in 1954, and after extensive remodeling, Morven became New Jersey's first official governor's mansion. It remains state property today, as a historic home and museum.

The land where Drumthwacket would be built went through three generations of the Olden family before Charles Smith Olden constructed what was to become one of Princeton's most stately mansions in 1835. Olden had lived for a time in New Orleans, and he was inspired by the plantation architecture of the Old South. The Drumthwacket that rose from the rolling fields of New Jersey was something of an architectural transplant, with the Greek Revival flair then popular in New Orleans's Garden District. The home had a massive portico with detailed Ionic columns. A newspaper description of the time aptly called it "baronial."

Charles Olden borrowed two Scottish Gaelic words for the name Drumthwacket. *Drum* means "hill," and *thwacket* is an ancient Scottish term best translated as "thicket or wooded area." Olden also entered politics, serving as the pro-Union Civil War governor of New Jersey. For four years, from 1859 to 1863, Drumthwacket was the unofficial executive residence.

Drumthwacket passed into the hands of Moses Taylor Pyne during the final decade of the eighteenth century. Ironically, Pyne's wife was a Stockton, of Morven fame, further linking the two historic homes. Pyne was a leading industrialist and banker who invested heavily in Drumthwacket. He first added a large, two-story east wing in 1893, and in 1900 he duplicated that addition to the west, expanding the home on either side of its distinctive porticoed central section. A landscape architect designed elaborate gardens, ponds, and pathways, including a formal seventeenth-century Italianate garden. Pyne constructed greenhouses and added a dairy operation, as well as a butler's home and a carriage house. By the turn of the century, the three-hundred-acre estate was the most elegant in Princeton.

Pyne's granddaughter Agnes inherited Drumthwacket in 1939. She subdivided portions of the grounds, which are now the sites of private homes. In 1941, Abram Nathaniel Spanel purchased the main house and twelve surrounding acres. Spanel's was a classic American success story: he was a Russian immigrant who worked his way to an engineering degree and achieved enormous wealth as an ingenious inventor and scientist. Among his many patents were latex products marketed under the Playtex brand.

Spanel sold Drumthwacket to the state of New Jersey in 1966, with the intention that it become the new official executive residence. Due to debates over costs, Morven remained the governor's mansion for another two decades, while Drumthwacket was used for conferences, special events, and even an art show. Finally, in 1981, the New Jersey State Historical Society raised funds to launch the rehabilitation of Drumthwacket and convert Morven into a museum. The extensive restoration of Drumthwacket addressed the smallest details. Preservation architects William Short and Jeremiah Ford III returned ceiling murals and the carved limestone Gothic mantelpiece in the library to their original splendor.

The Drumthwacket Foundation was created in 1982 to assume the curatorship of the house and its history, and to be responsible for loans, gifts, and acquisitions. Private-sector donations continue to support the Foundation today. The Foundation trustees, working with the Friends of Drumthwacket, have furnished the public rooms with eighteenth- and nineteenth-century antiques, focusing on New Jersey pieces. They have also rehabilitated the gardens, refurbished the private apartments, and completed the restoration of the Olden house, the eighteenth-century birthplace of the original owner of Drumthwacket.

Modern Drumthwacket invites visitors past Olden's six dramatic pillars spanning the portico into a broad central hall little changed since the original central portion of the

home was constructed in 1835. A centerpiece of the entry hall is the painting *Washington at the Battle of Princeton,* on loan from the Art Museum at Princeton University, depicting the historic event that occurred within walking distance of Drumthwacket. On the opposite wall is a 1765 Chippendale mirror that hangs above a Queen Anne dressing table. Chippendale Colonial walnut chairs flank the table, and the initial impression is solidly Colonial. A restored banistered stairway leads to a landing with a Palladian window, but visitors are inevitably drawn to the major public rooms on the ground floor, which extend into the two flanking wings that were added near the end of the nineteenth century by Moses Taylor Pyne.

To the left is the dining room, where the Sheraton mahogany table seats twenty-four. The table was originally selected for Morven, and the Georgian chairs were acquired by the Drumthwacket Foundation in 1984. Chinese hand-painted wallpaper covers the walls; each of the twenty-nine panels is distinctive in its depiction of birds, flowers, and butterflies. The room also contains the silver service from the U.S.S. *New Jersey,* the only battleship used during the Vietnam War.

Across the hall, in the parlor, visitors cross Tabriz Persian rugs to view

the 1797 Egerton tall case clock, two Egerton Pembroke tables, and a display of New Jersey porcelain.

Antiques fill the adjacent music room and the Tudor-style library, and in the latter is a candle stand with a unique heritage; the inscription gives its special origin: "Made by James Madison, class of 1771, president of the United States." The oak-paneled library also features an elaborately carved Caen stone fireplace and connects to a small horseshoe-shaped study with an oval desk, on which sits a Tiffany sterling desk set. Curved bay windows overlook the pond and formal gardens.

Above the library, the master bedroom suite features a circular entrance vestibule with a stained glass dome. The remainder of the east and west wing rooms include living quarters, kitchen, and service facilities.

The Drumthwacket grounds are more like a park than those of a residence, with terraces, broad walkways, fountains, and other remnants of the Pyne era. Mature trees dot the twelve-acre grounds. Wrought-iron entrance gates complete the impression of a stately manor house.

That landscape witnessed the battle for American independence. It has been home to families of achievement, and today it is the site of one of America's most historic homes, Drumthwacket, where New Jersey's first families are the most recent heirs to three centuries of tradition.

Visitors to Drumthwacket can stroll from the solarium into the formal gardens.

GEORGIA

THE GOVERNOR'S MANSION
ATLANTA

PHOTOGRAPHS BY KEN HAWKINS

Glory risen from the ashes . . .

I n 1864, it was Georgia's turn. Of all the states of the old Confederacy, Georgia was destined to suffer most grievously as the advancing Union armies moved closer to victory. Confederate general John Bell Hood lost the Battle of Atlanta in November, and his archrival, Union general William Tecumseh Sherman, pursued him to the state capital at Milledgeville, where Sherman lodged in the old governor's mansion to plan his next offensive, the legendary march to Savannah and the sea. Behind him, Atlanta lay in ruins. Ahead of him lay further devastation for the people of Georgia. For nearly a century, the state would remember 1864 with bitterness. But it would also rebuild. Today, Atlanta is one of America's great cities, host to the 1996 Olympic Games, and a symbol of the New South. It is also home to one of our most beautiful executive residences, one crafted where a century before there were only ashes.

Founded in 1733, Georgia was the southernmost of the original thirteen colonies and the last to be established. After it joined the united colonies in the War of Independence, its citizens moved quickly to establish the physical structures of government. The original mansion in Milledgeville would not be erected until 1837–38, but civic leaders had planned it in 1803 as they drew maps of the new capital city. They wrote Governor John Milledge, for whom the community would be named, "We have agreed on a place and laid it on the ground . . . one for a statehouse, one for a Governor's residence." The original mansion is a fine example of Greek Revival architecture, with two stories and a basement, a brick exterior, and a portico with four Ionic columns. Inside is a unique central rotunda, surrounded by an entrance hall, a drawing room, a library, a dining room, and a parlor. In the basement is a large banquet room, and there were four bedrooms at the top of the stairs. A railed, cantilevered balcony encircled the rotunda, which measured twenty-five feet in diameter and soared fifty feet to a skylighted dome. A spiral staircase connects the ground level and second floor.

Eight first families would live in the old mansion until General Sherman and his troops arrived. In 1861, Governor Joseph Brown had celebrated Georgia's secession there, but a few years later the mansion was occupied by Union troops, who destroyed or carried off most of its furnishings, and then converted for use as part of a girls' school. In 1965 the state began a major restoration. The old mansion, by then part of the grounds of Georgia College, was converted into a museum, a place for university functions, and a residence for the college president. Its public rooms were refurnished in English Regency and American neoclassical antiques.

Atlanta had already replaced Milledgeville as Georgia's capital city. As the region's primary rail junction, it had far outstripped the smaller

The Georgia Governor's Mansion and grounds.

community to the southeast in population and influence, and in 1868, as Georgia emerged from Reconstruction, the new legislature moved the capital there. The state soon purchased the John H. James mansion on Peachtree Street, and Georgia's governors lived in it until 1921. In 1925, the state acquired a third executive residence, known as the Ansley house, after its original owner. The house had been designed by Anthony Ten Eyck Brown and was constructed of Georgia granite. Its wide veranda and open reception areas made it ideal for public functions, but by the 1960s it had fallen into disrepair. One legislator called it "cold, gray, austere and medieval"—hardly the symbol of the New South.

In 1966, the state launched an ambitious project, the construction of the modern Governor's Mansion on the site of Woodhaven, an eighteen-acre estate owned by a former Atlanta mayor, Robert Foster Maddox. The site already included a formal terraced garden; what remained was to design and build a mansion that reflected Georgia's Southern heritage and Atlanta's increasing prominence. A fine-arts committee, including architects and art historians, took part in the planning and began assembling a collection of art and furnishings. Today, that collection is considered one of the finest of its kind in the world.

The mansion that rose on the old Maddox estate spanned nearly twenty-five thousand square feet behind thirty fluted Doric columns. The twenty-four-foot columns, crafted from California redwood trunks, rest on a wide brick porch and support an unadorned wooden cornice. Architect A. Thomas Bradbury chose to follow the Greek Revival style of the old Milledgeville mansion, but on a much grander scale. The thirty-room Governor's Mansion was completed in 1968.

Visitors approaching the Mansion enter through wooded grounds, where formal gardens, swimming pool, fountains, and reflecting pools remind them that this was once the site of one of Atlanta's grand estates. Concrete walkways and steps wind through the grounds, past hedges and grass pathways.

The dark mahogany front door stands more than eight feet tall. In the entryway, the Georgia state seal, in bronze, adorns the marble floor. The entrance opens into a reception area, where Bradbury borrowed a design feature from the old Milledgeville mansion, incorporating a circular stairway that serves the second floor. At the center of the circular hall is a huge eighteenth-century Italian gold-and-crystal chandelier. The circular hall contains two of the Mansion's most cherished artifacts. On the wall hangs a Samuel King copy of the 1776 Charles Willson Peale full-length portrait

The French porcelain vase bears a portrait of Benjamin Franklin.

The state dining room. The New England accordion table rests on a Sultanabad carpet. The chairs are reproductions of a set from the home of a former governor.

of George Washington as commander of the Continental Army. In the hall there is also an 1810 gilded Sèvres vase bearing a hand-painted portrait of Benjamin Franklin. Franklin represented Colonial Georgia at the Court of St. James's.

In the state drawing room, the Mansion's Federal furnishings are some of the house's finest. There are eight pieces attributed to Duncan Phyfe: a pair of Pembroke tables, four side chairs with bronze mounts, and two sofas, which are upholstered in different red and gold silk damask by Scala-

mandré. A pair of portraits by John Neagle are of Lieutenant and Mrs. John Marston of Philadelphia.

The smaller family living room is more relaxed and less formal. It is paneled in soft butternut and features a scroll sofa with winged-paw feet dating to 1815.

The library is paneled in cherry, with built-in shelves holding an important collection of books by Georgia authors about the state and its history. There are signed first editions by Joel Chandler Harris, Erskine Caldwell, Carson McCullers, and Flannery O'Connor, as well as a first edition of *Gone With the Wind,* autographed by Margaret Mitchell.

The state dining room seats eighteen at the mahogany table, attributed to John Seymour of Boston. The carpet is by Sultanabad and was made in Turkey around 1820. The sideboard dates to 1810 and holds the punch bowl from the U.S.S. *Georgia,* a battleship commissioned in 1907. The dining-room mantelpiece was crafted in England in white and green marble. It is topped by an Irish bull's-eye mirror from about 1810.

There is a first-floor guest bedroom in addition to other bedrooms and living quarters on the second floor. The guest bedroom is hung with nineteenth-century hand-painted French wallpaper and has an 1815 alcove bed and English needlepoint carpet, as well as an English writing desk. The upstairs presidential suite is used by presidents who visit the Mansion; Prince Charles of Great Britain was also once a guest there. The suite has a sitting room and separate aide's quarters. The Carter bedroom contains furnishings used by Governor Jimmy Carter before he was elected to the White House in 1976.

Ironically, Carter was among the most vocal opponents of the Mansion's construction when he served as a member of the Georgia state senate

Opposite:
The circular hall. Columns with Ionic capitals flank the doorway leading to the family dining room. The chandelier is of Italian design.

Above:
The dining-room fireplace.

in the 1960s. In 1992, when many of those who had served on the planning committee for the Mansion gathered for a reunion, Carter once again visited this splendid home situated in a city that had once been reduced to ashes. He recalled his futile efforts to stop the Mansion project three decades earlier.

"I'm glad I was voted down," the former president said. "[It] is not just a governor's mansion, but a museum for the South and the nation."

The state drawing room. The sofas were made in New York in 1810 and 1815, respectively. The Pembroke tables flanking the scroll sofa date from 1800.

CONNECTICUT

THE GOVERNOR'S RESIDENCE
HARTFORD

PHOTOGRAPHS BY ROBERT BENSON

The entrance hall. Corinthian columns flank the stairway and the guardian statue of Nathan Hale.

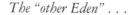
ifty years after Connecticut acquired its first official executive residence, Florence Berkman wrote of her unique connection to the house. She and her husband had moved into a small carriage house that was part of an original private estate that centered on a beautiful Georgian-style home. That was in 1941, and two years later, Connecticut bought the main house and converted it into the Governor's Residence. Some first families had done well by the old house, Mrs. Berkman said; others had not. But it still held the original charm she and her husband had first noted a half century earlier. It was, they decided, the "other Eden."

Connecticut residents are proud of their state's Yankee independence. The Fundamental Orders of 1639 constitute one of the first proclamations of democratic principles in the Colonial era; a century and a half before the ratification of the United States Constitution, the early settlers of Connecticut were declaring their faith in self-determination. It was Connecticut's Israel Putnam who told his troops at Bunker Hill, "Don't fire until you see the whites of their eyes!" Connecticut's Nathan Hale regretted that he had but one life to give for his new country. Connecticut's Colonial governor, Jonathan Trumbull, stood alone among the appointed governors of the thirteen colonies in supporting the cause of independence. With its self-reliant people (and its relatively small area), it was not surprising that Connecticut made no residential provisions for its elected governors between 1789 and 1943.

In the latter year, Governor Robert A. Hurley was living in a small Hartford house, unfit for entertaining or for state functions. A committee searching for a permanent executive residence viewed thirty-nine properties before it found Florence Berkman's "other Eden," the ancestral home of one of Hartford's wealthiest families. It rested on a hill, surrounded by six wooded acres. The site had been carefully selected in the first decade of the twentieth century, when Dr. George C. F. Williams decided he needed the best house his money could buy.

Williams (his friends said the initials stood for "comfortably fixed") was connected with a leading Hartford manufacturing firm. He had once been a physician, but when he fell from a horse and injured his leg while making a house call, Dr. Williams decided to shift careers. Ironically, he joined Capewell & Company, the country's leading maker of horseshoe nails. Williams hired the Boston architectural firm of Andrews, Jacques & Rantoul to design his new home, having been impressed with their work on the Revival-style Hartford Club. The Georgian design they created in 1908 for the Williams estate merged eighteenth-century American styles and the classical Greek themes so popular with the leading American industrialists, who sought to exemplify their prosperity in brick and stone.

It was constructed of brick with limestone trim and a towering slate roof. The three-story house had three tall chimneys and a railed second-story veranda. Williams would be closely identified with the elegant home over the years. In 1916 he added north and south wings to the original central house, and in 1927 the house grew once more, with the addition of an upstairs maid's room. The grounds also boasted a carriage house, a grass tennis court, and a greenhouse.

Dr. Williams was a cultured man who collected rare books and acquired the signatures of all seventy-six signers of the Declaration of Independence (the collection sold in 1926 for seventy thousand dollars). After Dr. Williams died in 1933, his son Staunton lived there briefly. The house was also used as a convalescent hospital, but by 1943 it stood vacant and in disrepair. The state purchased it for more than thirty-nine thousand dollars—money owed in back taxes—and began the extensive and expensive work of refurbishing it as Connecticut's executive residence. It was clearly a bargain, with its fifteen thousand square feet, nineteen rooms, nine fireplaces, a greenhouse, and a reflecting pool on acres of wooded grounds.

Governor Raymond Baldwin and his family moved in on September 14, 1945, an event noted in the paper beneath a headline that declared, "Residence Is Designed for Comfort . . . Eighteenth Century Motif Prevails Throughout Governor's Home." The house had nineteen rooms, the article said. It failed to note that structural restoration had absorbed most of the refurbishing costs. (When workmen had peeled the climbing ivy away from one exterior stairway, the stairway had fallen down.) Inside, the Residence's furnishings were what one official history calls "a con-glomeration of mismatched unrelated furniture in a myriad of styles." A local department-store owner came to the rescue, and through a combination of trades and new acquisitions, the Residence was soon decorated in eighteenth-century antiques and reproductions that matched its architectural style. Among the finest pieces were those created by Hartford cabinetmaker Nathan Margolis, who had previously executed commissions for the Rockefeller and du Pont families.

The first visitors to the Residence overlooked its inadequate furnishings to focus on the home's glorious design. In the entrance hall, adorned with Baroque wallpaper (later replaced), the stairway was flanked by Corinthian columns. On one side was the cozy, leathered library, adjoined by the living room, built around an unusual Duncan Phyfe sofa. The Mar-

The painting Connecticut Landscape *by Wilson Irvine hangs in the dining room above pieces from the U.S.S.* Connecticut *silver service.*

Right:

The dining room. The chairs and other furnishings were designed in eighteenth-century Chippendale style. The sideboard is Hepplewhite style.

Below:

The library. The woodwork is faux-painted burled maple. The tavern table in front of the fireplace dates from the late 1700s and is one of only three known surviving pieces by the cabinetmaker Amzi Chapin.

Opposite:

*The south entrance to the Residence
is reflected in a newly installed
swimming pool.*

Below:

*The south grounds include a pool,
cabana, fountain, and rose garden.
The view is from the sunroom.*

golis furniture added later included a dining-room table with twenty Chippendale-style chairs, each with carved and fluted legs and brass claw casters. Margolis also created a pair of claw-foot hall benches for the entrance hall, borrowing their design from a chair originally owned by Stephen Hopkins, one of the signers of the Declaration of Independence. Among other Margolis pieces were a pair of Hepplewhite inlaid plant stands, a mahogany two-drawer top-leaf table, and a pair of carved chairs copied from originals in the Metropolitan Museum of Art, New York. Margolis also designed a pair of Hepplewhite console tables with figured crotch mahogany fronts inlaid with satinwood and ebony.

Over the years, first families have added other touches. The dining room now contains a Hepplewhite-style sideboard, a Chippendale-style breakfront, and a sterling silver tea service. A Federal bull's-eye mirror hangs over the living-room fireplace, and there is an Empire-style tabernacle mirror from the 1830s with applied plaster rosettes and a burnished gold-leaf finish. Vases beside the fireplace date from around 1840 and are

of German origin. In the smaller family dining room are Hitchcock chairs acquired during the original restoration. The Residence is an eclectic mixture of pieces and styles: French Empire bronze candelabras decorate the entrance hall, while in the reception hall, early eighteenth-century scroll-top mirrors display unique hand-painted panels.

First Lady Francesca Lodge (1951–55) was among the most enthusiastic patrons of the Residence. She extolled its "simple elegance, typical of the best New England taste." Other first families were less thrilled, although one governor who chafed at the Residence's size later admitted that, after time, "we all had the feeling that it was our home." In later years, the state formed the Governor's Residence Conservancy to preserve the Residence. By the early 1990s, serious restoration efforts were under way, focusing on the primary downstairs public rooms. The Conservancy plans to continue adding to the collection of period Connecticut antiques.

The ongoing restoration efforts have also furnished the rooms in rattan items and added antiques that include a 1740 Connecticut maple and pine tea-and-tavern table, a 1790s cherry oval Pembroke table, and an 1850 brass skater's lamp. The sunroom mantel has been decorated with a collection of Connecticut-made pewter.

The Conservancy has also acquired a rare cherry Queen Anne breakfast table, which is used in the library. The table has an oversized molded and dished top, a turned bird-cage support, and elongated cabriole legs with pad feet. The table is one of only three known pieces in existence by the Connecticut cabinetmaker Amzi Chapin. Among other Conservancy acquisitions for the growing collection are a pair of 1795 andirons for the dining room and the antique silver service from the U.S.S. *Connecticut.* This thirty-six-piece set was created in 1906 and was reacquired for the state through the fund-raising efforts of Connecticut citizens and schoolchildren.

Loaned art displayed in the Residence includes works that reflect Connecticut landscapes and people, as well as portraits of historic figures like Silas Deane, America's first envoy to France; and Mark Twain, who called Hartford home during his most productive writing period.

On the Residence grounds, the Conservancy has added a swimming pool and cabana on the site of Dr. Williams's original wading pool. The Conservancy is also planning to restore the grounds and gardens to their 1920s state. The entrance hall has been improved with an inlaid version of the Connecticut State Shield. An 1898 Knabe piano, which once stood in the hallway, has been restored. The "other Eden" remains a work in progress.

Newspaper accounts of the first public reception at the Residence in 1945 quoted the ecstatic reactions of visitors. Said one: "It really is a great place, isn't it?"

The breakfast room. The Connecticut artist Barbara Lawless created the mural, depicting the state's landscape.

MARYLAND

GOVERNMENT HOUSE
ANNAPOLIS

PHOTOGRAPHS BY RICHARD LIPPENHOLZ

Government House.

nnapolis has always been identified with the sea. The United States Naval Academy is here, and the statehouse sits within blocks of the Chesapeake Bay. Maryland has an official state crustacean, the blue crab, and a state boat, the bay-skimming skipjack. This was a colony founded on shipping and trade, and in virtually every early etching of Annapolis or Baltimore, the sky is crowded with the masts of clippers. When the Colonial governor, Thomas Bladen, decided to build an official executive residence in 1742, he made the obvious choice: a plot near College Creek, on one of Maryland's innumerable fingers of land that jut into the bay.

Bladen was thwarted in his plans of grandeur by the rising Colonial objections to all things that smacked of British rule. His mansion was never completed, and it was eventually handed over to St. John's College. Later, Governor Horatio Sharpe leased Jennings House, a fine brick Colonial home with an English garden that ran to the water's edge, on the present grounds of the Naval Academy. Jennings House had been built sometime before 1750. "The governor's house is most beautifully situated," a contemporary account said. "This elevation commands an extensive view of the bay and the adjacent country. . . . There are but few mansions in the most rich and cultivated parts of England which are adorned with such splendid and romantic scenery."

The "adjacent country" and its inhabitants were through with British rule; Colonial governor Robert Eden, who had purchased Jennings House in 1769, fled aboard a British frigate in 1776, and the new state of Maryland confiscated his house for official use, renaming it Government House. For the next ninety years, it was Maryland's official executive residence, the scene of much history. There are homes in the East that proudly claim that "George Washington slept here," but Maryland's Government House could boast multiple visits by the first president. Of Washington's eighteen known visits to Annapolis, on nearly every occasion he recorded a visit to the governor's home. After the British surrender at Yorktown, Washington visited Annapolis in triumph. "The General's arrival was announced by the discharge of cannon," noted a *Maryland Gazette* account. "The evening was spent at the Governor's elegant and hospitable board with festive joy enlivened by good humor, wit and beauty."

Old Government House served Maryland's first families until 1866, when it was sold for twenty-five thousand dollars to the Naval Academy next door. The Academy used it for many years as offices for the superintendent and as a library. It was demolished in the early years of the twentieth century to make room for new midshipmen's dormitories.

In 1868, the state acquired land in the heart of Annapolis for the new Government House. Colonel R. Snowden Andrews of Baltimore designed

Opening page: The new colony of "Maryland" was named after Henrietta Maria, Queen of England (1609–1669), by Cecil Calvert, the second Lord Baltimore. This portrait of her adorns the entry hall of Government House.

a mid-Victorian brick home with a mansard roof, and in 1870 Governor Oden Bowie and his family moved in—without furnishings. It took an additional six years to finish the interior and landscape the grounds. Government House was extensively remodeled in the 1930s; architect Clyde N. Friz engineered a major renovation that included the addition of two wings flanking the original central section and conversion of the home into a five-part Georgian-style country house. Government House was further modified in the 1940s, with the addition of a powder room in the conservatory, and in the 1980s, under the auspices of the newly created Government House Trust, the home got a new skylight and grounds improvements. The Trust, established by the Maryland legislature, continues its effort to preserve and maintain the state's most historic home.

Visitors approach Government House over a lawn crisscrossed by wide brick walkways and colorful flower beds. The gardens extend around three sides of the house, with each garden section representing one of the state's three primary regions—tidewater, the piedmont, and rural western Maryland. The house is among trees. Wide white steps lead to the front door, framed by columns with Ionic capitals; to the right is a marking stone placed during construction of the house in 1868.

Visitors actually enter the second floor of the house. Downstairs are administrative offices and the kitchen. The main-floor entry hallway features Maryland and United States flags, plants on antique neo-Grecian walnut stands, and a Victorian damask wall covering by Scalamandré. The sofas are Chippendale-style reproductions, upholstered in silk. The entry hall contains several examples of the extensive Government House collection of historic art, and these establish a theme that is carried through each of the seven public rooms. The portrait of Cecil Calvert, the second Lord Baltimore, acknowledges Maryland's rich Colonial history. Another portrait is of Queen Henrietta Maria, wife of Charles I of Britain, for whom Cecil Calvert named the new colony of Maryland. Above the portraits, Waterford chandeliers light the entry hall, and below there is an antique Kurd Bijar Persian rug. Leading up the central stairwell are portraits of past Maryland first ladies. The stairwell runner is an antique Maylayer, and the unique clock was made in the late nineteenth century (the clock's movement is connected to a Regina music box, which plays a variety of selections). Above the stairway, the skylight added in the 1980s echoes the design and materials of the 1880s.

The main-floor reception room reflects the Federal period. The mantel, like others in Government House, was installed in the 1935–36 restoration, and it replaced the original Victorian marble mantels. A mirror in the reception room was created in the *verre églomisé* style, with painting on the reverse side; the

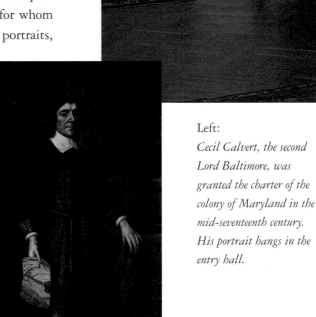

Left:
Cecil Calvert, the second Lord Baltimore, was granted the charter of the colony of Maryland in the mid-seventeenth century. His portrait hangs in the entry hall.

scene depicted is the burning of the British ship *Peggy Stewart* in 1774 by colonists protesting taxes on tea. Furnishings in the reception room include a 1780 drop-leaf table; a tall clock, made in the late eighteenth century, that once belonged to Governor Thomas Johnson, Jr., the state's first elected chief executive; and sofa seats and chairs in the Hepplewhite style. On loan from the Maryland Historical Society are a Federal lady's desk and a pair of Federal card tables. There are additional portraits of past first ladies here, along with a mural that is one of Government House's most treasured works of art. *The Last Moments of Command,* painted by Joseph Sheppard, depicts the scene on December 23, 1783, when General George Washington resigned his commission in the old senate chamber at the Maryland statehouse, where the Continental Congress was then in session.

The parlor reflects the Empire period. Furnishings include a Baltimore Empire sofa and Late Empire side chairs on loan from the Maryland Historical Society. A portrait of Thomas Johnson by Charles Willson Peale hangs in the parlor as well as additional first ladies' portraits. Tables in the parlor include an 1839 Empire pier table with a mirrored back, an Empire

Above:

The entry hall. Portraits lining the grand staircase are of past first ladies. The clock is a Regina.

Right:

The Victorian room. The parlor suite was made in Baltimore between 1865 and 1880 in the Renaissance Revival style.

Opposite:

The reception room. The mural is The Last Moments of Command, *depicting George Washington's final act as leader of the Continental Army.*

Below:

The state dining room. The Georgian banquet table seats up to twenty-two. Draperies are hand-loomed in nineteenth-century style.

center table, a pair of Baltimore Late Federal card tables, and a Baltimore Empire drum table.

The conservatory was one of the public rooms added in the 1935–36 renovation of Government House. Palladian windows give the room ample light, and the conservatory is filled with greenery. Furnishings here feature Maryland's artists and craftsmen. On loan from the Maryland Historical Society, the furniture displayed in this Maryland "regional showcase" represents various counties throughout the state.

The drawing room is used for large gatherings. The card table is of mahogany in the Federal style; the fifteen-hundred-piece Waterford chandelier adds to the elegance of this most public of Government House's rooms. As a tribute to Maryland's rich artistic history, the drawing room features changing displays of works from Maryland collections.

In the state dining room, guests sit around a Georgian-style mahogany four-pedestal table that seats up to twenty-two. The draperies here, as in many of the public rooms, are hand-loomed and reflect the styles of the nineteenth century. Two tabernacle mirrors bear the Maryland state seal; they were made for the house during the 1935–36 restoration. The ceremonial punch bowl also bears the state seal and was made in Baltimore by the firm of Samuel Kirk & Son. The room also houses a repoussé sterling coffee and tea service made by A. Jacobi & Company of Baltimore. A painting by Gawen Hamilton depicts the Sharpe family, including Colonial governor Horatio Sharpe, who first leased Jennings House as Maryland's governor's residence. Most of the state dining room furnishings were acquired by Governor Phillips Lee Goldsborough in 1912 and 1913 and made by Potthast Bros., a Baltimore firm that specialized in replicating early American designs. The original drawings are in the state archives.

The library retains the Victorian trappings of the original Government House, with its Renaissance Revival–style parlor suite, on loan from the Maryland State Historical Society and made in Baltimore between 1865 and 1880. The library also features Victorian wallpaper as well as panels and roundels from the house's original doors. The marble mantel matches those originally installed throughout the house, and there is a Victorian coal box beside it. The ceiling is decorated with plaster motifs from the historic 1870s Buckler House in Baltimore. On the wall is a photograph of Mark Twain standing on the front steps of Government House with Governor Edwin Warfield. The author visited Annapolis in 1907 for one of his final public appearances. An early nineteenth-century overmantel mirror in the library was owned by Governor Thomas Johnson, Jr.; it was presented to Government House in 1960 by his descendants.

The upper stories of Government House contain family living quarters. On spring nights when the windows are open and the breeze is right, Maryland's first families can scent the salt air from Chesapeake Bay and hear migrating geese honking overhead.

The conservatory. The sculpture is Lady with a Daisy *by Sanguinetti from about 1878. The Palladian-style windows were installed in the 1930s.*

SOUTH CAROLINA

THE GOVERNOR'S MANSION
COLUMBIA

PHOTOGRAPHS BY DOUG GILMORE

The South Carolina Governor's Mansion.

In a military tradition . . .

The history of South Carolina is filled with the heritage of the military. On June 28, 1776, South Carolina patriots scored the first decisive victory of the American Revolution. Barricaded inside a palmetto-log fort on Sullivan's Island, they repelled a British fleet and set the tone for later American successes at King's Mountain and Cowpens. Nearly eighty-five years later, South Carolina was the first of the Southern states to secede from the Union. South Carolinians fired the first shots of the Civil War, at Fort Sumter in Charleston Harbor. A cavalry sword dating to the War of 1812 is still a treasured symbol of the state; it hangs in the South Carolina senate chamber during sessions. The oldest monument on the statehouse grounds honors the members of the Palmetto Regiment who fought in the Mexican War. Confederate cavalry general Wade Hampton served as governor after the Civil War, and the state's current Governor's Mansion is a house that once served as home to the officers of a military academy, and which sits on a rise still called Arsenal Hill. During World War I, Governor Richard Manning hung a flag bearing five stars from the Mansion portico, to honor his five sons, all serving in France. One of them died there.

That proud military heritage dates to the Colonial period, when the very first home that could be called a governor's residence housed William Sayle, sent to govern the proprietary colony of South Carolina in 1670. The large frame home in the original settlement of Charles Town (later moved to Oyster Point and shortened to Charleston) was surrounded by a staked palisade and armed with four cannons to ward off Indians and Spanish trespassers.

The seat of government shifted several times prior to the Revolution. In 1712, the Colonial general assembly set aside funds to buy or build an executive residence, and by 1730 South Carolina had constructed a brick home on a plantation alternately known as Belvedere or the Point. While the first royal governor lived there for five years, subsequent governors chose other homes. In the 1740s, governors rented the magnificent Charleston home built by Charles Pinckney, one of the colony's leading citizens. But in 1786, following the War of Independence, the state capital followed South Carolina's growing population inland, to Columbia. There was no perceived need to build a new governor's residence, since chief executives were expected to live in Columbia only during the legislative sessions.

In 1842, the Arsenal Military Academy was established in Columbia to train officers for the state militia. Its buildings were erected atop Arsenal Hill, in a neighborhood dominated by the fine homes and mansions of South Carolina's planter elite. By 1855 the institution had grown, and the state invested more than thirteen thousand dollars in a residence for the

Arsenal faculty members. Although history has misplaced the architect's name, the two-story home was probably designed by George Edward Walker, renowned for his church and library designs. The contract, awarded to builders Clark Waring, Thomas Jefferson Goodwyn, and James S. Boatwright, specified "two Two-Story Brick Tenement Dwelling Houses" with a common wall. (A decade later, Goodwyn, as mayor of Columbia in 1865, would surrender the city to the Union troops of General William Tecumseh Sherman.)

Arsenal faculty members occupied the new home in 1856, and during the Civil War the school was merged with the Citadel, the state's other

Above:
The library. The book collection features titles by South Carolina authors.

military school. The tenements escaped damage when Sherman's troops burned much of Columbia. In 1868, Governor James L. Orr, prompted by the postwar housing shortage in the capital, suggested that the structure be set aside as South Carolina's executive residence. But he was not the first governor to live in the new Mansion. Robert Scott, the Union military governor, took up residence there in 1869.

Scott supervised an extensive remodeling to convert the Mansion from its original design as a faculty dormitory to a single residence. A central wall was removed and exterior doors were modified or sealed. Scott was so pleased with the results that he offered to buy the Mansion for twenty thousand dollars when his term expired, but the state refused. Subsequent governors alternated between living in the Mansion and leasing or buying private homes, and in the 1870s it was leased for a time to a private operator who used it as a boardinghouse. In the 1880s much of the front lawn was taken up by a vegetable garden, and there were cows and chickens roaming the grounds. In the decades that followed, different first families added their own touches—an iron fence, a fountain, marble flooring, and new dining-room furniture that was acquired in 1907 and is still in use

Right:

The family dining room. The nineteenth-century wallpaper by Jean Zuber depicts early America as seen through a Frenchman's eyes. The same paper was used by Mrs. John F. Kennedy when she redecorated the White House.

Below:

The state dining room. The wallpaper depicts South Carolina's state tree, the palmetto. The silver service is from the U.S.S. South Carolina, christened in 1908.

today. After World War I, the Mansion underwent yet another major remodeling, and a former stable was converted into a greenhouse. One first lady improved the grounds in 1924; another created new wooden mantels, one bearing the state seal in the years before World War II.

The Mansion was reborn yet again in the 1950s. Major structural repairs upgraded the building between 1956 and 1959, and during the Ernest Hollings administration (1959–63) a rear porch was converted into new first-floor dining and guest-room areas. Ceiling beams were replaced in the 1960s, and further renovations and additions gradually created the Mansion visitors see today. As the Mansion's needs outgrew the available space, the state acquired two adjacent antebellum homes. The Lace house, built around 1854, is used for guest lodging and entertainment; the Caldwell-Boylston house, dating from the 1830s, contains offices and the Mansion gift shop. Both are venerable old Columbia residences that boast a long, shared heritage.

The South Carolina Governor's Mansion has had a diverse group of guests throughout its history. Presidents from Franklin Roosevelt to George Bush have overnighted or dined there, as have religious leaders from Billy Sunday to Billy Graham. Leonard Bernstein once played the piano all night in the parlor.

The staircase still greets visitors as they enter the narrow, high-ceilinged central hallway on the ground floor. To the right are the large drawing room and the state dining room; to the left, the small drawing

Opposite:
*The large drawing room. The lyre
tables flanking the fireplace date to
1815 and match one presented to
President Andrew Jackson.*

Above:
*The small drawing room. This
room has become known as the ladies'
parlor, where a portrait of the
current first lady usually hangs.*

room and the library. Those four rooms—the heart of the Mansion's public area—retain an aura of the Old South that carries into the upstairs bedrooms and family room.

In the large drawing room are two lyre tables from 1815, and there is
an English crystal chandelier donated by South Carolinian Bernard
Baruch. The tables, which flank the carved fireplace mantel, match one
once owned by Andrew Jackson and now in his legendary home, the Hermitage, in Tennessee. There is also a grand piano left to the Mansion by
Governor James F. Byrnes.

In the state dining room, the silver from the U.S.S. *South Carolina* is
displayed around the table and chairs acquired in the first decade of the
twentieth century. The room's wallpaper and a matching hand-painted
screen incorporate motifs of flowers and birds. The smaller family dining
room at the rear of the Mansion is less formal, but it still features a
chandelier designed in Philadelphia and Jean Zuber wallpaper depicting
nineteenth-century American scenes. The same wallpaper was used by
Jacqueline Kennedy to redecorate the White House in 1961.

In the library, floor-to-ceiling shelves line the wall behind a comfortable Chippendale sofa and two chairs. In each of the public rooms, paintings and antiques continue the antebellum theme. Portraits include one of Andrew Jackson, born in Waxhaw.

The ground floor also features the Signers' Room, where overnight guests sleep on unique canopied beds, hand-carved with motifs of rice sheaves, beneath embroidered hangings and spreads. The beds, like so many of the Mansion's furnishings and artifacts, were acquired or donated by past governors. Many of the Mansion's treasures bear the name of a past chief executive or other prominent South Carolinian: Governor Manning's chair, a 1916 mahogany Chippendale armchair; the Pickens secretary, an American Empire piece that belonged to a Civil War governor; the Middleton bed, which was once owned by Arthur Middleton, a signer of the Declaration of Independence. Others are known by their makers: the Lannuier card tables; the unique Milliken sideboard, a 1790s Hepplewhite piece made in New York by Mills and Deming. Every room reveals a treasure.

The Middleton bedroom. Arthur Middleton signed the Declaration of Independence for South Carolina and later fought in the Revolution. The four-poster mahogany bed served him in the field.

The Mansion sits on nine acres in the heart of Columbia's most historic district, with the Lace and Caldwell-Boylston houses looming alongside. The front portico of the Mansion is flanked by flower beds. Throughout the grounds, flowers and overarching trees provide shade and colorful surroundings to strollers.

The Mansion that grew out of an officer's dormitory remains a work in progress. More governors and first families will add their personal treasures to the home built on Arsenal Hill.

NEW
HAMPSHIRE

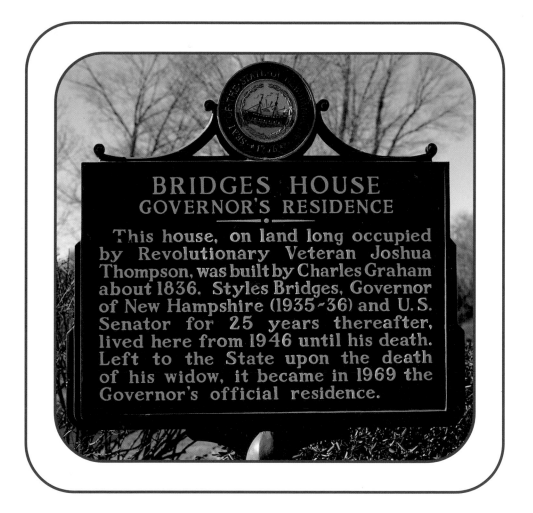

BRIDGES HOUSE
GOVERNOR'S RESIDENCE

This house, on land long occupied
by Revolutionary Veteran Joshua
Thompson, was built by Charles Graham
about 1836. Styles Bridges, Governor
of New Hampshire (1935-36) and U.S.
Senator for 25 years thereafter,
lived here from 1946 until his death.
Left to the State upon the death
of his widow, it became in 1969 the
Governor's official residence.

BRIDGES HOUSE
CONCORD

PHOTOGRAPHS BY GARY SAMSON

Bridges House.

Captain Ebenezer Eastman established his ferry service on the east side of the Merrimack River around 1727, on land that would one day be part of Concord, New Hampshire. Captain Eastman had built a house there, with musket slits and sturdy walls to hold off expected assaults. The Eastman land passed from descendant to descendant for decades in a series of tangled transactions typical of the Colonial and Revolutionary periods, with new houses being built here and old ones burning down or being abandoned there. Eventually, ten acres of the original Eastman land fell to Stilson Eastman, Ebenezer's grandson, and in the early 1780s he sold it to Lieutenant Joshua Thompson, one of the certified heroes of the American Revolution. Thompson had been an aide to Lafayette at Valley Forge. In postwar retirement, he lived in a small house on the land until 1831, when he sold it to Joseph Whidden. Three years later, Whidden passed it on to Charles Graham, and Graham built a house that would one day become the home of one of New Hampshire's greatest citizens and, ultimately, be designated its official executive residence.

Graham was a carpenter and joiner, and it is likely that he did most of the interior work on his new house, which was one of the first in the area to be faced with brick. It fronted southeast, well back from the dirt road; its gabled ends, reminiscent of Greek temple pediments, overlooked passing horse and cart traffic. Graham built well: the granite lintels above the doors came from Rattlesnake Hill, across the river in Concord, and they were precisely sized by convict-artisans from the state prison. The wooden front and rear cornices had crown moldings that also carried the Greek Revival theme, as did doorway sidelights framed by narrow pilasters. Graham was at his best inside, where the single-run staircase, interior doors, and fireplaces all exhibited elegant craftsmanship. The Norfolk-type thumb latches on the doors were probably imported from England. Graham was equally meticulous with the pine stairway rail, with its maple newel and angle posts. It was a livable house, meant to outlast its builder.

Graham remained there until 1846, when another skilled carpenter, Charles T. Seavey, bought "the homestead where I now live" for $1,187.50. The papers still exist, detailing the property boundaries that abutted those of "the Widow Hoit" and Eliphaz W. Upham. Seavey moved on in 1850, selling the house and land to Herman Sanborn. The Sanborns remained there for three generations, raising sheep, and in 1908 the venerable old home was sold to Alfred Bath, owner of a stone monument company. In 1946, the house was acquired by its next-to-last owner, a man who would give it a name and a purpose, and who left a vibrant mark on the history of New Hampshire.

Styles Bridges had served as governor from 1935 to 1937, when he was

Below:
The library. The "north of Boston" chest of
drawers dates from the early 1800s.

Right:
A mahogany chest presented to a New
Hampshire official by the president of
Pakistan sits atop the chest of drawers.

elected as New Hampshire's most enduring member of the United States Senate. Bridges and his wife, Deloris, decided they needed a home in Concord, and they purchased the old Graham house in the same year he went to the Senate—where he would remain until his death in 1961. Mrs. Bridges lived on in the house until she died in 1969. Her will expressed a dream she and Senator Bridges had long shared: the house, she wrote, would be left, "with all household furnishings and equipment . . . to be used and maintained exclusively as the official residence of the governor of the state of New Hampshire."

Like its small neighbors Vermont and Rhode Island, New Hampshire had never seen fit to build or buy an executive residence. Especially after the advent of the automobile, few places were far from Concord, located in the populous south-central part of the state. Past first families had lived at home, with the governors commuting to the state capitol building or renting nearby quarters. But the offer of what had become known as Bridges House had nostalgic, as well as utilitarian, value. It was one of New Hampshire's most historic homes, and it had long been occupied by the state's most illustrious leader. Senator and Mrs. Bridges had enlarged the dining room and added a sun porch. The furnishings and artifacts that were part of the bequest to the state included valuable antiques. There were rooms filled with late eighteenth- and early nineteenth-century American

Opposite:
The dining room.

Above:
*The living room. A portrait
of Styles Bridges hangs above
the fireplace.*

pieces—chests, tables, chairs, a sideboard, a Concord clock, Queen Anne
chairs from Portsmouth, even a yellow-painted rocker made by Abijah
Wetherbee of New Ipswich. Mrs. Bridges also left a large English Georgian silver collection and a set of diplomatic china, bearing the American
eagle, that reflected the senator's Washington service. The Bridges had
remodeled the study with the addition of raised pine paneling in the pre-
Revolutionary style. Bridges House was a gem—and it was free.

Subsequent first families have made some changes, but the only major
structural work has involved an enlargement of the kitchen. A detached
barn was converted to meeting space in the 1970s. The study is now home
to an extensive collection of books by New Hampshire authors, but other
alterations have been largely confined to minor matters of personal taste,
reflecting each first family.

During the 1980s, new sofas and chairs were added to the conference room, and donors presented a new set of sterling silver flatware for the dining room. Carpeting was removed and many of the original wood floors were refinished. First Lady Nancy Sununu added new draperies and curtains. Her redecoration efforts brought a sunny look to the living room, where needlepoint displayed the state flower, the purple lilac. A portrait of Styles Bridges was hung above the fireplace, assuring that the home's most famous owner would remain a part of his widow's bequest. Mrs. Kathy Gregg later also oversaw the restoration of the dining-room table in the Federal style, added new wallpaper, and adorned the windows in rose-colored draperies and valances. The table matches the Chippendale chairs and sideboard. Private donors also added a silver cabinet to the dining room, where built-in shelves hold the house's silver and china collection, as well as specially commissioned crystal glassware.

The screened sun porch was furnished in white wrought iron, and an Oriental runner was added to the staircase. In the master bedroom upstairs, morning glory stenciling circles the walls, and a bouquet of flowers is stenciled above the fireplace. Upstairs floors are of wide pine boards.

The house was originally designed as a private residence, and it retains that flavor today. The downstairs living room, dining room, and study and the upstairs bedrooms are warm and inviting, but they are too small to lend themselves to public entertaining or large state functions on a grand scale. In the barn, remodeled as a conference center, there is a stone fireplace in the center of the room and ample space for larger gatherings, but the New Hampshire governor's mansion has never been intended as the center of activity and social events other states enjoy in their much larger executive residences. Instead, it is a solid, balanced two-story brick home with a legacy that dates to the 1830s, when it was created as what it remains today—"the homestead where I now live."

VIRGINIA

THE EXECUTIVE MANSION
RICHMOND

PHOTOGRAPHS BY KATHERINE WETZEL

The Virginia Executive Mansion.

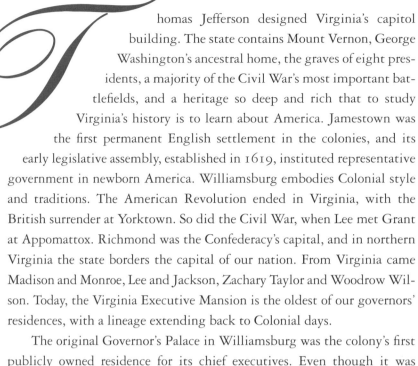

homas Jefferson designed Virginia's capitol building. The state contains Mount Vernon, George Washington's ancestral home, the graves of eight presidents, a majority of the Civil War's most important battlefields, and a heritage so deep and rich that to study Virginia's history is to learn about America. Jamestown was the first permanent English settlement in the colonies, and its early legislative assembly, established in 1619, instituted representative government in newborn America. Williamsburg embodies Colonial style and traditions. The American Revolution ended in Virginia, with the British surrender at Yorktown. So did the Civil War, when Lee met Grant at Appomattox. Richmond was the Confederacy's capital, and in northern Virginia the state borders the capital of our nation. From Virginia came Madison and Monroe, Lee and Jackson, Zachary Taylor and Woodrow Wilson. Today, the Virginia Executive Mansion is the oldest of our governors' residences, with a lineage extending back to Colonial days.

The original Governor's Palace in Williamsburg was the colony's first publicly owned residence for its chief executives. Even though it was destroyed by fire in 1781, the Palace remains a part of Virginia's myth and lore, and it has been reconstructed at Williamsburg in painstaking detail. When the royal governors fled at the outset of the Revolution, the Palace was occupied by Virginia's first Continental governor, Patrick Henry. Thomas Jefferson succeeded Henry in 1779, and that most eclectic of America's leaders issued his architectural verdict on the Governor's Palace: it was "capable of being made an elegant seat." Jefferson's sketched suggestions for remodeling the Palace survive, but the building did not. In 1780, the new state's seat of government was moved to Richmond.

Governor Jefferson rented the Turpin house there, and it became Virginia's temporary executive home. He had to flee twice when British troops, led by Benedict Arnold, threatened the city. A year later, as victory loomed at Yorktown, Virginia acquired its second official executive residence, a four-room frame-and-brick house previously owned by William Marsden. It stood approximately on the site of the present-day Executive Mansion. Governor Benjamin Harrison was the first to live there, and he was followed by twelve other chief executives, although not all of them chose to occupy the house. It required constant effort to keep the old home in trim condition: whitewashing the walls, patching drafty windows, and adding new outbuildings. Governor James Wood inventoried the furnishings in 1796 and found them "ruined . . . old and many of them [chairs] broken." Still, George Washington often dined there, and the house was a part of the seat of government of new America's most dominant state. Governor Henry ("Light-Horse Harry") Lee lived there; his son would be named Robert E. Other famous residents were James Monroe, a future president;

and John Tyler, Sr., whose own son would one day live in the White House. The younger Tyler organized a mansion dinner in 1809, to honor Jefferson's retirement as president. "Two plum puddings, John?" his father marveled at the extravagance. "This is rather extraordinary!" Young John agreed: "But it is an extraordinary occasion!"

The old house was far from extraordinary, and in 1811 Virginia's general assembly authorized construction of the home that would serve as the state's executive residence for most of two centuries. The legislature appropriated twelve thousand dollars, the old Marsden home was finally demolished, and the first family moved to rented rooms as work began on the new residence. The plans were created by Alexander Parris, a product of his Massachusetts and Maine upbringing, and he brought a love for antiquity and the Greek Revival style that one of his mentors, Benjamin Latrobe, was also applying to the design of public buildings in the new national capital at Washington. Parris was also profoundly influenced by Boston architect Charles Bulfinch. Bulfinch had successfully adapted eighteenth-century neoclassicism to American needs, using red brick and wood in place of stone. Parris added a touch of England and a dash of Boston to Richmond as he designed the Virginia Executive Mansion. It would be one of his most enduring monuments.

Sadly, Governor George William Smith, who had taken a keen interest in the construction effort, did not live to occupy the house. Smith died in a fire on December 26, 1811, and it was his unexpected successor, Governor James Barbour, who oversaw completion of the Mansion. He moved in during March 1813, while young America was again at war with Britain. On one occasion, Barbour called out the militia to defend Richmond and his new home against a threatened British incursion.

His successors made minor modifications to the Executive Mansion, and over the decades much of the original interior design faded into dim memory. But by 1830 the exterior looked much as it does today. In that year a parapet was added along the roofline, and builders constructed a new portico and "three porches and a front door." A newspaper said the house was "now entitled to the appellation of elegance."

The Executive Mansion still had much history ahead of it. General Lafayette dined there in 1824. Slaves lived in the home's kitchen house as household servants in the 1840s. An elegant statue of George Washington on horseback was added to Capitol Square in 1858; it was clearly visible from the Mansion. Like other states torn by the secession decision in 1861, Virginia for a time had two governors, and as the war

unfolded, pro-Union counties split away to form the new state of West Virginia. General Lee conferred with governors in the Mansion during the 1862 Peninsula Campaign, and when Union troops finally captured the Confederacy's capital in 1865, a bucket brigade labored through the night to save the Mansion from fire. In that same year, Mathew Brady stood at the end of the tree-lined mall leading to the Mansion's front portico and photographed the historic house. (Confederate president Jefferson Davis chose another Richmond home as his Southern "White House.")

After the war, Union general David Hunter Strother lived at the Mansion during Reconstruction, as did a brief series of carpetbagging chief executives. Civilian governors returned in 1870, including James Kemper, who had been one of George Pickett's brigade commanders in the general's famous charge at Gettysburg. It was probably Kemper who built a small fish pond in front of the Mansion. Robert E. Lee's nephew Fitzhugh also served as governor. By the turn of the century, Governor Andrew Jackson Montague took a renewed interest in the Mansion, and in 1906 Governor Claude Swanson sponsored a major interior restoration that made the ground-floor rooms more public in nature. Twin parlors were combined into a large ballroom, and an oval dining room was added at the rear of the first floor. Ornate woodwork gave a monumental style to the public rooms. In 1914, the final major expansion added upstairs bedrooms and living areas above the new dining room. In 1926, the resident first family barely escaped a fire that damaged the rear rooms (First Lady Helen Trinkle and her son, Lee, had to jump from an upstairs window), but the damaged rooms were soon restored. Structural repairs followed in the 1930s, and in the 1970s the Mansion collection was expanded with the addition of many historical antiques. In 1989, the Mansion once more underwent an exterior renovation, returning it to its 1847 appearance.

From the front, it is compact, simple, and austere, its symmetry focused on the columned central portico. But inside, the Mansion expands down the broad central hall, beneath carved arches to a view of the elegant oval dining room, where a portrait of Thomas Jefferson hangs over a marble-top sideboard from about 1800. On either side of the main hallway are the ballrooms and the old governor's office and ladies' parlor, each with period fireplaces. Unobtrusive staircases lead to the second-floor living quarters; the Mansion does not have the grand central stairway common to so many executive residences.

Everywhere the walls are carved, corniced, or papered in styles that reflect the Mansion's rich past, and portraits of great Virginia historical figures adorn each of the public rooms. Most of the furnishings,

Below:
The Lafayette bedroom. The Marquis de Lafayette, hero of both the American and French Revolutions, dined at the Mansion in 1824. The guest bedroom has borne his name ever since.

Right:
The south ballroom. The columns continue from the front portico throughout the Mansion.

Opposite, below:
John Letcher, governor during the Civil War, made crucial decisions in this Mansion office, including the appointments of generals Robert E. Lee and Stonewall Jackson.

though they include a wide selection of antiques, have been in the Mansion for less than sixty years, since the collection and restoration efforts of the twentieth century. There are a number of relics of past first families, including furniture that belonged to Governor Barbour, the first governor to reside at the Mansion.

Upstairs are an open sitting area, two front rooms that correspond to those downstairs, and a hallway leading to family bedrooms and living areas. There is a library here, as well as a family dining room. A single set of stairs leads to the Mansion's small attic. In the basement, modifications over the years have added offices, storerooms, and a kitchen. Staff members can walk through a covered area linking the basement to the detached original kitchen building, constructed when the Mansion was first built in 1811–13. The roof of the covered area is railed and serves as a walkway connecting the main-floor porch and the Mansion's south entrance. The kitchen building still has its original brick floor.

A late nineteenth-century brick carriage house sits at the rear of the Mansion's grounds, along with a greenhouse, and the rear grounds also contain formal gardens bordered by brick walls added in the 1950s.

Virginia's Executive Mansion has changed and grown through its nearly two centuries of service. It has seen war, housed great names, and justified the faith of those who built it—it has endured. Occasionally, a modern visitor will notice what appear to be scratches on one of the Mansion's glass windowpanes. Take a closer look: they are the initials of the children of Governor Fitzhugh Lee, the collateral descendants of Robert E. Lee, carved there with a diamond in the 1880s—the smallest but by no means the least of history's marks left on our oldest executive residence.

The ladies' parlor. The Mansion has two downstairs parlors, from the era when gentlemen and ladies adjourned to separate rooms after dinner.

NEW YORK

THE GOVERNOR'S MANSION
ALBANY

PHOTOGRAPHS BY ROBERT BENSON

The drawing room. New York governors are traditionally administered the oath of office in front of the drawing room's fireplace shortly before midnight on New Year's Eve.

President Grover Cleveland once lived here, before he became the only American ever elected to two nonconsecutive terms in the White House. Also resident here were the distant Roosevelt cousins, Theodore and Franklin, who held the presidency for a combined total of nearly twenty years. Nelson Rockefeller, another occupant, became vice president, and four other New York governors—Samuel Tilden, Charles Hughes, Al Smith, and Thomas Dewey—won their parties' presidential nominations between the nation's centennial year of 1876 and the 1940s. The Mansion, which celebrated its own centennial in 1975, has housed more presidents than any American residence except the White House itself. So significant is the New York Governor's Mansion that one of its tenants, Levi P. Morton, served as vice president, then came home and ran successfully for governor.

This cradle for leaders was a hundred years too late for the first New York governors, who traditionally arrived in Albany in need of lodgings. Future president Martin Van Buren lived in a private home. So did Governor William H. Seward, who became one of President Lincoln's key Cabinet officials. In 1837, New York thought to buy its chief executives a home, but the downtown row house the state purchased was deemed unsuitable; governors refused to live there, and a newspaper account said it was ultimately "ridiculed out of existence." There were other efforts to find an executive residence, but each was scuttled by legislative fears of high cost. Finally, the answer materialized on a site southeast of the state capitol building. It bore the unlikely name of Gallows Hill.

Successful Albany businessmen Thomas Olcott and George Hoyt had constructed neighboring homes on Gallows Hill in the 1850s. Olcott later sold his two-story home to Robert L. Johnson, who converted it from a simple, austere house to a Victorian showpiece with cupolas, a mansard-roofed tower, and multiple porticoes and verandas. Johnson liked to entertain, and he added an elegant porte cochère out front. His unusual, eclectic home became the governor's residence before it was the Governor's Mansion. Governor Samuel J. Tilden rented the house when he arrived in Albany to take the oath of office in 1875. His tenure was successful (he won his party's presidential nomination), and his successor, Lucius Robinson, convinced the state to buy the house in 1877 and designate it as New York's official executive residence.

In the 1880s, architect Isaac G. Perry, one of the designers of the new state capitol building, was asked to remodel the Mansion. He trimmed away the Victorian ironwork, replaced the mansard-roofed tower with Romanesque battlements, and added a new north wing, complete with extra bedrooms and a grand reception room. The house now had more than thirty rooms, and it had been converted to an approximation of the Queen

Opposite and above:
The Princess Suite, named in honor of Princess Beatrix of the Netherlands, after her visit in 1959.

Anne style, with wide interior spaces and a central living hall. The adjacent Hoyt house was removed to make room for the Mansion's sprawling, ornate expansion.

The Mansion remained virtually unchanged until a 1961 fire caused by aging wiring heavily damaged the ground floor and produced extensive losses upstairs. There were calls to demolish and completely replace the damaged structure, but it was decided to rebuild instead. One of the first discoveries made by workmen as they stripped away the charred rubble in the entrance hall was the original brickwork installed by Olcott. The restoration went well beyond repairs from the fire, and if the Mansion that emerged remained true to its combined Olcott-Perry design, it was also somehow more pleasing and coherent. Perhaps the public's architectural eye had changed as well. Whatever the reason, a Mansion that had been derided and discounted for almost a hundred years rose, phoenix-like, as a modern treasure.

The New York Governor's Mansion has hosted some of the most imposing and fascinating characters in American history. Within a month of his inauguration, Governor Tilden invited poet and editor William Cullen Bryant to spend a week there. Grover Cleveland, who hated what he called "flummery," often walked to work from the Mansion to the state

capitol building. He went fishing the day after he was nominated for president. Teddy Roosevelt refereed boxing matches for his sons and their friends in the third-floor hallway. Al Smith built a private zoo on the Mansion grounds, where he kept bears, monkeys, and elk. The polio-stricken Franklin Roosevelt installed an elevator. Albert Einstein was a guest there, and so was Harry Truman, who planted a sugar maple on the grounds, where it still grows. Nelson Rockefeller displayed his private art collection during his tenure as governor, a fabled collection that included works by Henri Matisse, Vincent van Gogh, and Pablo Picasso.

The modern Mansion is also a repository for fine and historic art, most of it drawn from the nineteenth century. The John Rogers bust of George Washington is displayed in the entrance hall, and other works include Albert Bierstadt's *Autumn Woods,* four etchings by James M. Whistler, a Frederic Church painting titled *New England Scenery*, and *The Marriage of Pocahontas* by Henry Brueckner, which served as a source for the many engravings of this event. The Presidential Medals of the two Roosevelts and Grover Cleveland are also on permanent display.

Visitors to the Mansion are immediately aware of their historic surroundings. In the entrance hall, a Frank Fowler portrait of Samuel Tilden overlooks a Victorian table and the Washington bust. In the aptly named memorabilia room, created by F.D.R., are a Louis XV marquetry table owned by Governor Roswell Flower (served 1892–94) and china from Governor Tilden's era.

Opposite:
The drawing room, used for parties, conferences, and family gatherings.

Below:
The reception room. Once used as an office by governors, the reception room displays prints by James M. Whistler, a portrait of Christopher Columbus once owned by Theodore Roosevelt, and inaugural medals in honor of New York governors who have become president or vice president.

Right:
Twin four-poster beds make the Princess Suite comfortable for overnight Mansion visitors.

Main-floor rooms open off the main hall, which is furnished with Renaissance Revival chairs and a settee that was probably in the Mansion when it was purchased in 1877. A Roosevelt portrait looks on from above the drawing-room fireplace, where New York governors have traditionally taken their oath of office at midnight on New Year's Eve. The drawing-room mirrors are reproductions of the William and Mary style in *verre églomisé,* painted on the back of the glass. Governor Rockefeller donated the cut-glass chandeliers, a 1735 Georgian table, and an Adams oval mirror.

One of the room's most unusual objects is the Tiffany dragonfly lamp on loan from the New-York Historical Society. The broad drawing room has two separate furniture groupings and ample floor space, suited to a variety of functions.

The dining room has a trestle table in early Renaissance Revival style that can be extended to seat thirty-two guests. Over the mantel is a triple framed mirror dating to 1720, and the mantel itself has been restored to its original cherry wood. It is flanked by nineteenth-century sconces from India. The candelabras on the mantel are bronze, porcelain, and glass; they were made by Wedgwood and date to 1785. The Mansion's silver collection is on display in the dining room. It is Tiffany silver, bearing the state seal, with some pieces dating to 1885.

A less formal breakfast room was once part of the Mansion's broad porch and was converted to its current function in 1917. More Mansion silver is displayed here, as is part of the Mansion's extensive and eclectic china collection. One plate bears an early version of the state seal, which was modified in 1882. The breakfast room opens into the library, which doubles as a family room and houses an oil painting, *A View of the Hudson River,* by Frank Anderson. The Dutch-influenced Albany city seal adorns the mantel.

The staircase leading to the second floor is adorned with artworks, including Gilbert Stuart's portrait of Robert Livingston, who administered the oath of office to President Washington in 1789. If the Mansion resembles a museum, that impression is reinforced on the second floor, where each governor is invited to decorate a gallery. The gallery has been home to displays as diverse as Rockefeller's collection of modern art, Hugh Carey's New York sports collection, and a selection of items representing each of New York's sixty-two counties. The gallery also holds an eagle-based trestle table that belonged to Franklin Roosevelt, as well as his wheelchair and ashtray.

Other second-floor rooms include the Princess Suite, named for Princess Beatrix of the Netherlands, who stayed here in 1959. The suite contains a sitting room and adjoining bedroom. In the sitting room, domed sculptures of Venus and Mars sit atop the mantel; they were original to the Mansion in 1877. The mahogany four-poster beds date to 1890, as does the mahogany dressing table.

The Mansion grounds feature a Civil War cannon, a tennis court, an indoor therapeutic swimming pool built for F.D.R., and a formal rose garden. There are trees on the grounds with histories as diverse as the rooms inside. One, a weeping elm, was planted by Governor Charles Whitman to celebrate his son's birth. A Doyenne Boussock pear tree is the sole survivor from an orchard that stood on Gallows Hill prior to the 1800s.

It is a roomy, rambling house, one that past residents have cherished. When Al Smith relinquished it and the governorship to Franklin Roosevelt in 1929, more than a thousand people stood by the gates to witness the historic transfer of power. "We've got the home fires burning," Smith declared, "and you'll find this is a fine place to live."

The Princess Suite guest bathroom.

NORTH CAROLINA

THE GOVERNOR'S MANSION
RALEIGH

PHOTOGRAPHS BY CHARLIE JONES

The North Carolina Governor's Mansion.

North Carolina is a state that has frequently reinvented itself. As one of the original thirteen colonies, it was the first to instruct its delegates to the Continental Congress in favor of independence. North Carolinians agonized over the secession decision in 1861, then supplied more troops to the Confederacy than any other state. In the twentieth century, it led a Southern trend away from agriculture and toward industry, creating a renowned "research triangle" centered on three great universities and a trio of modern, thriving cities. Its executive residences have changed with the times as well. From a home that housed the last royal governor of pre-Revolutionary North Carolina to the Governor's Mansion that celebrated its centennial in 1991, the state has had four official governor's residences, each distinct and different, each a reflection of its own era.

When royal governor William Tryon erected Tryon Palace in New Bern in the late 1760s, Colonial farmers who were beginning to fan the winds of independence regarded it as yet another example of British excess, especially when Tryon increased their poll taxes to finance the two-story Georgian home. After the Revolution, Tryon Palace was used for a time as the new state capitol building, but its central portion was destroyed by fire in 1798. (Tryon Palace has been reconstructed as a museum and historic attraction.)

In 1792, the North Carolina legislature shifted the capital to Raleigh, and five years later the state purchased a frame home for its governors in that growing city. It proved inadequate, and what was to be known as the Governor's Palace won legislative approval in 1813. Construction stretched through the War of 1812. When it was completed, the Governor's Palace was an impressive two-story Classical Revival brick home. Twenty governors lived there from 1816 until the Civil War. But when General William Tecumseh Sherman led his Union troops from Mississippi, where he had occupied another prewar governor's mansion, through Georgia and into North Carolina in 1865, the Governor's Palace was doomed. Sherman made the home his military headquarters; by the end of Reconstruction it was a wrecked and neglected shell, and in 1885 it was razed.

Postwar North Carolina chief executives lived in private homes until Governor Thomas J. Jarvis (served 1879–85) complained that "it does not comport with the dignity of the state for the Governor to live at a hotel." The legislature agreed, as long as the new mansion could be constructed with inexpensive prison labor. Architect Samuel Sloan began the project but soon died. His brilliant assistant, Adolphus G. Bauer, then assumed control. Bauer caused considerable scandal by marrying an Indian princess and ultimately took his own life. But Bauer's vision was to outlive him.

Known for his flamboyant Queen Anne–style structures, he poured all of his art into the design of the house that was to embody that "gingerbread house" mode of construction. It was finally completed by Colonel William Jackson Hicks, who held the dual positions of architect and warden at the North Carolina State Penitentiary. As construction of the Mansion continued for eight years, prison laborers worked inside a stockade erected around the site, which was scornfully called "Jarvis's Folly" by its critics.

Many of those critics fell silent in 1891, when Governor Daniel G. Fowle and his family moved into the splendid high-Victorian Mansion and promptly hosted a grand opening gala for two thousand citizens. They marveled at its steeply pitched roofs, its inviting pillared porch, and its stained glass windowpanes. There is an appealing delicacy about the North Carolina Governor's Mansion that remains virtually unchanged today.

The Mansion has undergone a number of partial renovations in its first century of life, including a 1925 neoclassical interior redesign that toned down much of the original high-Victorian appearance and a 1970s project that included a full rewiring and refurbishing of all brick, mortar, and trim. But the architects have always remained true to the Mansion's genesis; when the 1925 designers removed Victorian columns from the entry hall, they promptly replaced them with columns in the Corinthian style. This mixture of Victorian and neoclassical styles still defines the

Above:
The ballroom. Guests can dance, dine, or visit between the twin fireplaces.

Opposite, above:
A burled walnut chest-on-stand dates from 1714 and is of Queen Anne design.

Opposite, below:
The gentlemen's parlor. The rug design refers to historic events from North Carolina history.

Mansion's character, which later systems and structural refinements hardly touched, and which served to make life there a continuing delight for one first family after another and for their guests. North Carolina's Mansion is ideally designed for entertaining groups, which have ranged from the small cluster of editors who sampled a 1929 "stay at home" feast, featuring such local products as corn pone, to the black-tie throngs attending elegant recitals in the ballroom. So homey is this house that an oil and real-estate heiress visiting there during World War I took a bumpy ride down the grand staircase—on a dishpan.

The Mansion's most recent restoration came as its centennial approached in 1991, when the slate roof was replaced by a replica of the original design. What began as "Jarvis's Folly" has found a place in North Carolina's heart, admired as one of the oldest executive residences in the country originally designed for that purpose.

Originally the grand hallway, which first greets a Mansion visitor, was designed with dark wood columns and wainscoting. Today it is a bright and spacious expanse with Corinthian columns halfway between the front door and the freestanding grand staircase. The staircase is constructed of native pine; its brilliant crimson and gold runner matches the broad hallway carpet designed to mark the Mansion's 1991 centennial. Along the walls hang portraits of many of the chief executives who have lived here, and two cut-crystal chandeliers light the hallway and its furnishings, which include a Baroque Revival pier table, a carved mirror, a Directoire cabinet, and two Scottish 1830 Regency sofas. The massive newel posts are carved with an acorn and oak design, recalling Raleigh's earlier name, City of the Oaks.

The downstairs public rooms include two throwbacks to an earlier era when the sexes often socialized apart from one another. The gentlemen's parlor is decorated in Chinese Chippendale. Heavy chairs and sofas sit on a handmade rug adorned with scenes from North Carolina's past: Hernando de Soto exploring the area in 1540, Sir Walter Raleigh founding a colony in 1585, the founding of the first state university in 1795, and the Wright brothers' flight at Kitty Hawk in 1903. There is an ornate mirror over the

The rose room. The rose room, or east bedroom, is the Mansion's official guest accommodation. It is the only room in the Mansion decorated in Victorian style.

Above:
The library. The conference table is leather topped, and the woodwork is stained heart pine.

Above, right:
The ladies' parlor. The chandelier and the mirror match those in the gentlemen's parlor.

mantel, and a Steuben crystal urn features a likeness of Blackbeard the Pirate. The burled walnut chest against the wall is a Queen Anne piece from 1714. Furniture in the ladies' parlor consists of Southern period antiques, with the exception of a Louis XVI gilded console table. The cut-crystal chandelier and overmantel mirror match those in the gentlemen's parlor.

The ballroom is one of the Mansion's most spectacular rooms, with its polished wood floor and matched pairs of French mirrors and Sheffield chandeliers. The original ballroom was on the second floor, immediately above the present first-floor ballroom. The room was first known as the music room, and its history includes service as a temporary barracks for sixty American soldiers who passed through Raleigh during World War I. The ballroom's mahogany Victorian suite is part of the original Mansion collection and once sat in the gentlemen's parlor.

The cozy library features a leather-top conference table and dark heart pine paneling and fireplace moldings. The library was restored to its original 1891 design during the second term of Governor James B. Hunt, Jr.

The San Domingo mahogany table in the dining room seats up to twenty-four guests on Chippendale chairs with hand-worked needlepoint cushions. Overhead, a nineteenth-century Austrian crystal chandelier lights this bright, high-ceilinged room, with its fireplace and gilt-framed mirror, its white ceiling, and its pale blue walls that seem to demand elaborate floral arrangements.

For more informal events and private moments enjoyed by the first family, the morning room features light wicker furniture and broad, tall windows that overlook the grounds. The room was an open porch until it was enclosed in the 1980s; it complements the south porch, a covered exterior deck that wraps around the south side of the Mansion and also features wicker, and it has a direct view into the Victorian formal garden. Visitors strolling in the garden can look back at the Mansion's four chimneys, its decorated tile roof, and the wide, inviting porch up two flights of brick steps.

The family sections of the Mansion include a more modern living and dining area, a richly furnished den, and six upstairs bedrooms, each in its own unique style. The east (or rose) bedroom, at the top of the grand staircase, is the Mansion's official guest room, and it is the only bedroom fully decorated with Victorian furnishings. President Harry Truman slept there in 1948. Other bedrooms feature Chinese decor, a Victorian rosewood bed owned by Governor Fowle, a canopied bed that matches one in the White House, and elegant Tabriz rugs.

The south porch wraps around the Mansion and looks down two flights of brick steps to the hedge-lined grounds.

North Carolina's temperate climate invites Mansion residents and visitors outdoors, where the grounds are lush and green, planted with masses of native azaleas and rhododendrons and widely scattered beds for annuals that bloom at least nine months of the year. A small kitchen garden provides herbs and vegetables used by Mansion chefs, and there is a wandering walkway that leads through a rose garden with a central sundial.

On summer nights visitors can hear the chirping of locusts and watch fireflies among the trees. And as the lights come on in one window after another, outlining the small twin second-story balconies and the colored tile decorations beneath the third-floor windows, the Mansion becomes a warm and welcoming cottage in the woods.

KENTUCKY

THE GOVERNOR'S MANSION
FRANKFORT

The Kentucky Governor's Mansion.

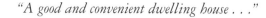
*A*merica first moved west through Kentucky. Daniel Boone penetrated the Cumberland Gap as early as 1768, and the early forts and settled outposts sent back word to the coastal colonies: Here is open, free land, waiting for the plow. One of the first acts of the new Virginia general assembly was to create Kentucky County, in 1776.

Three years after the Constitution took effect in 1789, Kentucky joined the Union. Frankfort was chosen as the capital; it was close to the river, and there was plenty of wood for building. Kentucky later produced John C. Breckinridge, vice president in the years before the Civil War. That war was notably hard on Kentuckians, residents of a border state where many owned slaves. More than seventy-five thousand Kentuckians fought for the North, while some thirty-five thousand went with the South. In few other regions were there more instances of brother battling brother between 1861 and 1865.

In 1796 Kentucky's legislators appointed a committee "with full power and authority to purchase a good and convenient dwelling house, together with such necessary out houses as would be sufficient for the accommodation of the Governor." The state bought a lot in Frankfort. Robert Letcher, son of the brick contractor, helped build the house. So did the stoneworker Thomas Metcalfe. In a development unique in American history, both men would ultimately live in the mansion they helped create: Metcalfe served as governor in 1828–32 and Letcher in 1840–44.

The home—known today as the Old Governor's Mansion—was called "The Palace" when Governor James Garrard hitched four black horses to his coach and rode up to the limestone front steps to take possession in 1798. In the next one hundred seventeen years a total of thirty-three first families would live in the Federal-style home, later modified to reflect Georgian influences. As originally built, it had a portico, an entry hall, a cozy parlor, an office and a dining room downstairs, and a covered porch. The Mansion was remodeled in 1859, and gas fixtures were installed after the Civil War. There were three fires over the years—one in 1899 nearly gutted the interior—and as the decades passed, both the Mansion and its surrounding neighborhood decayed. After the new Mansion was built in 1914, the old one served as an office building until it became a barracks for Kentucky state troopers in the 1930s, and finally sat vacant for many years. In 1946 it was declared unsafe and condemned; there was discussion of demolishing it, but leaders who intervened noted that there was still life left in the old house. Over a ten-year period, restoration work resulted in a complete interior renovation and extensive redecoration. The intent was apparently to preserve the old Mansion as a historic site, but so thoroughly was it restored that it seemed foolish not to put it to work once again as a residence. Today the old Mansion is the official residence of Kentucky's lieutenant governors. As it celebrates its first two hundred years in public service, the old Mansion is the oldest home in America built as a state executive residence and still in use as one.

The new, and current, Mansion is next door to the state capitol building. Begun in 1912 and occupied two years later, it displays a grand French theme. When it opened for public inspection on January 20, 1914, Governor James McCreary welcomed a thousand guests, who were dazzled by its elegance and scale. The Mansion, designed by E. A. and C. C. Weber of northern Kentucky, is in the Beaux-Arts style, openly copied from the Petit Trianon, the villa near Versailles once occupied by Marie Antoinette. It is an imposing structure, some eighty feet wide and two hundred feet long, with twenty-five rooms. The front formal gardens are perhaps the most elaborate of those for any American executive residence. It may have been the old Mansion that was called "The Palace," but it is the new one that clearly merits the name.

The new Mansion underwent extensive remodeling and redecoration in 1980 after the state fire marshal declared it unsafe. Governor John Y. Brown and his family moved to a private residence and launched a three-year, multimillion-dollar renovation project, which included completion of the formal gardens, designed in 1912 but left unfinished. The Mansion today is largely the product of that ambitious renovation, made possible by a combination of public and private funding as Kentuckians answered the call to "Save the Mansion."

The Mansion's broad formal gardens are split by a central walkway that leads guests past stone benches and tall black lampposts, up a series of short steps to the spectacular front portico, with its four pairs of stone Ionic columns soaring two stories above the balustrade and terrace. The gardens form a mall that frames the Mansion's limestone face. Echoes of Versailles are everywhere, from the colorful flower beds and sculptured hedges to the stone balustrades.

Inside, the Mansion's public first floor continues the French theme. One wing is occupied entirely by the huge ballroom. The other wing contains the sun parlor, reception hall, and guest bathrooms. In the main central portion of the structure are the state and family dining rooms, the governor's reception room, and the first lady's parlor, separated by two wide main halls. The transverse hall runs from the side entrance past the sun parlor and reception hall to the ballroom at the opposite end. The shorter main hall bisects the Mansion and leads from the main entrance to the split central staircase. Upstairs are the first family's private living quarters. There is the great room, created from several smaller rooms (a den and living area) during the 1980 renovation, and on the third floor are a small reception area and bedrooms. The upstairs areas also include two studies, two state bedrooms for guests, and the governor's bedroom suite.

The ballroom.

Above:
The governor's reception room. The furnishings are arranged in conformity with eighteenth-century principles.

Right:
The sun parlor is furnished with antique wicker furniture found in central Kentucky.

But it is downstairs, on the public floor, where the Mansion displays its French decorative style, brought to Kentucky just a century and a half after Daniel Boone first explored the wilderness territory. The foyer is lit by a brass and cut-crystal chandelier. On each side of the stairs are large Chinese vases, which were among the more expensive items acquired during the 1980 restoration. To the left is the governor's reception room, the Mansion's most formal room, decorated in cream and gold. Furnishings are in the Louis XVI style, and the ornate plaster, chandelier, and hand-carved Kentucky yellow-poplar mantel all date from 1912. Draperies and upholstery are in Kentucky blue, and the Aubusson-style carpet is by Schumaker. A French clock and twin black-marble candelabras adorn the mantel.

The ballroom is the most public room in the Mansion, and guests are inevitably drawn to it down the long central hall. It can seat up to eighty-two for dinner or serve as a spacious area for receptions and dances. The parquet floor was replaced during the 1980 restoration, but the three chandeliers—each with more than four thousand glass beads—and the delicate woodwork are original. Fourteen oval-back Louis XVI–style chairs decorate the ballroom, and there are in reserve two hundred spindle-back chairs specifically designed for the Mansion. The ballroom's design gives the Mansion a slightly asymmetrical appearance from the air: its semicircular windowed north wall contrasts with the squared-off design of the south wing.

The state dining room shares the north end of the Mansion with the ballroom and the governor's reception room, and like the ballroom it has a bow-end shape, extending out from the back of the building. The table and chairs are in the neo-Georgian style. Ceiling lights are mounted in rosettes, creating a halo effect. The state dining room's walls are painted in pastel shades, and the room contains three pieces of silver from the U.S.S. *Kentucky,* launched in 1898, and a pair of candelabras once owned by the family of Isaac Shelby, Kentucky's first state governor and a hero of the Revolution.

The first lady's salon is at the front of the Mansion, opposite the governor's reception room. It is decorated in 1890s French style with a rug by Schumaker. Colors follow those used in the Mansion in 1914: cream and pale gray-green. The center table is Napoleon III, and the room also contains inlaid tables made by the French cabinetmaker Millet in the early twentieth century. A Louis XVI reproduction console is modeled after one from the Palace of Versailles, and there is an 1880s Louis XV–style rolltop desk. Wall sconces are by Edward Caldwell of New York and date to 1910.

The first-floor sun porch was originally designed as a study and library. The 1980 remodeling created a study upstairs, and the original sunroom, which gave way to bathrooms in 1980, was re-created here. It is an informal sitting room decorated in wicker furnishings and adorned with photographs of past first ladies. Among the wicker pieces are a rare 1898 fan-back chair and a 1900 wicker Victrola. The sun porch is also decorated with works by Kentucky artists and craft masters, including a 1920s quilt.

The main stairway.

The final public-floor room is the family dining room. Its walls and mantel are in Kentucky poplar with a mahogany stain. It is designed more in the English style than the other, French-flavored rooms of the first floor, with a red-painted ceiling and stenciling characteristic of the Greek Revival and high-Victorian styles. The table, chairs, and sideboards were acquired for the Mansion in the 1930s.

The downstairs hallway is as impressive as the rooms it serves. Its two *bombé* chests date from the 1930s, and there is a pair of mirrors acquired in the 1940s. The children of past governors were said to have roller-skated in the hallway, before the hardwood floors were replaced in 1980 by parquet to match the ballroom.

TENNESSEE

FAR HILLS
NASHVILLE

PHOTOGRAPHS BY JED DEKALB

Far Hills.

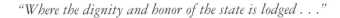

t first, Tennessee wasn't quite sure of its name. The eastern portion of the territory was called Franklin (after Benjamin), and it was not until the long, narrow strip of land to the west of North Carolina joined the Union in 1796 that the name Tennessee—from the Cherokee village name *tanasi*—came into general use. For nearly fifty years there was equal uncertainty about the location of the capital. It migrated from Knoxville to Kingston, back and forth between Nashville and Knoxville, and finally settled in Nashville in 1843. There, Tennessee's governors bought or rented quarters for another half century. Among them was Governor Andrew Johnson, Abraham Lincoln's vice president in 1864 and his successor in the White House. It was the postwar governor Robert L. Taylor who raised the issue of an official executive residence. "The honor in being called to such a high station is ample compensation," Taylor explained in a message to the legislature, "but the state should surround its executive with facilities for maintaining the dignity and the reputable honor of the commonwealth." Governor Taylor had defeated his brother in the only U.S. gubernatorial race to pit sibling against sibling, and he believed that Tennessee should provide him and his successors with a place to live.

The legislature disagreed. There had been discussions about a possible executive residence in the 1850s, and one proposal even suggested that the first family could find lodgings "at the lunatic asylum." Then, these discussions were interrupted by the Civil War. The last of the eleven southern states to secede, Tennessee was a major battleground. Bloody engagements were fought at Shiloh, Stone's River, Chickamauga, and Chattanooga. Nashville fell to advancing Northern troops in 1864, giving Tennessee an earlier start than many of the other states in the Confederacy on the painful road through Reconstruction. The last state to secede in 1861 became the first to be readmitted to the Union in 1866.

In 1907 the Tennessee legislature finally authorized the purchase as a governor's residence of a three-story stone house built in 1890 and owned by John Gray, Jr. It was a roomy home, with a large parlor, a conservatory, and a third-floor ballroom—all typical of the opulence of the Gilded Age in which it was conceived. Six first families would live in the Gray house, from 1907 until 1923. The house that had waited until after the wounds of one war healed was destined to fall victim to the needs of another conflict.

After World War I, Tennessee searched for a suitable site for a memorial park honoring state residents who had fought and died in Europe. The old mansion site fell within the boundaries of the chosen acreage. In 1923 it was razed and the resident first family moved into rented quarters. This house was described as "a fine and imposing structure . . . fronting the park and grounds of Vanderbilt University." It was the Tate house, owned by W. R. Tate, and it was soon acquired by the state as Tennessee's second executive residence. It was smaller than the Gray house, with two stories and a compact brick facade. The house had been constructed by a wholesale grocer in 1910. It was of neoclassical design, with a one-story Ionic portico. Five first families would occupy the home until 1949, when legislators deemed it "no longer suitable for occupancy." Tennessee went house hunting once again.

Soon Far Hills was found. Built by William Ridley Wills in 1929, Far Hills was emblematic of the pre-Depression comfort desired by the nation's business leaders. Wills was the founder of a major insurance company based in Nashville. He contracted with the architectural firm of Hart, Freeland, & Roberts to create a fifteen-thousand-square-foot Georgian home on an elevated ten-acre site, and the result was inviting and attractive. Far Hills had stone arches that contrasted with a jutting pediment, flat pilasters, and stone columns. The state paid one hundred fifteen thousand dollars for the house, and Governor Gordon Browning moved his family into the new mansion after his 1949 inauguration.

Far Hills is a symmetrical three-story mansion with a large formal drawing room, a sunroom, a combination library and office, a state dining room, and an elliptical staircase leading to three bedrooms, two staff offices, and the private governor's rooms on the second floor, as well as a large third-floor room now used as a family recreation area. The legislative resolution designating Far Hills as Tennessee's new executive residence referred to it as "a place where the dignity and honor of the state is lodged."

The residence today is home to an impressive collection of Tennessee art and antiques. There are original fixtures—sconces, unique "egg and dart" moldings—first installed by Wills in 1929. As an insurance company president, Wills was concerned with fire safety. Far Hills was built of reinforced concrete with masonry walls. Its interior flooring is of marble or white oak planking.

In the residence's foyer, visitors are greeted by unique peacock door knockers specially ordered by Wills, who then ordered the manufacturer to destroy the mold. The elliptical stairway is made of solid Indiana limestone and concrete, with banisters of wrought iron topped by a carved walnut rail. So precise were the building standards demanded by Wills that the builders had to install and remove the staircase seven times before he approved. Foyer furnishings include a rare New York Sheraton table, probably by Duncan Phyfe; a Baltimore mahogany table from about 1790; and antique lamps once owned by Virginia's famous Custis family, related by marriage to both George Washington and Robert E. Lee.

The dining-room table is a Sheraton mahogany of pedestal design. It seats up to twenty-two guests on Chippendale chairs, precise replicas of a set of Randolph chairs in the Philadelphia Museum of Art. Former First Lady Honey Alexander led a group of volunteers who created the

Below:
The family dining room.

Right:
The foyer. The elliptical stairway was installed and removed seven times before the builder was satisfied.

Opposite, below:
The state drawing room. The portrait over the mantel is of Andrew Jackson, painted from life by Samuel Waldo after the Battle of New Orleans.

needlepoint cushions, which depict Tennessee flora and fauna. The dining room also contains a Hepplewhite mahogany sideboard made in New York soon after the Revolution. The sideboard retains its original finish and brass fixtures and is known to have once belonged to Robert Livingston, the American ambassador to France who negotiated the Louisiana Purchase. It was original to the house and holds silver from the armored cruiser *Tennessee,* commissioned in 1906. The silver later saw service aboard the battleship *Tennessee,* which was badly damaged at Pearl Harbor in 1941, was

Left:
The recently redecorated sitting room displays Tennessee art.

Right:
The dining-room sideboard was made shortly after the American Revolution and belonged to Robert Livingston, the American ambassador to France who negotiated the Louisiana Purchase. A portrait of John Sevier, Tennessee's first governor, hangs above the sideboard.

repaired, and saw battle service in the Coral Sea, at Midway, and in the Solomon Islands during World War II. Also in the dining room are a New York Federal mahogany breakfront from about 1800; a portrait of John Sevier, Tennessee's first governor; and a nineteenth-century English supper service. The breakfront has a fascinating pedigree: the glass in its doors came from New York's Cooper Union, the building where Abraham Lincoln delivered his famous "house divided" speech, and the eagle decorating its top was said to have been in the presidential residence in Philadelphia before the nation's capital was moved to Washington, D.C.

The smaller family dining room is furnished in items donated to the residence by the citizens of Greeneville. A portrait of Sam Houston decorates the governor's office. Although Houston is best known for his association with Texas, he also served as the seventh governor of Tennessee. An inkwell on the desk remembers another famous Tennessean forever linked with Texas—woodsman and onetime congressman Davy Crockett. The inkwell is made from a stone collected at the Alamo in San Antonio, where Crockett fell at the head of a group of Tennessee volunteers.

The sitting room features a Chippendale-style mahogany secretary from about 1780, which is said to have belonged to President Woodrow Wilson. Just outside the sitting room is a new addition to the furnishings, a cherry and tulip poplar sideboard attributed to the cabinetmaker James Hicks and made about 1815. In the state drawing room is a portrait of Tennessee's most famous son, President Andrew Jackson, painted from life by Samuel Waldo after Jackson's victory at the Battle of New Orleans. When the rare portrait was put up for auction in 1971, the White House entered an early bid, but soon withdrew in favor of Jackson's home state. The drawing-room wall covering was hand-painted in Hong Kong and features the Tennessee state flower, the iris.

First families can entertain in less formal surroundings in the sunroom, furnished in cane with a tile floor. The residence's grounds, designated as an arboretum, include many native Tennessee trees as well as a formal water garden and numerous flower beds.

As modern Nashville has grown to surround its wooded grounds, the house that became Tennessee's executive residence has remained "a place where the dignity and honor of the state is lodged."

One of eleven plates of the Rockingham china dessert set, c. 1840, each with a different flower. This plate depicts Tennessee's state flower, the iris.

OHIO

THE GOVERNOR'S RESIDENCE
COLUMBUS

PHOTOGRAPHS BY DAN LEE

The Ohio Governor's Residence.

"What could a minister do with twenty rooms?"

hen Ohio became a state in 1802, its original constitution vested most state power in the legislative body. The first governors had few powers or responsibilities, and there was no need to build an executive residence. In 1812, when the state capital was moved from Chillicothe to Columbus, the Ohio legislature appropriated funds for a capitol building and a prison—but not for a governor's mansion. Several early governors boarded at nearby taverns.

As the years passed and the state grew, Ohio assigned more duties to its chief executive, and the governorship came to be seen as a springboard to national political prominence. When Governor William McKinley won the presidency in 1896, after former Governor Salmon P. Chase had gone on to become a key Lincoln Cabinet member and chief justice of the United States, Ohioans began to take their chief executives far more seriously.

The decision to build the first Ohio governor's mansion grew out of the plight of Governor-elect James M. Cox. Cox and his family arrived in Columbus in 1916, eager for his inauguration, but the house they had hoped to rent was already taken by the incoming secretary of state. The Cox family retired to a hotel, and among the first bills he proposed was one to acquire a permanent executive residence. In 1917, Ohio purchased the Columbus home of Charles H. Lindenberg.

Lindenberg had amassed a fortune in the manufacture of fraternal garb and ceremonial regalia in an era when such groups as the Masons and Knights of Columbus were immensely popular. In 1904, he commissioned a local architect to build a spacious château-style red-brick home for his family, but when the state came calling in 1917, Lindenberg happily sold it. Ohio immediately set to work converting the house into a governor's mansion. Inmates at the state prison crafted furnishings in the Sheraton and Hepplewhite styles. Horticulturists from Ohio State University suggested an elaborate landscape and garden design. The house had a broad central staircase, stained glass windows, and rich woodwork. A vast ballroom spanned the third floor, and there was a skylighted palm room that made the mansion ideal for entertaining. As work on the newly acquired mansion progressed, the Cox family waited for moving-in day.

Governor Cox thought the mansion delightful, but he was destined to spend less time there than he had hoped. He was nominated for president in the fall of 1920. It was an all-Ohio election, with Cox facing a home-state senator, Warren G. Harding. Harding won, and Cox returned to Columbus to serve out the remainder of his term as governor. He moved his family to the mansion in December, and over the next thirty-seven years, the Lindenberg mansion on historic Broad Street was home to ten first families.

Above:
The great room.

Opposite:
The garden room provides access to the patio and the wisteria-covered pergola.

By the mid-1950s, the original mansion was decaying, and the estimated cost of repairs was seen as too extensive to be practical. Ohio's search for a new governor's mansion happily coincided with a family's decision to donate its historic home.

In 1925 the industrialist Joseph Jeffrey decided to reward his son Malcolm, a World War I veteran, with a new home in Bexley, an emerging community east of downtown Columbus. The elder Jeffrey chose the architect Robert Gilmore Hanford to design the Jacobean Revival residence, which replicated the comfortable, sprawling style long associated with eighteenth-century English manor houses. The Jeffrey home featured stone walls, brick chimneys, steep gables, a slate roof, interior wood paneling, and leaded-glass windows—a taste of fine country living transplanted to Columbus. Visitors approached up a wide curving driveway to reach the recessed front door, within a carved limestone entry. Inside was a large entrance hall and a wide carved staircase leading to the second floor. Downstairs was a broad living room, with a bay window and leaded-glass doors leading to the adjacent garden room, along with a music room, a dining room, and a kitchen, which was modernized in later years. The second floor boasted nine rooms and six baths, with balconies overlooking the grounds and gardens from the master bedroom and a second room that was later to become a study for the resident first families. The spacious third floor had nine more bedrooms and three baths, and the home's basement, originally used for storage and utilities, is today a large recreation area.

Malcolm Jeffrey lived in the home with his family until his death in 1930. His widow sold the house to her sister-in-law, Florence Jeffrey Carlile, Malcolm's younger sister. Mrs. Carlile died in 1955, and her daughter Janet inherited the Jeffrey mansion. Janet Carlile had married Charles U. Harris, who became Episcopal bishop of Chicago.

"What," Bishop Harris wondered, "could a minister do with twenty rooms?" He understated the number of rooms in the palatial home by five, but his intentions were clear. The Chicago clergyman contacted Ohio officials, offered the house to the state as its new governor's mansion, and in 1957 signed an agreement transferring the home and much of Mrs. Carlile's personal artifacts and antique furnishings to the state of Ohio. On March 2, 1957, Governor C. William O'Neill and his family moved in. The old Lindenberg house was transformed into a repository for state historic archives, and some years later it was sold to a private owner.

O'Neill and several subsequent chief executives added modern furnishings, paint, and carpet to the new mansion, diluting the original country-manor-house atmosphere. As the changes accumulated, there was a general decline in the appearance and condition of the house. One 1970s first family declined to live in the mansion. By the time of the Richard Celeste administration in the early 1980s, the mansion was in a state of disrepair similar to that which had caused the state to abandon its first executive residence three decades earlier.

This time, the outcome was different. Ohio launched a major restoration project for the historic home. The home's official title was changed: it was now called the Governor's Residence. A private foundation, Friends of the Governor's Residence, launched a long-term restoration and preservation effort, and over most of the next decade much of the Residence was restored to its original glory. Beginning in 1984, the foundation, in concert with the state, coordinated a major grounds improvement project that added a large patio and a fish pond. Reconstituted under Governor George Voinovich as the Governor's Residence Foundation, the group has also worked to replace the Residence's roof with slate approximating the original.

The Foundation's new mission has been to restore the public rooms to the Jacobean Revival theme created by Mr. Jeffrey. Among those contributing to this historic effort was the Harris family, which unearthed detailed photos of the major public rooms taken in the 1930s or 1940s. Gradually, with painstaking care, the Residence has been restored to a close approximation of its earlier appearance. One governor found an original gilt mirror in the attic. A pair of Louis XVI gilt torchères was traced to the Lindenberg house. Other artifacts, from rugs and paintings to a stained

Opposite:
*The Residence has a small
herb garden.*

Below:
The governor's study.

glass transom window once used in a state prison office, were unearthed in storage warehouses or retrieved from private collections. In some cases, the Foundation commissioned replicas of historic furnishings.

Today's Governor's Residence is a trove of new and historic objects brought together in a restored manor house that, while never precisely mirroring the original, has in many ways surpassed it. Its original twenty-five rooms, twelve bathrooms, six fireplaces, and hand-cut oak ceiling beams create a warm, intimate setting, even in the largest of the public rooms. Arranged throughout are antiques collected or restored to match the original atmosphere of the home, or newly commissioned pieces that reflect that same style. When planners sought to furnish the drawing room, they designed a settee, three armchairs, two side chairs, and four stools in Honduran mahogany to match the Jacobean Revival style; but where seventeenth-century designers might have placed ornate oak leaves, Residence designers substituted the trademark Ohio buckeye's leaves and fruit. Then they added an antique A. H. Davenport sofa to complete the "old and new" pairing of similar styles and designs.

The Harris family also participated in the restoration effort, donating items that included a seventeenth-century oak court cupboard that had once stood in the living room—and which stands there today, just as it did in old photographs. So meticulous were these restoration efforts that small

crystal items and objets d'art once owned by the Jeffrey, Carlile, and Harris families were retrieved and placed in their original locations. Eight pieces from the U.S.S. *Ohio*'s silver collection are also displayed in the Residence, and there is a first-floor display of fine Ohio pottery.

First there was the old mansion, then the new mansion, and now there is the Governor's Residence, in a state that resisted the very concept of an executive residence for more than a century. Now the state has avidly embraced the restoration of a home that proved too large for a minister but just right for Ohio's first families. As Bishop Harris noted when he handed the keys to the state of Ohio, his mother-in-law "wanted the house in some way to give a great deal of pleasure to people." Finally, it does.

Ohio artist Howard Chandler Christy painted The Summit *in 1943. Today it hangs above the Residence's grand staircase.*

LOUISIANA

THE GOVERNOR'S MANSION
BATON ROUGE

PHOTOGRAPHS BY ROBERT M. COLEMAN

The Louisiana Governor's Mansion.

In the spirit of Oak Alley . . .

Louisiana's original executive residence was built shortly before the Civil War in Baton Rouge by Nathan King Knox, a leading local businessman. In 1887 the state acquired the large two-story Knox home and designated it the governor's mansion. For forty years chief executives and first families came and went in an orderly succession—until Huey Long won the governorship in 1928. Best known as the Kingfish, Long was determined to modernize Louisiana, starting with its public buildings. He first approached the legislature, complaining that the old mansion was decrepit and unfit for habitation. When it balked at a new mansion, he assembled a gang of convict laborers and simply demolished the old house—a fait accompli that was difficult to dispute.

A new mansion, strongly resembling the White House at 1600 Pennsylvania Avenue, was erected in 1930. Governor Long occasionally visited but never actually lived in this two-story neoclassical home, which had a full basement, four thirty-foot Corinthian columns, a carved pediment, and a slate mansard roof with open balustrades and fourteen dormers. Downstairs was a six-car underground garage, which was later converted for use as an auditorium. The Long mansion had large public rooms on the first floor and family bedrooms and living rooms on the second, including an oval-shaped sitting room again reminiscent of the White House design. Much of the interior was designed on a grand scale. The dining room had floor-to-ceiling windows, and in the library a nine-foot cypress mantel bore the carved image of a pelican, from the Louisiana state seal. After Long's assassination in 1935, the old Louisiana mansion, like the state's political environment, returned to normal. First families lived there for nearly thirty years.

By 1960 there was growing sentiment in favor of replacing the Long mansion with one more representative of Louisiana's rich architectural heritage. Few other states had as many fine examples of the historic antebellum plantation homes, and one of the most impressive was Oak Alley, downriver from Baton Rouge. Like many elegant homes built between 1830 and 1860, Oak Alley was designed in the Greek Revival style. It became the model and inspiration for the present Louisiana Governor's Mansion, created by the architectural firm of Annan & Gilmer of Shreveport. Under the administration of Governor Jimmy Davis, construction of the new Governor's Mansion was completed within fifteen months. When Governor and Mrs. Davis moved in, only a few months remained in his term of office. The old Long mansion was soon converted for use as an arts and sciences museum.

The new Mansion omitted Oak Alley's second-floor veranda and added Georgian influences. White Doric columns line it on all but one side.

Opposite, above:
The antique silver service was presented to Governor Murphy J. Foster in 1893. A century later his grandson, Governor Mike Foster, brought it back to the Mansion.

Opposite:
The dining room. The twenty-one-foot table can be broken down into six individual tables. The 1830s mantel is made from marble quarried in Philadelphia.

Above:
First families can retire to the small family dining room, located behind the main state room. The brass chandelier was once installed in the main dining room at the old mansion.

The exterior is faced with white brick, with a green slate roof and matching slate paving on the wide porches. Outside, the Mansion retains the plantation-home atmosphere, with a wide lawn, flanking trees, and lampposts. The lampposts were imported from Plymouth, England, and are topped by antique copper lanterns from Europe. The parking area is ringed by brick walls with cast-iron railings in the New Orleans style.

The Mansion contains twenty-five thousand square feet of space in three floors and a basement. Upper floors are served by an elevator, which like most of the ground floor is easily reached from both family and public areas. The Mansion designers sought and achieved a level of convenience that blended the public and semiprivate living quarters almost seamlessly. Depending on the event, the downstairs living areas can be opened or sequestered by closing strategically located doors.

There is a private entrance for the first family downstairs, with access to both the basement and the ground floor, which contains security and service areas and a six-car garage. On the state floor, the main entrance is an inviting combination of influences—a fanlight paneled double door hints at plantation design but also borrows from the main doorway of the

Opposite:
The governor's office. The paneling is tidewater cypress.

Opposite, above:
The vestibule light fixture is adorned with the state seal.

Above:
Doorways lead to the surrounding porches from the main state room.

antebellum Ohio home of the late Senator Robert A. Taft. In the entrance vestibule, the state seal is etched on the crystal globe of the light fixture. It and an Adam lamp in the grand stair hall were removed from the old Long mansion. The main reception hall and the stair hall are both paved in Italian marble, with a slab bearing the state seal in the center of the circular stair hall. The artists, who took more than two months to complete the seal, used more than twenty-five hundred separate pieces of inlaid stone, and added their own special touch, a magnolia blossom, which is not part of the official seal.

The main-floor state rooms flank the reception hall. The drawing room to the west and the dining room to the east feature matching five-foot, thirty-branch crystal chandeliers that date from the 1830s. Secondary doorways lead onto the porches from each large public room, much as in Oak Alley and other plantation residences.

The twenty-one-foot dining-room table can be extended to twenty-five feet. It is an eighteenth-century reproduction with a top created from an English antique, and it can also be broken down into six individual tables capable of seating six guests each. The room also contains a pair of large marble-topped serving consoles from the old Long mansion. Adjacent to the dining room are the butlery and the kitchen, the former housing the state china, crystal, and silver. These service areas are paired with a smaller family butlery and kitchen that serve the daily needs of the first family.

The downstairs family living area includes breakfast and dining rooms. In the family dining room, an eighteen-branch brass chandelier hangs above the table; it was removed from the original mansion, stripped of its silver plate, and rehung here. The governor's office is paneled in tidewater cypress.

Second-floor rooms include additional family and guest bedrooms, which overlook the front veranda. The master bedroom continues the plantation theme with a copy of the wood mantel once used in a Louisiana bank building. In the north wing are guest bedrooms, including a large sitting room and the state bedroom. The first lady's office is also located on the second floor. Upstairs, on the third floor, are three additional guest bedrooms, storage areas, and a large family recreation room.

The Louisiana Governor's Mansion is also home to a large art collection, expected to become the core of the new Ogden Museum of Southern Art in New Orleans. The theme of the collection is Louisiana history and scenery, and many paintings depict arching trees lining bayous or plantation scenes.

INDIANA

THE GOVERNOR'S RESIDENCE
INDIANAPOLIS

PHOTOGRAPHS BY RICH MILLER

The Indiana Governor's Residence.

Home at last . . .

Opening page:
The garden fountain on the grounds of the residence.

One of the most important moments in the early history of America came in 1795. The Treaty of Greenville opened lands in what is now the Midwest to white settlement, following the Battle of Fallen Timbers, fought August 20, 1794, near modern Toledo, Ohio. The Treaty of Greenville set a precedent that would prevail for the next seventy-five years as white America pushed westward and absorbed Indian lands bit by bit. Had it not been for that battle and the rarely recalled treaty that followed it, much of what became Indiana could have remained in tribal hands, delaying settlement, territorial status, and statehood, which came in 1816.

Indiana's second territorial governor, William Henry Harrison, was also a general, and in 1811 he defeated the powerful Shawnee confederacy at the Battle of Tippecanoe. His victory would eventually propel Harrison from rented gubernatorial quarters in Indiana to the White House, but it was not until the year of statehood that the first state governor, Jonathan Jennings, lived in what was called the governor's mansion in Corydon. Indianapolis replaced Corydon as the state capital in 1825, and for the next century and a half, Indiana's first families would call a variety of places home, including four more official executive residences and a number of rented quarters.

There was a governor's mansion at Market and Illinois Streets between 1837 and 1861, called "damp and unhealthy" by one first family; a governor's mansion on East Twenty-seventh Street from 1924 through World War II (it has since been demolished); and yet another home called the governor's mansion on historic North Meridian Street from 1945 until 1974, when the present Indiana governor's mansion was acquired. One proposed mansion was never occupied. When the wife of Governor James Brown Ray (served 1825–31) saw the house that the state had allocated for her and her husband, she refused to live there. The neighbors, she complained, would be able to inspect her Monday washing as it hung out to dry. A Civil War governor, Oliver P. Morton, reported residential experiences typical of many of his fellow chief executives over the years; according to records compiled by the Indiana Historical Society, Morton began his tenure at the Market and Illinois Streets mansion, then "boarded at the Bates House . . . boarded at 54 Circle . . . [and] resided at 149 North Pennsylvania." Between 1816 and 1974, the state's first families stayed in at least thirty-six separate residences, hotels, and boardinghouses, often logging as many as four different addresses during a single term in office.

By the 1970s state officials were seeking a thirty-seventh address to call home. The governor's mansion on North Meridian in Indianapolis was deemed unsuitable, and attention soon turned to a fine English Tudor home on more than six acres not far from the old mansion. Built in 1928

Below:
A large metal bird-cage gazebo decorates the Residence grounds.

Right:
The Residence's patio overlooks the grounds.

by local resident Scott Wadley, it had been sold to C. Severin Buschmann, who was willing to sell it to the state as the new mansion. The house, now the Governor's Residence, has a living room, a dining room, a sun porch, a library, an informal dining room, staff offices, and a large kitchen. Upstairs are three bedrooms, a sitting room, and a den on the second floor and a third-floor extra bedroom with attic space. It also has a basement with laundry facilities and a recreation room. Outside is a private backyard garden, a fountain, and herb, flower, and vegetable gardens.

"The state of Indiana," a newspaper account said in 1975, "has a gracious new Governor's Residence." Remodeling and redecorating spanned two years, and when Governor Otis Bowen moved in with his family, they found what was described as "glowing silver and crystal, rich leather, handmade crewel and fine old Oriental rugs." Many of the rugs and other furnishings had been moved from the previous mansion, and the original porte cochère was glassed in to form a portico. Craftsmen also installed large hundred-year-old wooden front doors removed from an old state hospital, and throughout the Residence, decorators created an eighteenth-century atmosphere emboldened with rich colors.

Today's Residence remains largely unchanged from the 1974–75 remodeling, although a wrought-iron gazebo on the south lawn was added in the 1980s. Successive first families have turned to private donors for a growing collection of period antiques and have planted new trees on the already wooded grounds, adding stands of dogwood and Japanese cherry. In 1980, the Indianapolis Garden Club created a large flower garden in honor of the state's many renowned authors; there are thirty-six markers identifying plants with quotations from different Hoosier writers, such as Booth Tarkington, James Whitcomb Riley, and Kurt Vonnegut.

A wall hanging in the sun porch recognizes the diverse history of Indiana's many executive residences. Created by local artists using screenprinting, appliqué, embroidery, and hand-quilting, the tapestry depicts the original mansion in Corydon (1816–22) and the four Indianapolis mansions that followed. It is striped in colors that match stained glass windows in the foyer and which were originally installed in the skylight at the state capitol building. In the foyer there is also a silver punch bowl from the service of the U.S.S. *Indiana;* it still bears a dent from a piece of an exploding shell that struck the battleship during the Spanish-American War.

The hallway leading from the foyer to the first-floor public rooms is decorated with a French Rococo mirror bearing gilt cherubs and dating to

Above:
The grandfather clock in the front hallway was made by William Harris of London in 1702.

Opposite, above:
The stained glass window in the foyer was originally part of the skylight at the Indiana state capitol.

Opposite, below:
The living room. The unique electrically operated player piano was given to the Residence by the Trimble family, the original owners of the former executive residence.

the 1870s. A Queen Anne clock made by William Harris of London in 1702 also adorns the hallway, along with a William and Mary chest with marquetry inlay on walnut.

The wood-paneled library displays books by Indiana authors or about the state. Also displayed in the library is a crystal Statue of Liberty, a gift to the state from France. Traditionally, incumbent first families display family photographs and memorabilia in the library.

The living room centers on a 1920s Steinway piano, one of the first electrically operated player pianos ever manufactured. It was brought from the old North Meridian Street mansion and was inherited by the state from the Trimble family, previous owners of that residence. The Trimbles were patrons of the arts and, around 1933, had the piano elaborately hand-painted. The living-room breakfront is from the estate of Lord Devon of Sussex and was made in 1770. The Chippendale piece still has its original hand-blown glass panes and holds additional pieces from the U.S.S. *Indiana* silver service, along with historic china.

The dining room has a Lalique crystal chandelier, given to the Residence by former neighbors, and a three-pedestal Sheraton cherry table which seats up to eighteen guests. An 1875 English tall case clock is of oak and mahogany, and the case still bears part of the original paper label identifying the maker, Isaac Stokes.

Outside, the Hoosier Heritage Garden has been enlarged with new brick walkways and added hedge borders.

After a gypsy existence that lasted nearly two hundred years, the first families of Indiana are home at last.

MISSISSIPPI

THE GOVERNOR'S MANSION
JACKSON

PHOTOGRAPHS BY GIB FORD, JR.

The Mississippi Governor's Mansion, seen from the east garden.

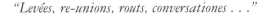

They named the city Jackson, after the president who embodied the democratic ideal of the common people. As capital of the new state of Mississippi, it had a population of less than three thousand, and it was not seemly that the governor and his family should be forced to rent rooms. So in 1833, Mississippi's fledgling legislature passed one of its first bills, an appropriation of ten thousand dollars for the "erection of a suitable house for the Governor in the town of Jackson." For various reasons, state architect William Nichols could not set to work until 1839. As the new home rose, a reporter wrote that "much is anticipated by the elite here . . . when the Executive Mansion shall be ready. . . . Levées, re-unions, routs, conversationes, déjeuners, and soirées, will be the order of the day." By February 1842, with six rooms ready and the rest nearing completion, Governor Tilghman Tucker and his family moved in. After two major restorations and the Civil War, the Mississippi Governor's Mansion is the second oldest continuously occupied executive residence in America.

The modern Mansion remains true to the original Nichols design, a classic Greek Revival home of two stories with a spacious basement. Out front, stone steps lead visitors to the semicircular portico with four fluted Corinthian columns that echo the ancient Monument of Lysicrates in Athens. The theme continues inside, where heart-of-pine floors, handcrafted cornices, lintels, and ceiling friezes preserve an era of elegance. There is much of the Old South in this home, and much history as well.

In the 1850s, the Mansion's parlors witnessed angry debates over secession. During the Civil War, with the coming of the Northern invasion, Jackson was evacuated in 1863, and the Mansion housed wounded Confederate soldiers for a time. Later it served as headquarters for the victorious General William Tecumseh Sherman for a few days. After the war, the Mansion was occupied alternately by elected Mississippi governors and occupying Union officers. In 1868, General Adelbert Ames forcibly evicted Governor Benjamin Humphreys after Humphreys declined a suggestion that the competing officials live there jointly. "Old Ben Humphreys . . . will long live in the memory of his people," proclaimed the local paper. In 1884, the former Confederate president, Jefferson Davis, made one of his last public appearances at the Mansion, by then restored to the custody of Mississippi's elected first families.

In the new century, modern plumbing, electricity, and telephone service were added to the venerable old Mansion, which was for a time considered for sale or even demolition. But Mansion supporters convinced the legislature to preserve "what Sherman would not burn," and in 1908 the state launched the first of two twentieth-century restoration efforts. The project added a matching two-story annex, which replaced a family cottage originally erected to the north. Designers also added a rectangular porte-cochère entrance to the hallway connecting the original and new wings and removed Nichols's original central grand staircase, replacing it with a more conventional flighted stairway. There were exterior modifications as well, including a new brick facing and grounds improvements. Among the first visitors to give their approval was President William Howard Taft.

Mississippi's twentieth-century chief executives have been a colorful group. One Mansion legend involves Governor Earl L. Brewer, who eased an unsophisticated dinner guest's potential embarrassment when the visitor mistook a finger bowl for lemonade: Brewer led his other guests in squeezing lemon into his own bowl, adding sugar, and sipping the makeshift concoction. Another first family observed an unexpected tradition: in 1941, Governor Paul Johnson, Sr., hosted his son's wedding at the Mansion; twenty-four years later, Governor Paul Johnson, Jr., held his daughter's wedding in the same parlor. Governor Ross Barnett was known for his hospitality; he once lent a Mansion bedroom to a hitchhiking college student.

By the 1970s, structural problems made the Mansion unsafe. Architectural historian Charles Peterson and restorationist Edward Jones, who had redecorated several sections of the White House, undertook the second major restoration effort, beginning in 1973. The work spanned two years and included the re-creation of the style of the original Nichols staircase and an intensive effort to locate and acquire furnishings, chandeliers, and other items that reflected the taste and sensibilities of the 1840s. Private funding from garden and school groups also added a new formal garden to the Mansion grounds. At the Mansion rededication in 1975, visitors from across Mississippi lined up to view their historic home in its renewed splendor.

In the octagonal foyer, an Empire Argand chandelier from 1825 hangs overhead, and in the center of the foyer there is a Philadelphia pedestal table in the style of A. G. Quervelle from about 1825. Visitors are drawn to the restored staircase, framed by Corinthian columns.

The front sections of both the first and second floors are restored public rooms, while the rear sections house family living quarters, kitchen, and private studies for the governor and the first lady. Downstairs, visitors can tour the state dining room, where carpeting was added in the 1975 restoration. The carpet was woven in England and based on a design from the 1830s. The main dining table seats sixteen and is one of the few more modern pieces retained during the restoration. Against the wall stands a mahogany sideboard in the style of Duncan Phyfe.

The ground floor also features a pair of distinctive connected parlors on one side of the central foyer and staircase, opposite the state dining room and a third parlor. The front rose parlor carries a red theme throughout, from

Opposite:
A fall-front desk by Michael Allison, New York, c. 1827.

Above:
*The front rose parlor. The crystal chandelier matches the
parlor's red and cranberry color scheme.*

The state dining room. The carpet was created in England and is based on a design from the 1830s.

the cranberry-overlay crystal chandelier above to the gilt Grecian couch from the 1820s and the window hangings. A unique Philadelphia work table in the front rose parlor is perhaps the Mansion's rarest piece. Its gilded supports and feet take the form of dolphins and winged eagle legs. The table dates from the first half of the 1820s.

The back rose parlor continues the carpet theme and contains a wide selection of fine antiques, including an octagonal pedestal table and four gondole chairs. The ornate carved architraves that span the connecting doorway between the parlors replicate the originals.

The gold parlor connects to the state dining room and is a center for Mansion entertainment, with treasured Empire furnishings and a méridienne and companion sofa in the style of Duncan Phyfe.

The public areas on the Mansion's second floor are equally elegant and historic. From the sitting hall, a narrow double door flanked by sidelights opens onto the upstairs balcony. The hall also features an 1880s square piano, a Grecian sofa, and a dark wood secrétaire à abattant. The upstairs bedrooms are all lighted by distinctive chandeliers and have as their themes the colors that give them their names: the gold, green, cream, and pumpkin bedrooms.

In the gold bedroom, Victorian furnishings date from the pre–Civil War administration of Governor William McWillie, whose daughter Annie was the first Mansion bride. The canopied mahogany bed was hers, as was a lacquered and stenciled English writing desk. The green bedroom features a fireplace with the original 1841 carved wooden mantel. In the cream bedroom, the Renaissance Revival half-tester bed has hosted Mansion visitors, who included John F. Kennedy while he was a senator from Massachusetts. The hand-carved four-poster bed in the pumpkin bedroom was donated to the Mansion by a San Antonio, Texas, family.

Family areas of the Mansion are securely separated from the public rooms and include bedrooms, a kitchen and dining area, den, living rooms, offices, and a small conference room. This condominium-style rear section of the Mansion was completely rebuilt in the 1970s restoration effort. The Mansion's basement, which extends beneath both the original and the 1975 front and rear sections, also contains service and staff areas.

The gold bedroom. The bed belonged to Annie McWillie, daughter of a former governor and the first to be married in the Mansion.

The Mansion grounds, too, were extensively renovated in the 1970s. Walkways and flower beds lead to a small gazebo, and in the rose garden are the genetic descendants of a specially bred rose named the Mississippi. The Mansion and its grounds, which are in a developed business area of Jackson, are surrounded by a brick fence and iron gates.

After more than one hundred fifty years, America's second oldest executive residence is still a place for "levées, re-unions, routs, conversationes."

The gold parlor. Empire furnishings are featured in this, the Mansion's primary room for entertaining.

ILLINOIS

THE EXECUTIVE MANSION
SPRINGFIELD

PHOTOGRAPHS BY MATT FERGUSON
AND MARS CASSIDY

The Illinois Executive Mansion.

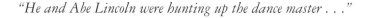

"He and Abe Lincoln were hunting up the dance master . . ."

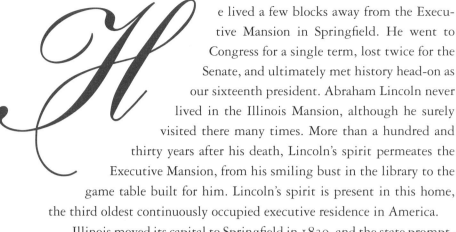

He lived a few blocks away from the Executive Mansion in Springfield. He went to Congress for a single term, lost twice for the Senate, and ultimately met history head-on as our sixteenth president. Abraham Lincoln never lived in the Illinois Mansion, although he surely visited there many times. More than a hundred and thirty years after his death, Lincoln's spirit permeates the Executive Mansion, from his smiling bust in the library to the game table built for him. Lincoln's spirit is present in this home, the third oldest continuously occupied executive residence in America.

Illinois moved its capital to Springfield in 1839, and the state promptly bought a house one block north of Lincoln's home. In 1853, the state sold the original mansion and acquired a lot several blocks away. Called Cook's Grove, the two-and-three-fourths-acre site had often been used by deer hunters. To design a new mansion, officials hired Chicago architect John Murray Van Osdel, who was credited with creating some of America's first steamboats and served as editor of the magazine that would become *Scientific American.* Van Osdel was at work by 1854, and early in 1855 a local editor wrote of the partially built Executive Mansion, "It will be a noble and handsome structure worthy of the state." Governor Joel A. Matteson moved in late in the year, and on January 10, 1856, he hosted the first official reception. It was a bitterly cold day; the gas lines froze and Governor Matteson lit the Mansion's rooms with candles. On the following evening, a second party included dance music, which drew John Todd Stuart, Lincoln's former law partner. It is not known for certain whether Lincoln attended the event, but Stuart wrote of himself two days later, in the third person, that "he danced all evening . . . next day he and Abe Lincoln were hunting up the dance master."

Van Osdel's Mansion was created in modified Georgian style, with the interior done in pure Greek Revival style by the designer Thomas Dennis. This two-way contrast often puzzled later Mansion residents, who were unsure what style of furnishings would best suit the Mansion. A major restoration and enlargement in the 1970s finally settled the matter; today the residence is decorated with English Regency furnishings.

The Illinois Mansion has been home to some colorful families. Mrs. John Riley Tanner (first lady in 1897–1901) loved red and painted the interior woodwork to suit. Governor Henry Horner (served 1933–40) had a pet deer, and Governor Dwight Green (served 1941–49) owned a pet pig that roamed the Mansion grounds. Florence Fifer, the twelve-year-old daughter of Governor Joseph Fifer (served 1889–93), once rode her pet pony through the front hallway; she later became the first woman to serve in the Illinois state senate. Governor William Bissell (served 1857–60) died in the Mansion. Lincoln was a good friend and visited his bedside on March 17, 1860, just months before being nominated for the presidency.

The Executive Mansion has been renovated several times over its long life, beginning in the late 1800s, when a high mansard roof was added and the front steps were divided. Earlier, a kitchen wing had been added to the rear in 1886. There were further renovations and efforts at preservation between the two world wars, including a 1930 project that enclosed the southwest porch and created a library, but by 1965 an architect was warning that "no dancing be done on the first or second floors . . . and that large gatherings be distributed as much as practicable." Experts were so worried that the Mansion might collapse that when large groups were invited for dinner, workers jammed temporary braces under the state dining room's floor. In 1970, Governor Richard Ogilvie and his family moved out of the Mansion to make way for the most extensive restoration project in the house's history.

The elliptical stairway is similar to the original.

Workers soon found some surprises: twenty-seven distinct coats of paint were identified on the woodwork, and scrapers uncovered the original recessed window shutters, which had apparently been repeatedly painted over until they were forgotten. The project also included a large addition to the rear of the Mansion, with public areas and new living quarters for the first family. The addition was built over and replaced a series of earlier additions that had begun in the 1800s. In 1972, the nonprofit Illinois Executive Mansion Association was created to oversee long-term restoration and preservation projects. The Association has acquired a number of one-of-a-kind artifacts. The Mansion collection is of museum quality and includes rare Lincoln artifacts.

Visitors to the modern Illinois Executive Mansion see a replica of the original elliptical stairway, which had been modified in the late 1890s to a rectangular format. In the first-floor entrance hall, the chandelier is original. The front doorknobs are markedly lower than usual, apparently to remind butlers in an earlier era to bow as they welcomed visitors. The front entry doors are rounded, to allow women wearing the ponderous hooped skirts of the 1850s to pass through easily. There are four parlors grouped around the entrance hall and stairway. The entrance also displays a portrait of Lincoln by an unknown artist, along with two petticoat consoles.

The carpet throughout the Mansion bears oak-leaf designs, for the Illinois state tree. The east and west parlors are furnished in Regency style and have matching Baccarat French crystal chandeliers. A vitrine in the west parlor holds a piece of Mary Todd Lincoln's china, a tureen from the original state china, dating to 1855, and the current official state china, manufactured in Illinois.

There are two other parlors surrounding the entrance hall, vestiges of a time when homes featured separate rooms for entertaining men and women and different classes of guests. In the northwest parlor, pole screens stand next to the fireplace. There are a Regency hunt table and an English mahogany secretary from about 1810. The square grand piano in the east parlor is at least two hundred years old and was made by Broadwood & Sons of London, which started in business in 1728. The east parlor features a portrait of Patrick Henry and also one of Edward Baker. Baker—Lincoln's close friend and his son's namesake—died in the Battle of Ball's Bluff in 1861; Mrs. Lincoln presented the portrait to the Mansion after her husband was assassinated in 1865. A second piano is also kept in the east parlor; it is more than one hundred twenty-five years old and was once in the old state capitol building. The northeast parlor complements the northwest parlor in decor.

The state dining room spans the rear of the Mansion's original front wing and contains one of the most unusual artifacts in any executive residence. Peter Scott Glass of Sheboygan County, Wisconsin, completed a table in 1864 that he hoped to present to President Lincoln. It was created with more than twenty thousand pieces of inlaid wood and

The Lincoln table, created in 1864.

The library.

bore the carved faces of Vice President Andrew Johnson and the Civil War generals Ulysses S. Grant and Benjamin Butler. Glass charged people twenty-five cents to view the table in order to raise the funds required to transport it to Washington. After the president's death, the Lincoln table was donated to the Mansion, where it is on display today. The state dining room also includes other touches of history. Two vases displayed here once belonged to John Todd Stuart, who had gone with Lincoln in search of the dance master after the Mansion opened in 1856. There is a breakfront holding silver made for the U.S.S. *Illinois.* The state dining room also contains a number of items bequeathed to the Mansion by former chief executives.

The hall leading from the state dining room into the rear wing has been named the Hall of the First Ladies, where photos of past first ladies adorn the walls, along with one of the Mansion's treasures, a portrait of Mary Todd Lincoln, painted from life by Francis B. Carpenter. Carpenter had also painted the famous *First Reading of the Emancipation Proclamation,* and he lived in the White House for six months while completing that work. Mrs. Lincoln asked Carpenter to do her portrait as a surprise gift for the president, but Mr. Lincoln was killed before it was completed. Mrs. Lincoln ordered Carpenter to destroy the unfinished painting, but he did not do so, and it was reacquired by the Lincoln family in 1930 and donated to the state.

The library also contains Lincoln memorabilia. The Lincoln bowl is said to have been used in the White House between 1861 and 1865. The Lincoln bust here is by Thomas D. Jones, for whom Lincoln posed at the St. Nicholas Hotel in Springfield before traveling to Washington to assume the presidency. It is one of the few likenesses of Lincoln with a smile.

The Margaret Van Meter ballroom was previously called the south room and was part of the 1971 expansion of the Mansion. In 1996 it was renamed for the founder of the association that supports Mansion preservation efforts. The ballroom was modeled after the White House's East Room, with pressed glass chandeliers custom designed for the room, a twenty-one-star American flag (Illinois was the twenty-first state), and portraits of Lincoln, George Washington, and Captain Meriwether Lewis, co-leader of the 1803 expedition to the West.

The Mansion's second floor includes historic rooms at the front and more recent family living quarters at the rear. The Kankakee room is a second-floor parlor, with French block-printed wallpaper. The Bartels suite is named for William Bartels, who carved the nineteen pieces of meticulously decorated furniture in the room; Queen Victoria of England once offered to purchase the items for one million dollars. Another bedroom has furnishings used by Governor Richard Yates, who served during the Civil War.

In the Lincoln bedroom are a bed and dresser presented to the president after his

The state dining room.

election in the tumultuous fall of 1860. He and Mrs. Lincoln placed it in storage in Springfield when they left for Washington, intending to use it on their return. It is there today in the Illinois Executive Mansion, where Abraham Lincoln may have once danced the night away, and where he continues to live for a state and its people.

The Lincoln bedroom. The bed and dresser were presented to the new president in 1860 and were intended for his use after he left office.

ALABAMA

THE GOVERNOR'S MANSION
MONTGOMERY

PHOTOGRAPHS BY ROBERT FOUTS

The Alabama Governor's Mansion.

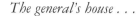

rom statehood in 1819 until the second decade of the twentieth century, Alabama's chief executives had no official residence. That changed when the state acquired the Montgomery home of wealthy merchant Moses Sabel, and Governor Emmett O'Neal moved in in 1911. The Sabel house had been constructed in 1906, and it was an imposing and luxurious residence for its time. The Beaux-Arts brownstone house had a marked French touch. But the two-story stone structure was hardly spacious enough for entertainment and public functions, and for the next four decades it suffered from what one state official politely called "a minimum of maintenance." By 1947 Alabama was searching for a new mansion.

It turned out to be a few blocks away, and from the same era as the Sabel house. Robert Fulwood Ligon, Jr., was the son of a Confederate veteran. His father had later served as Alabama's lieutenant governor, and the younger Ligon followed a predictable path for the offspring of a Southern gentleman in the era after the Civil War. He became a lawyer, married well, and eventually became clerk of the state supreme court. Mr. Ligon was also Colonel Ligon of the Alabama National Guard, and in 1903 he achieved the rank of brigadier general. Forever after he would be known as General Ligon, and the home he built in Montgomery in 1907 was "the general's house."

The architect, Weatherly Carter, chose the prevailing style of the era— neoclassical, a mixture of Southern plantation and classical Greek elements. Out front were four fluted columns topped by Corinthian capitals, supporting a large entablature. The second-story balcony had ornamental balustrades, and the entire facade was designed to reflect the bright Southern sun; the home gleamed. Hailed as "one of Montgomery's finest homes," the house was filmed in 1914 for a silent movie about the city.

General Ligon entertained frequently. When he died, in 1939, his widow remained in the home until her death in 1950—a time when state officials were searching for a new mansion. Because Governor Jim Folsom had lived nearby in the Sabel home and often walked through the neighborhood, he knew of the general's house. Folsom had, in fact, visited with Mrs. Ligon during one of his strolls. He told her the house might make a wonderful governor's mansion—"It looked so Southern." Folsom was among those promoting the acquisition of the house when Mrs. Ligon's daughter, Emily, offered it to the state. Alabama took title to the house in October 1950.

As the Governor's Mansion, the house was renovated and redecorated, and a new kitchen, utilities, and a rear marble terrace were added. The upstairs rooms were even more extensively remodeled. Today the Mansion is a blend of old and new, with original wall sconces and chandeliers in rooms with more modern drapes and carpeting. Sadly, the state did not choose to retain many of the Ligon-era Victorian-style furnishings, which were sold as antiques. Only four original items remain in the Mansion today. Still, the 1950 renovation was not without its benefits. A newspaper story of the time said that the designation Governor's Mansion "fits as well as opera gloves." As might be expected, others complained at the renovation's cost of one hundred thirty-two thousand dollars. "The state," another paper complained, "had bought a pig in a poke and to make matters worse it was an old pig in a poke."

Meanwhile, the original Sabel home was sold to a private owner, eventually reacquired by the state, and demolished in the 1960s to make room for a highway.

In the 1950s the state purchased a lot and house adjoining the Mansion, where a later administration constructed a swimming pool in the shape of Alabama and extended the Mansion grounds. Governors who followed added a brick wall and gatehouses and restored much of the interior woodwork. In 1972, a fire damaged the rear servants' quarters, prompting additional renovations. But the Mansion was generally regarded as "dilapidated" by the mid-1970s, and in 1974 a major restoration of the architectural shell was undertaken. In the 1980s, a private group dubbed Friends of the Mansion launched an effort to furnish the Mansion in styles associated with the nineteenth century.

General Ligon would still recognize his house today. In the main foyer, triple-layer molding and pilasters frame the doorways leading to the ground-floor rooms, which include living, dining, and breakfast rooms, as well as studies for the governor and first lady. The main staircase, modified since the general lived here, soars two full stories and splits into twin staircases that separate at the second floor.

The living room retains much of the original flavor of the house, with features such as floor-to-ceiling gold-leaf mirrors, a grand piano, and a pink marble fireplace. The adjacent sunroom is an enclosed porch, furnished in light wicker with hanging plants; windows extend around three-fourths of the room, offering views of the rear and side gardens. The Mansion's open grounds have been reduced by the addition of the swimming pool and other exterior modifications over the years, but the rear white-marble terrace, added in 1950, and a tennis court add a cozy, self-contained feeling to the grounds.

The ground-floor first lady's room is a classically furnished parlor that features a Colonial blue damask sofa and chairs in cranberry, blue, and golden yellow. Brass and crystal candelabras decorate the marble fireplace mantel. From the first lady's room, visitors enter the formal dining room, which seats eighteen on chairs with covers created by the Mountain Brook Needlepoint Guild, illustrating flags and Alabama historic scenes. The dining room also has a marble fireplace, and an antique buffet and breakfront

The main foyer. The grand staircase splits into a pair of winding stairways that lead to the second floor.

Below:
The dining room. The Amari china was acquired in 1979, while the mahogany dining table dates to the early 1900s.

Right:
The breakfast room. The wall covering illustrates the vine and olive culture pioneered by eighteenth-century French immigrants to Demopolis, Alabama.

The first lady's parlor.
The furnishings reflect the
Mt. Vernon style.

Inset:
Among the Mansion's artworks
is Mountain Tops in the
Snow, *by Thomas Moran.*

face each other from opposite walls. The Czech crystal chandelier counts 1,368 elements. The room also contains silver goblets from the U.S.S. *Alabama*—a touch that perhaps the general himself would have appreciated.

Family members often dine in the small breakfast room, just off the remodeled modern kitchen. The decorative wall fabric here is in the Demopolis design, depicting scenes from Demopolis, Alabama's French "vine and olive colony" from the early 1800s. President Thomas Jefferson had encouraged émigrés fleeing the French Revolution to settle there. The fabric matches the black-and-white tiled floor, which leads visitors onto the

The governor's den. The Mansion's most comfortable room is a good place for reading.

white-marble terrace, with its wrought-iron railings and awnings. Also adjoining the breakfast room is the governor's study, where Alabama's chief executives can find solitude for reading and work.

The Mansion's second floor includes four bedrooms, the first lady's office, a study, and five bathrooms. Most historic is the yellow room, which contains Governor James ("Big Jim") Folsom's oversize bed. The blue room is decorated as its name implies, and the large master bedroom is traditionally decorated to fit the preferences of the resident first family. In the study, the materials are leather and fabric, with an outdoors or hunting theme.

MAINE

BLAINE HOUSE
AUGUSTA

PHOTOGRAPHS BY BRIAN VANDEN BRINK

Blaine House.

A rambling old sea captain's house . . .

In the historical novels of Kenneth Roberts, Mainers are portrayed as stalwart tamers of the sea and of the wooded frontier, for Maine's shores are rocky, its forests dense and seemingly limitless. Other New Englanders call Maine "Down East," and it is indeed a different sort of land, full of challenges and deep woods. In the nineteenth century, it took grit to settle here and endurance to stay.

In 1830 Captain James Hall of Bath acquired a plot of land along the Kennebec River in Augusta, and there he built a sturdy square-frame house at the corner of State and Capitol Streets, across from the new Bulfinch-designed state capitol building. Hall added to the house before he died, and his wife lived there for a time before selling it to Greenwood Child, a local merchant. When he died in 1855, the old house once again went on the market.

Seven years later, James G. Blaine gave his wife, Harriet, five thousand dollars for her birthday. A native of Kentucky, Blaine had settled in Augusta as a newspaperman. He had joined the new Republican Party in 1858; he became speaker of the Maine statehouse, and he won a seat in Congress in the same month he gave Harriet her birthday present. She promptly bought the old Hall house, and over the years the Blaines remodeled and enlarged it several times, in keeping with James Blaine's growing political career. Blaine went on to become a United States senator, a secretary of state, and, in 1884, the unsuccessful Republican nominee for president. For most of the last third of the nineteenth century, he was Maine's most prominent public figure. Blaine died in 1893, and Harriet ten years later. One governor, John F. Hill, had rented the house during his term, and young members of the state legislature later leased it during sessions. In 1917, the family gave the house to Walker Blaine Beale, grandson of the long-dead political patriarch. He, in turn, joined the U.S. Army to fight in France and lent the house to the state. Maine coordinated its war effort in Blaine House by installing the state's Committee on Public Safety there. When young Lieutenant Beale died at Saint-Mihiel, his mother mailed the deed to Governor Carl Milliken. Her "first and strongest desire," the bereaved mother wrote, was that Blaine House be "used and maintained as the official residence for the Governor of Maine." She asked only that a plaque be placed in the front hall recalling her son's sacrifice in the Great War. That plaque is there today.

The house bears James G. Blaine's name, and his study is still preserved there, although he never served as governor. Such is his legacy that more than a century after his death, Maine's executive residence is universally known as Blaine House. The state gratefully accepted Mrs. Beale's offer, bought up adjacent lots to expand the grounds, and in 1919 hired the architect John Calvin Stevens to remodel the old mansion.

By 1920, Stevens was finished. His goal was to restore Blaine House to something like its original simplicity. Captain Hall had constructed his house in a combined Federal and Greek Revival style, with a hipped roof, a broad facade, and a door in the center. The rooms fanned out on either side of a central hall, with the kitchen out back. The porch adapted Greek Revival elements, including Ionic columns. By 1872, the Blaines had given the design an Italianate flavor and expanded the house by adding a conservatory, a cupola, a porch, and a second section that mirrored the older portion of the house. Here Blaine placed his study and billiard room. He also had parquet floors put down, added wainscoting, and remodeled the first-floor rooms in the original section, knocking out walls and installing Corinthian columns to create larger dining and reception rooms.

Stevens linked the original and newer parts of the house together. He painted the whole exterior white, added green shutters, and built a new two-story wing at the rear of the house, angled off from the newer section. This wing contained service and servants' areas and greatly expanded the home's total space. Stevens gave the interiors their respective colors: blue and gold in the reception room, green and silver in the state dining room. Other rooms were papered in Louis XIV Alsatian patterns. A sunroom, a large family dining room, and larger bedrooms were added. Outside, Stevens modified the cupolas and restored much of the original Federal and Greek Revival appearance. Blaine House today is essentially as Stevens intended, although restoration efforts in the 1950s repaired the roof and floors. In the late 1980s, under Governor John R. McKernan, Jr., and his wife, Senator Olympia Snowe, the Blaine House Restoration Fund guided additional restoration efforts, including a project to restore the grounds to their original state, using the 1920 landscape plans.

The reception room. The drapery fabric and colors are similar to those used in 1919. James G. Blaine imported the black Italian marble fireplaces.

Blaine House is a rambling house with few of the trappings one associates with an executive residence. First families have almost always reported feeling comfortable from their first moments there. Some have kept unusual pets, including baby lambs and a pair of alligators. There is a simple waist-high wooden slat fence around Blaine House, and visitors can approach the front door as they would a neighbor's. Inside, the narrow entrance hall still stretches the length of the house, as Captain Hall intended. The Beale plaque hangs beside Colonial sconces. Upstairs, at the curve of the staircase, a plaster statue of the goddess Minerva stands in a hallway niche. It is a relic of the Blaine occupancy, as is the bust of the poet Lord Byron in another niche over the hall doorway.

The reception room is blue and gold. A paint analysis done for the 1980s restoration has resulted in some new tints here—moss-green walls and ivory woodwork that approximate original hues. Draperies also match 1919 photos of the room. The gilded overmantel mirrors date from the early nineteenth century. Twin fireplaces, vestiges of this room's having

The sunroom. The sunroom was originally an open porch, enclosed during the 1919 remodeling of Blaine House.

originally been two separate chambers, are of Italian black marble and date from Blaine's ownership of the house. The reception room also displays scenic paintings of Maine.

In the state dining room, the color scheme of green and silver is intended to symbolize Maine's forests and lakes. The striped wallpaper was printed in Cincinnati in 1908, and the woven vine border is a reproduction of a Brunschwig & Fils design. The Priscilla Turner rug is based on an 1870s design; it was created in Auburn, Maine. A portrait of James G. Blaine looks down from over the white mantel. A reproduction of a Chippendale cabinet holds the cobalt-blue state china, which bears Maine's state seal. Perhaps the most historic items in the state dining room came from the ill-fated battleship *Maine,* sunk in Havana harbor by an explosion, the 1898 incident that triggered the Spanish-American War. The ship's silver service was salvaged and used aboard the second U.S.S. *Maine* until that vessel was decommissioned in 1922. Today, Blaine House continues to "Remember the Maine."

A smaller family dining room adjoins the larger state dining room. It contains a simple Hepplewhite table, chairs, and sideboard. A doorway opens onto the garden.

The sunroom, added in the 1919–20 remodeling, was originally an open porch and retains its long, narrow dimensions. The room's windows overlook the state capitol building, and the trellis-patterned draperies add an outdoor motif to the room, which has a granite fireplace and comfortable furnishings that include a grand piano and an Empire sofa.

The Blaine study has been carefully restored and furnished with the mahogany chair and desk that James G. Blaine used on the floor of the Senate. The wallpaper is a reproduction of the paper Blaine hand-copied from the wall of Abraham Lincoln's study in the White House. Books line one wall opposite the dark stone fireplace, and a second desk bears a large inkwell and a statuette of Shakespeare. Over the fireplace is an engraving of the Francis B. Carpenter painting of Lincoln reading the Emancipation Proclamation to his Cabinet. A glass frame attached to Blaine's Senate desk holds a handwritten card dated April 7, 1865; in the closing days of the Civil War, it authorized "the bearer Mr. Blaine to pass from City Point to Richmond and return," and it is signed "A. Lincoln."

The Blaine study. Senator Blaine used the desk and chair during his service in Washington. The overmantel painting is a copy of Francis B. Carpenter's famous work The First Reading of the Emancipation Proclamation.

The family dining room. First families enjoy easy access to the outdoor garden.

The game room is also much as Blaine left it, with a restored two-tone mahogany and birch floor, a World War I—era pool table, and two Tiffany-style hanging lamps. The first family photograph collection also hangs here, depicting past residents of Blaine House, and there is a display cabinet filled with Blaine campaign buttons and other memorabilia.

Blaine House is aptly named. It is as if the great man still lived here, just down the hall in one of the house's comfortable rooms. One governor, after casually tossing his hat on a chair in the study, heard touring visitors commenting on how immediate and lifelike the room was; when the guide told them that the room was just as Mr. Blaine left it, decades earlier, a young tourist said, "See, Mother, even his hat!"

Above, left:
The state dining room. Over the mantel is a portrait of James G. Blaine donated to the house by his daughter.

Above, right:
Made in 1895 for the U.S.S. Maine, *these silver serving dishes have been exhibited in the state dining room since 1922.*

MISSOURI

THE GOVERNOR'S MANSION
JEFFERSON CITY

PHOTOGRAPHS BY HUGO H. HARPER,
NEIL W. SAUER, ROGER BERG, AND
ALISE O'BRIEN

"A handclasp with history . . ."

From its early history, the ownership of the area now known as Missouri has frequently changed hands. First the French recognized the land's value, founding St. Geneviève on the Mississippi River in 1735 and St. Louis in 1764, which soon became a fur-trading center. Then control of the area west of the Mississippi went to Spain in the 1760s, following the French and Indian War. A secret treaty in 1800 transferred control of the region back to France. The vast territory that included St. Louis and went by the name of Upper Louisiana was finally purchased by President Thomas Jefferson in 1803. Even before the purchase was completed, Jefferson chose Meriwether Lewis and William Clark to explore the region. Their expedition left from St. Louis in 1804 and returned twenty-eight months later.

Fittingly, both Lewis and Clark were later appointed territorial governors of the area known as the Territory of Louisiana and later renamed the Territory of Missouri. It was Clark who established the first official executive residence for the Missouri Territory. His home in St. Louis had a long room called the council chamber, where he met with the chiefs of the Indian nations, who were coming into increasing contact with westward-bound white trappers and settlers. Clark was an indefatigable collector; the council room became a kind of museum, jammed with canoes, various artifacts, and even excavated mastodon bones.

Missouri was the major jumping-off point to the Far West, and with its growing population merited statehood in 1821. St. Charles was its first capital, but the legislature decreed that the permanent seat of government should be located on the Missouri River somewhere near the center of the state. It chose well on geographic grounds, but envisioning Jefferson City as the capital took some effort in 1821. It was a river stop with but one official resident, a saloonkeeper. But build it they did: by 1826, Missouri's first official building, a two-story brick structure, had risen on the bluffs. The state senate met upstairs, the house of representatives downstairs, and the governor—a bachelor named John Miller—lived in two cramped corner rooms. At night the officials of the new state could hear wolves howling at the edge of town and smell the campfires of Indians come to parley.

In 1832 the legislature set aside funds for a more permanent executive residence in Jefferson City. It was a limestone-block house with a two-story portico situated on the south of the same block as the state capitol building, where Governor Miller had lived in tiny rooms. The mansion soon took on a new social importance as Governor Lilburn Boggs, who had married Daniel Boone's granddaughter, Panthea, began entertaining state officials. They said the mansion was too small, which it may have been, but even with its stone construction it did not escape the threat of fire. In 1837

Opening page:
The Missouri Children's Fountain, by sculptor Jamie G. Anderson, on the grounds of the Mansion.

Opposite:
The Missouri Governor's Mansion

the state capitol burned, and rescuers narrowly saved the mansion by covering its roof with wet blankets.

Later residents included First Lady Lavinia Marmaduke, whose family tree may be the most intriguing of any state first lady's in American history. Her father, Dr. John Sappington, was an entrepreneur who used quinine as a secret ingredient in his special pills that treated malaria; her mother was a sister of Kentucky's governor; each of her three sisters, one after another, married Claiborne Fox Jackson, who became governor of Missouri in 1861; and her son, a Confederate general, also won the governorship.

During the memorable year 1857, four different governors served within a twelve-month period, one with a tenure of only fifty-three days, the shortest term in the state's history. In the turbulent Civil War period, Missouri was a key border state. While remaining exclusively under Union control during the war, Missouri was the site of a number of significant battles. The old mansion sat vacant through the war as governors came and went. In 1871, crowds avoided the reception hosted by a new governor because they were afraid the neglected mansion's upper floors were unsafe. The same year, the Missouri legislature appropriated fifty thousand dollars for a new mansion, to be built on the site of the first structure. The architect George Ingram Barnett designed a three-story Renaissance Revival home with Italianate and French influences. Three days after it was occupied, on January 23, 1872, the people of Jefferson City greeted the home's first official visitor, Grand Duke Alexis of Russia, who was on a hunting expedition to the West.

The Missouri Governor's Mansion was an architectural gem. Built of red brick, it featured light-colored stone quoins at the corners as well as stone frames surrounding the windows and doors. It was topped by a mansard roof with iron grillwork. Four pink-granite columns supported the portico. Double doors, fourteen feet tall and hand-carved from walnut, opened for the Grand Duke upon his arrival at the Mansion. The first floor was designed with guests in mind, and the sweeping grand stairway had a walnut railing carved by a Swiss artisan. Downstairs were the great hall, the library, the double parlor, and the dining room. Upstairs were seven bedrooms on the second floor and six more on the third, along with a ballroom.

Subsequent first families have made changes to portions of the Mansion. Glass doors were added to the front entrance in the 1880s. By 1900, it was traditional for each departing first lady to leave an oil portrait of herself at the Mansion. In

1903, a sheltered south entrance, called a porte cochère, was added. The Mansion was further modified after a 1905 chimney fire spread to the second floor. When the state capitol, too, burned, in 1911, the original records of the Mansion were lost in the fire. By the 1930s, a new state capitol had been dedicated, but the Mansion was showing its age. The roof leaked and the grand stairway was sagging. During the administration of Governor Lloyd Stark, the Mansion underwent its most extensive renovation to date, including construction of a kitchen wing in place of the old south entrance and installation of a new roof.

There were additional redecorations and modifications through the 1950s, but in each case, the goal was primarily crisis management: a sagging wall here, a leak there. Several first ladies—Juanita Donnelly in the 1950s and Geraldine Dalton in the 1960s—encouraged the legislature to initiate a program for the Mansion's care, but to no avail. First Lady Betty Hearnes launched the exterior restoration in 1969 by taking all the paint off the bricks. However, it was not until First Lady Carolyn Bond's work in the 1970s that the Mansion came under the auspices of a comprehensive historical preservation effort. For the next two decades, Missouri Mansion Preservation, Inc., oversaw the Mansion's preservation, joining private funds for restoration with state appropriations for structural repairs.

Above:
The double parlor, two rooms used as one and divided by marbleized columns.

The focus of the preservation effort between 1976 and 1983 was the first floor and its public rooms, which today are considered among the nation's finest examples of Renaissance Revival restoration. Visitors entering the great hall encounter one of the Mansion's nine fireplaces and a rich Victorian color scheme that continues throughout the public rooms. The stairway winds gently upward past the oil portrait of First Lady Margaret Stephens, who started the tradition of placing first ladies' portraits in the Mansion, and an ornate brass-and-crystal Archer & Pancoast globed chandelier. The great hall features a ten-piece parlor suite that was part of the Smithsonian Institution's 1876 centennial exhibition of Renaissance Revival furnishings. Each of the first-floor rooms soars seventeen feet from floor to ceiling, making the public areas of the Mansion among the most spacious in America.

Huge doorways open from the great hall into the library, the double parlor, and the dining room. In the double parlor, craftsmen have created a ceiling stencil adapted from period color studies and confirmed by an 1872 oil painting of a similar setting. Draperies complement the ceiling colors—gray-blues, ivory, rose, and burgundy accented with gold leaf—and the double parlor also features a bordered Wilton carpet, a fringed circular ottoman, and a large period parlor suite attributed to the nineteenth-century furniture maker John Jelliff. The ornate overmantel mirror was a gift from the Bond family; throughout most of the twentieth century, departing first families have presented a major gift to the Mansion.

The double parlor's name reflects its two connected wings, one rectangular and the other half-oval. They are separated by marbleized Corinthian columns. From the 1889 Chickering piano to a center table with apsidal ends that mirror the exterior design of the Mansion, the impression is one of roomy elegance and hospitality.

The dining room was originally two rooms that could be divided by a partition. The combined room still retains two marble fireplace mantels. Furnishings here include a sideboard acquired for the previous mansion in the 1840s and silver-service items from the U.S.S. *Missouri,* the battleship

Above:
The library, decked out for the holidays.

Left:
The dining room. On the table is the silver service from the U.S.S. Missouri.

on whose deck the Japanese surrendered in 1945, ending World War II. The Empire mahogany table dates from the 1830s. A unique mirrored pier table was designed to reflect candlelight.

The library is inviting, with dark green wall coverings, a vast over-mantel mirror, and plush chairs arranged around a tea table. Most of the furnishings—including matching bookcases and chairs from the famous Jedediah Willcox mansion in Connecticut—are of walnut, a native Missouri wood.

Upstairs, restoration efforts have focused on the Stark bedroom on the second floor. The room features a mahogany Rococo Revival half-tester bed and matching dresser and a six-light Mitchell-Vance ceiling fixture from 1870.

On the third floor, the restored ballroom spans the full width of the Mansion. Its ceiling is decorated in tripartite design: gold filigree in the frieze, the wall field in Pompeian red, and a dado formed of decorative square panels in brown. Mirrors reflect from every angle and give an impression of added space and activity, while overhead are 1880 Cornelius & Baker brass and crystal chandeliers. The furnishings include a suite of gold-leaf ballroom furniture exhibited at the 1904 World's Fair in St. Louis, an 1885 billiard table, and a Renaissance Revival ebonized upright piano from about 1881.

On the Mansion front lawn, a bronze sculpture of children playing on a fountain commemorates the Mansion's one hundred twenty-fifth year. The idea of the Missouri Children's Fountain was conceived by First Lady Jean Carnahan and is the work of Missouri sculptor Jamie G. Anderson.

One of Missouri's first ladies, Geraldine Dalton, first encountered the Mansion when her husband was inaugurated in 1961. She said that the experience of entering through those huge front doors seemed to offer "a handclasp with history." This was a Mansion first lit by candles and oil lamps, and it still has something of that golden light, preserved for a second century.

ARKANSAS

THE GOVERNOR'S MANSION
LITTLE ROCK

PHOTOGRAPHS BY MIKE TIBBIT

The Arkansas Governor's Mansion.

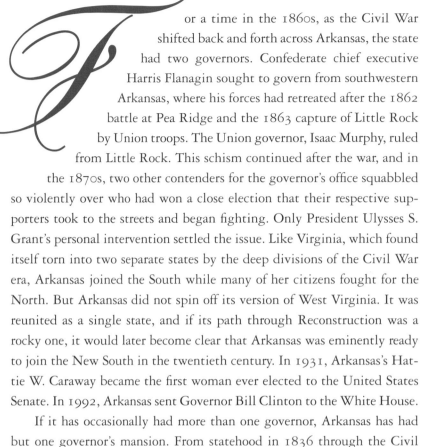

or a time in the 1860s, as the Civil War shifted back and forth across Arkansas, the state had two governors. Confederate chief executive Harris Flanagin sought to govern from southwestern Arkansas, where his forces had retreated after the 1862 battle at Pea Ridge and the 1863 capture of Little Rock by Union troops. The Union governor, Isaac Murphy, ruled from Little Rock. This schism continued after the war, and in the 1870s, two other contenders for the governor's office squabbled so violently over who had won a close election that their respective supporters took to the streets and began fighting. Only President Ulysses S. Grant's personal intervention settled the issue. Like Virginia, which found itself torn into two separate states by the deep divisions of the Civil War era, Arkansas joined the South while many of her citizens fought for the North. But Arkansas did not spin off its version of West Virginia. It was reunited as a single state, and if its path through Reconstruction was a rocky one, it would later become clear that Arkansas was eminently ready to join the New South in the twentieth century. In 1931, Arkansas's Hattie W. Caraway became the first woman ever elected to the United States Senate. In 1992, Arkansas sent Governor Bill Clinton to the White House.

If it has occasionally had more than one governor, Arkansas has had but one governor's mansion. From statehood in 1836 through the Civil War and Reconstruction and into the twentieth century, the state had no official executive residence at all. In 1944, the Arkansas Federation of Women's Clubs began lobbying state officials on behalf of a mansion, but initial legislative efforts to build one were rejected. Finally, in 1947, the Arkansas legislature created a Governor's Mansion Commission, and by December of that year Governor Ben T. Laney was laying the Mansion's cornerstone on property near the state capitol building.

The site of the Governor's Mansion has had a rich history. When Arkansas became a state, the federal government issued a grant of five sections of land in Little Rock to help provide for a capitol building. The land was later sold—first to Chester Ashley, who became a U.S. senator, and later to a railroad executive, Roswell Beebe. The land ultimately passed to the Fulton family. William S. Fulton had served as the final territorial governor of Arkansas, and he later represented the new state in the United States Senate. His home, Rosewood, described as "a fine place a mile or so south of town," was just west of the present Mansion's site. After Fulton died in 1844 the property passed to his widow, and after her death the state's School for the Blind moved to Little Rock and leased Rosewood. In 1869 the school added seven adjoining acres, bought from the Fulton estate, and there it erected several buildings to house students and classrooms. The site afforded a grand view of the capitol, and trustees of the school were pleased.

The dining room. The walls are covered with hand-painted silk paper from England.

"The surface of the ground is so cut and laid as to present a plat of great beauty and utility . . . most enchanting," wrote one of the trustees.

In 1939 the School for the Blind moved to a new facility and its buildings were left empty. So they remained until 1947, when the site was rededicated as the location of the new Governor's Mansion. The architects, Frank J. Ginocchio, Jr., and Edwin B. Cromwell, used three hundred thousand bricks from the old school buildings to build the Mansion, which they designed in a symmetrical Georgian Colonial style. On January 10, 1950, the Mansion was formally dedicated, and as many as a hundred eighty thousand citizens filed through it during the next three days to view the new home of Arkansas's first families.

The two-story Governor's Mansion has a north formal portico with four columns. The original iron balconies and interior circular stairways incorporated railings that matched those in the old capitol building, known as the old statehouse. The iron stairway has been replaced by a hand-carved wooden staircase, with the state seal carved in the first-floor banister. The central portion of the Mansion extends east and west into semidetached wings that form individual guest houses, each with its own living room, bedrooms, and baths. The wings are linked to the main house by walled walkways, a feature borrowed from the design of many Virginia homes of the eighteenth century. The Mansion also has a rear, or south, terrace and a large entry hall. The inside circular staircase extends from the basement to the second floor, and at the landing a large Palladian window affords a view of the south Mansion grounds.

On the first floor, east of the main hall, is the formal drawing room, a spacious twenty-five-by-thirty-five-foot room for entertainment and state functions. The windows reach to the floor and are separated by ornamental plaster panels. There is a large fireplace in the formal drawing room, with an impressive nine-foot mantel. Guests step down into a smaller east room, also called the morning room.

The ground floor also includes the state dining room, its walls covered with hand-painted silk paper from England above wainscoting. A large French crystal chandelier lights the room. A smaller private dining room is at the rear of the Mansion; a bay window overlooks the grounds; and the rear service stairway gives the first family private access to the upstairs living quarters. In the west wing on the first floor are the kitchen and utility rooms. The upstairs living quarters include four bedrooms and four baths, as well as a study for the chief executive. First families have traditionally furnished these rooms to fit their personal tastes.

The Mansion's furnishings have a distinctive Arkansas flavor. The decorated chair seats in the state dining room were created by residents of Pine Bluff in 1972. The historic subjects and themes depicted on them include Indian tribes, Arkansas's French and Spanish Colonial heritage, its place as part of the Louisiana Purchase, the Civil War era, the state seal, and examples of the state's scenic beauty. The room also holds the silver

Left:
The U.S.S. Arkansas *silver service is displayed in the Mansion.*

Below:
The dining-room chair seats display scenes from Arkansas's past.

Right:
The Arkansas state seal is hand-carved into the banister in the great stairwell.

service from the U.S.S. *Arkansas,* which was presented to the Navy in 1919 and returned to the state after World War II. The chandelier is of French origin, of crystal and ormolu, and the four-part banquet table is a mahogany and satinwood reproduction in an English Chippendale style. The antique sideboard has a unique brass gallery.

The entrance gates to the Mansion were originally crafted of iron and donated to the state's Confederate veterans' home by former Governor George W. Donaghey (served 1909–13). When the home was relocated, the gates were added to the Mansion's entrance.

The interior of the Mansion is decorated in an eighteenth-century period motif. In the entrance hall are two brass chandeliers and hurricane sconces, replicas of those used in official buildings in Williamsburg, Virginia. The drawing room's furniture includes reproductions in eighteenth-century styles, as well as an English antique mahogany chest and a rug that is a handmade copy of an old French Aubusson. In the dining and drawing rooms, the color scheme is based on sea-foam green.

The first floor also has a den, or informal living room, furnished in a less formal Colonial style, and the family dining room is done in early American pieces. In the guest house, the theme continues, with period reproductions again in a less formal style. It is decorated in Empire antiques and reproductions from the 1836 statehood period.

Artworks in the Mansion include a portrait of General James Miller, a hero of the War of 1812. The Mansion also contains a grand piano donated by Mrs. Agnes Bass Shinn, a leader of the women's-club effort that led to the construction of the Mansion, and a seven-foot grandfather clock presented in 1976 by former First Lady Margaret F. Cherry in honor of Governor Francis B. Cherry (served 1953–55).

Today, Arkansas has one governor and one mansion—a destiny that was not always certain.

MICHIGAN

THE GOVERNOR'S RESIDENCE
LANSING

PHOTOGRAPHS BY DENNIS CRAFT
AND THOMAS GENNARA

The Michigan Governor's Residence.

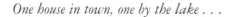

here is no place in Michigan more than eighty-five miles from one of the Great Lakes. Those vast inland bodies of water have determined Michigan's destiny since Etienne Brulé, a French explorer, first landed at the future site of Sault Sainte Marie, the oldest city in the Midwest. The French, the English, and the Americans came to Michigan for furs, lumber, trade, and empire; Major Robert Rogers led his fabled Rangers to Detroit during the French and Indian War; Lieutenant Oliver Perry defeated the British on Lake Erie in a key battle of the War of 1812.

In 1837, Michigan became our twenty-sixth state. Ten years later, the state capital was shifted from Detroit to Lansing, but until 1969, Michigan's first families had no official residence in the capital city. It says much about Michigan and its intricate bond with the vast waterways that surround it that governors had an official summer house, on Mackinac Island, more than two decades before the state purchased them a home near the capital.

The Governor's Residence, established in 1969, was not the state's first attempt to give first families a place to live. When Governor Epaphroditus Ransom was inaugurated at Lansing in 1848, he found the town to consist of little more than a sawmill and a handful of log buildings. There are dim historical accounts of a house constructed for the Ransom family's use, but his successor is said to have found it too small. At least one lieutenant governor later lived there, and the house was eventually abandoned.

Governors continued to visit Lansing during legislative sessions and live at home the rest of the year until the 1880s, when Governor Russell Alger became the first to move his family permanently to the capital city. Subsequent chief executives rented or bought houses in Lansing. It was a quadrennial ritual: the new governor would arrive to set up his administration, while the new first lady hunted for a house. In 1969, Howard Sober, a trucking executive who apparently felt the state's first families deserved better, offered to donate his Lansing home to the state of Michigan as its chief executive's residence.

Sober had built the house in 1959. It was a single-story, L-shaped, ten-room ranch house on a three-and-one-fifth-acre lot, designed by the architect Wallace Frost. It sprawled over more than ten thousand square feet and presented a low, modern profile. Inside, it had large living and dining rooms, atriums, and other areas well suited to hosting large groups. Sober and his wife had entertained frequently here, and the house was designed to comfortably accommodate sizable parties. Sober was willing to donate the house but asked that the state pay for its furnishings, which had been designed to match the original construction. Governor William Milliken and his family promptly moved in, and they soon enclosed a rear screened

The formal dining room. The crystal chandelier is original to the Residence. The bordered carpeting reflects Michigan's native flowers and birds.

The library.

terrace in glass to provide a place for meetings. The Sober house had quickly become the Governor's Residence.

The Residence was redecorated under the auspices of the newly formed Friends of the Governor's Residence in the 1980s, but its basic design is largely as the Sober family intended. It has large, central public rooms dividing the kitchen and living wings. Ceilings are fifteen feet high; the spacious living room was clearly designed for large groups. There wide windows provide a direct connection to the outdoors, and the house could be transplanted to Southern California with minimal modifications. There are modern built-in bookshelves in the den and a distinctive Federal-style aura to the dining room. The house was designed to be functional, yet welcoming to guests. The living room is sunken, with a full wall of windows on the garden side. A hall leads discreetly to the bedrooms and living areas. So far, the Residence resembles what it was built to be, a 1950s suburban home of more than usual size.

The formal dining room, though, is elliptical, with the same floor-to-ceiling windows that adorn the living room. Surfaces are curved here, creating a sense of ease in strong contrast to the more formal and heavy decor of the dining areas in most other executive residences. The furnishings included in the original Sober home were a mixture of Oriental, French, English, and Spanish, with a scattering of antiques, and many of those items remain today, although subsequent first families have added refine-

The living room. The fireplace is often used during chilly Michigan winters.

ments. One 1975 newspaper headline summarized the overall impression: "Governor's Residence Blends Elegant, Modern." Another said, "Guv's Mansion, er, Residence," as if neither term were a precise fit. First families have found the Sober house functional over the years, and if it lacks much of the grandeur of other mansions, it also has the advantage of being relatively modern.

More traditional is the Governor's Summer Residence on Mackinac Island. First families had often vacationed here when it was a national, and later a state, park. There were old homes on the island, many built in the 1870s to house the officers of old Fort Mackinac, and in 1935 the Michigan legislature designated the former post commander's house as a summer retreat for the first families. Ten years later, to help host a meeting of the National Governors Conference on the island, the legislature acquired the former Scherer house, which ultimately became the Summer Residence.

The Mackinac Island house was built in 1901–2 by the Lawrence

The living room. The foyer has floors of Italian marble, and separating the foyer from the living room are marble planters.

Young family of Chicago, and was sold to Clara Scherer of Detroit in 1926. Young was a wealthy lawyer and railroad man who also played a role in developing the island as a tourist resort. The home's three stories and twenty-four rooms made it one of the island's finest summer homes. It was built almost entirely of wood, with a native white-pine shingle exterior. It was constructed on a foundation of native limestone boulders, which were also used in making the chimneys. The residence is all dormers and flaring eaves, with a large and airy porch that wraps around three of its sides, and an upstairs veranda affording a hilltop view of the shipping channel below.

Today the Summer Residence is administered by the Mackinac Island State Park Commission. Presidents John F. Kennedy, Gerald Ford, and George Bush have visited the home, and President Ford stayed overnight in one of its eleven bedrooms. The living-room walls and ceiling are paneled in dark walnut. Furnishings are a varied mix of modern and Victorian, and in the dining room a canopied, octagonal dark wood ceiling arches over the fireplace and oval table. The Summer Residence is delightful and relaxing, from its cozy interior rooms, like those in a north-woods hunting lodge, to the sunny veranda overlooking the distant Mackinac Bridge, the longest anchorage-to-anchorage suspension bridge in America. "Time," a former governor said of the house, "slows down so much here, no one even looks at their watches."

So popular has the island retreat become with Michigan's first families that two former governors built their own vacation homes there after they left office, and one asked that he be buried there.

Michigan is unusual in having not one but two official executive residences. In Lansing, it is the modern, spacious, and functional Governor's Residence, a place for public receptions and official meetings. And on Mackinac Island, close to the waters that have created so much of this state's character, there is the rambling, relaxed Summer Residence, now attracting increased public interest as a historic home in its own right as it approaches its centennial.

The best, it would seem, of two distinct worlds.

FLORIDA

THE GOVERNOR'S MANSION
TALLAHASSEE

PHOTOGRAPHS BY ROBERT M. OVERTON

The Florida Governor's Mansion.

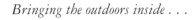

Opening page:
The U.S.S.
Florida's twelve-
gallon sterling-
silver punch bowl
was crafted
in 1911.

lorida's peninsula was among the first areas of North America to be discovered and mapped by European explorers. The venturesome Spaniards of the early 1500s said they had "gone to occupy Florida," and ever since, in wave after wave, people have had the identical idea. Few states have grown as consistently, and none has surpassed Florida as a destination for vacationers and retirees. The clear reason is the climate, coupled with close proximity to the ocean. It is no surprise, then, that for the state dining room of the Florida Governor's Mansion, the designers chose two central elements: a mural alive with the peninsula's palms, blue skies, and colorful foliage; and a silver set from the U.S.S. *Florida* that had ranged the wide seas.

The expanding United States acquired Florida from Spain in 1821. Commissioners named to choose a new capital included residents of both the territory's east and west coasts, and in the traditional spirit of compromise they selected what was to become Tallahassee, inland. The first territorial governor lived on a boat in St. Marks Harbor until a log cabin—designated the official governor's residence—was constructed in Tallahassee, beside a stream and within the walls of an old Spanish fort. But for eighty-three years, until 1907, Florida's territorial and state chief executives made their own living arrangements.

In that year the state completed its first official governor's mansion, a two-story Georgian Colonial white clapboard home. It served fifteen first families until 1955, when it was thought to be structurally unsound and was demolished. Over the next two years, the state built the present residence, which stands ten blocks from the state capitol building.

The Governor's Mansion blends European historical styles with a sense of the scenic beauty native to Florida, as if an elegant drawing room had been transported into a garden. Andrew Jackson served as territorial governor in 1821, after his military service in the local Indian wars and before he ascended to the White House. As a tribute to Jackson, the new Greek Revival mansion was designed to reflect the Hermitage, his legendary Tennessee home. It has a two-story central portion fronted by six cast-stone Corinthian columns and a broad balcony. On either side are single-story wings, and a basement houses offices and service and staff areas. The Mansion occupies the center of a city block, and part of its spacious grounds adjoin those of the Grove, the historic home of one of Florida's territorial governors, now owned by the state.

Inside, furnishings and accessories have an eighteenth-century flavor, spiced by colors that reflect Florida's scenery and the myriad brilliant vegetation that grows there: peach-blossom fabric on chairs; rugs bearing flowers and shells; shrimp and salmon pinks and tropical blues. Florida's

Mansion brings the outdoors inside without obscuring the deep streams of history that flow through the house.

In the ground-floor entry hall, past the double doors of Honduras mahogany, visitors walk on marble that hints at the elegance to come. There are Wedgwood-blue and cream moldings, glass and brass wall sconces, and a Chippendale mahogany side table. Two works of art combine the Mansion's dual themes: a portrait of two Scottish lassies, *The Sisters,* looks on from the far wall as guests admire the Edward Marshall Boehm porcelain *Western Bluebirds on Wild Azaleas.* The mansion has benefited from an obscure 1698 English law that required clock makers to inscribe their names on their products: the Chippendale clock standing against the wall bears the name of Jonathan Lees, who designed and built it around 1770. Three pieces on the entry hall's east wall suggest the Colonial air that dominates the Mansion's furnishings. The table surprises visitors with its "bird cage" mechanism, which allows it to spin like a lazy Susan or nestle against the wall. On one side of the table is a Martha Washington chair from around 1790; on the other, a chair copied from one in the George Wythe house in Colonial Williamsburg.

The state dining room's mural is actually scenic wallpaper. The scene represents Lake Maggiore in northern Italy and is a reproduction of an 1840s French design, created by using a total of 742 different woodblocks and eighty-five distinct colors. French in design, Italian in inspiration, the wall covering remains a perfect expression of Florida, with its blue skies and brilliant colors.

The Mansion also contains the silver service from the U.S.S. *Florida,* one of America's first modern battleships. The silver was presented to the ship by the people of Florida in 1911; when the ship was decommissioned in 1930, the silver was returned to the state. The forty-five pieces, including a twelve-gallon punch bowl, are decorated with the Florida and Navy seals, but as with most works of art, the delight lies in the details. On one side of the bowl is a rendering of Juan Ponce de León, on the other, a Seminole Indian. The base is a seashell supported by alligators, and on the ladle's handle is a portrait of the Indian chief Osceola, one of Florida's most famous early figures.

The central state dining-room table seats twenty-four, and diners are surrounded by a 1790 Hepplewhite sideboard, a George III mahogany butler's secretary topped by a china cabinet, a Queen Anne–style love seat, and other objects of unique design. Overhead is an ornate cut-glass chandelier from a 1760 French castle; on the floor is a 1910 Heriz Persian rug, dominated by cobalt blues and brick reds; along with a Kashan rug in the entry hall, it sets the color scheme for the entire Mansion.

The reception room is the Mansion's largest. With the entry hall, it dominates the home's central section. The room is designed around a huge fifteen-by-twenty-five-foot Heriz rug. Paintings on loan from the Ringling Museum of Art decorate the walls. Guests are surrounded by such

The entry hall. The Chippendale clock was designed and built around 1770 by the English craftsman Jonathan Lees.

Right:
The state guest bedroom. The Regency X-back chairs have needlecrafted seats decorated in a Florida wildflower motif.

Below:
The Florida room. A wall of windows gives this 1985 Mansion addition access to the gardens.

The state dining room. The scenic wallpaper is a reproduction of an 1840s French design. It was created using 742 different woodblocks and eighty-five colors, and represents Lake Maggiore.

furnishings as a baby grand piano, a mahogany Chippendale chest and desk bookcase, Hepplewhite chairs, and a pair of 1740 Queen Anne card tables. The black-marble fireplace is flanked by 1770 Chippendale console tables; the andirons are antiques, dating from the 1840s.

The reception room also contains an 1852 tea service created by the renowned mid-nineteenth-century silversmith William Gale and a clock that is one of the Mansion's most notable artifacts. The brass tabletop clock was manufactured in Austria in 1820 and brought to America in 1850 by Edmond Lafayette, nephew of the Marquis de Lafayette, who had inherited land granted to the marquis by an America grateful for his service in the Revolution.

The ground-floor guest bedroom has two canopy beds with Pratesi bed linens from Ireland. The dressing mirror on the eighteenth-century table was designed to swing up, for inspecting one's hair, or down, for checking the proper alignment of petticoats. An 1800 Regency mahogany Canterbury was originally designed to store sheet music and sit beside a piano, but it is now filled with books for Mansion guests.

In 1985, the state converted a brick patio adjacent to the central wing into the Florida room, a modern, windowed entertainment and living area that combines the Mansion's traditional elegant antiques with more modern furnishings. Modern sofas and glass tables contrast with a Chippendale walnut side table and an 1835 engraving by John James Audubon. The room contains miniature portraits of Florida's first ladies, housed in an Empire display cabinet, and it opens onto a bright garden and patio where Hugh Nicholson's sculpture *Manatee Dance* celebrates Florida's state marine mammal.

The Florida Mansion centers on the central state rooms; there are four private bedrooms upstairs, and the south wing of the main floor includes private living and dining rooms and a kitchen, all for the first family's use. Outside, the grounds extend the Mansion's public character. French doors open from the Florida room onto a patio surrounded by flower beds and burgeoning greenery. The garden has a lily pond where bullfrogs live. Florida's native flowers—roses, caladiums, marigolds, petunias, pansies—speckle the area with year-round color. The trees are equally in Florida's spirit: palms alternate with moss-draped live oaks and dogwoods. Brick walkways convey visitors to the pool, tennis courts, and greenhouse, where many of the ground's plants are grown.

The people of Florida spend much of their time outdoors, enjoying the balmy climate and open skies. The state Governor's Mansion has captured that essential characteristic of its citizens.

Texas

The Governor's Mansion
Austin

The Texas Governor's Mansion.

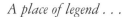
Texas is a land deep in history. Three states (Virginia, Mississippi, and Illinois) have older governors' mansions, but like most things Texan, the one that sits diagonally across from the state capitol building in Austin can justifiably claim to be unique. Several state executive residences have been the homes of future presidents, but only Texas has had a governor who was a president first. Governor Sam Houston (served 1859–61) was the first president of the Republic of Texas, a dozen years before he moved into the Governor's Mansion as its third gubernatorial resident. Houston's bed dominates an upstairs room today, and as with many mansions where legends have lived, there are those who believe his ghost lingers, too.

Built between 1854 and 1856, the Texas Governor's Mansion reflects the passion for the Greek Revival that dominated so much of our nation's public architecture, and indeed its thought, throughout the first two-thirds of the nineteenth century. The Mansion is as much a soaring piece of oratory as a building, a statement of principles in brick and columns. Americans of that era viewed their nation as a modern Athens, a reincarnation of the Greek ideal of democracy. When the orator Edward Everett planned his remarks at the dedication of the Gettysburg cemetery in 1863, he chose Greek Revivalism as the theme of a two-hour stem-winder that might be remembered today, had not Lincoln followed him with 272 short and simple words that proclaimed the same democratic ideal.

The builder Abner Cook chose the Greek Revival style for the Texas Mansion, and like so much that came to the West in the years before the Civil War, it was a style that adapted well to local standards. The two-story residence was constructed of locally produced bricks, with a broad veranda and an upstairs balcony. Cook chose sturdy pine for the six thirty-foot fronting columns. It is hardly a coincidence that the Mansion closely resembles Andrew Jackson's famous Nashville home, the Hermitage; Cook lived in Nashville before journeying west to Texas in 1839, and he may have apprenticed to the architects who designed the Hermitage.

As originally completed in 1856, the Mansion was built around a central entry hall, a grand, U-shaped staircase, and an upstairs hall, with four rooms on each floor, all opening to the center. A smaller, semidetached kitchen wing at the rear housed servants. A major addition in 1914 replaced the kitchen wing with a more modern kitchen, a second family dining room downstairs (now the conservatory), and additional upstairs rooms that have become part of the family living quarters. This L-shaped addition carefully preserved the Mansion's original roofline and exterior appearance even as it expanded the floor space from six thousand to nearly nine thousand square feet and increased the number of rooms from eleven to

Opening page:
Robert Jenkins Onderdonk's Fall of the Alamo *hangs in the Mansion entry hall.*

twenty-one. In 1979, the Mansion was thoroughly restored and remodeled, with the addition of an impressive collection of artworks and artifacts, but it remains remarkably true to Cook's original 1854 design.

It is a house meant to be visited. There are ten original fireplaces, one in each of the eight primary rooms and two in the main dining room. (Another fireplace was added in the modern era in the private family living quarters.) The spacious entry hall has a sixteen-foot ceiling; the dark wood staircase railing winds up and to the left past a window that, until the 1914 addition, opened to the rear of the Mansion. Beneath the ornate chandelier, above the heavy wide-plank pine flooring, is Robert Jenkins Onderdonk's painting *Fall of the Alamo,* one of many tributes in the Mansion to Texas history. Although the painting is of museum quality, this is nonetheless a home, where real people have lived for more than a hundred and forty years. Indeed, there are still nail holes in the staircase railing where a former governor hammered in tacks to dissuade his children from taking the tempting slide down it each morning.

To the right, the small parlor (originally called the reception suite) focuses on the elegantly carved mantel and the overmantel mirror. Houston's portrait hangs on one wall, a Federal-period girandole mirror on another. The room is furnished with a superb collection of nineteenth-century antiques, including a pianoforte in an ornate mahogany case and a Sheraton serving table attributed to the Salem, Massachusetts, furniture maker William Hook.

The small parlor opens into the large parlor, traditionally the site of the Mansion's formal ceremonies and events. It, too, displays cherished antiques: an 1810 Empire card table, two Sheraton sofas, an Empire breakfront, and a silver tea service on a tray bearing the heraldic arms of John Jay, a signer of the Declaration of Independence and the first chief justice of the United States. Cove ceiling molding accents the original keyhole window molding. In both parlors, coordinated rugs reveal the rich pine flooring common to all four original ground-floor rooms.

Across the central hallway, the library is truest to the original design. Traditionally decorated in shades of green, it displays a portrait of Stephen F. Austin—the "Father of Texas"—as well as the Austin desk, given to the state

Below:
Texas yellow roses bedeck the small parlor.
Philadelphia armchairs from about 1830
are on each side of the fireplace.

Right:
The small and large parlors. The adjoining
parlors allow guests to circulate easily.

in 1923 by his descendants. A library sofa belonged to the Pease family, the first Mansion residents.

The state dining room also retains its original function. The oval mahogany Sheraton Regency table seats eighteen beneath a unique six-branch brass chandelier bearing a patent date of 1843. Chairs attributed to Duncan Phyfe line both sides of the table, and there is a low-manteled fireplace at each end of the room.

The 1914 Mansion addition originally added a family dining room to the first floor. Today that room is the conservatory, a sunny entertainment room featuring a rug that displays the seals of the six nations that have ruled Texas, interspersed with native wildflowers. This room is still used by the first family for dining. At the rear of the Mansion, the back entry hall has a rug bearing the seldom-seen reverse side of the state seal.

Upstairs, rooms open off the broad central hallway beneath chandeliers that originally decorated the downstairs parlors. The hallway also doubles as a central sitting room.

The Sam Houston and Elisha Pease bedrooms serve as state bedrooms. In the Pease room, named for the first governor to live in the Mansion, are

two beds and a desk that belonged to the Pease family. On top of the desk is an invitation to the first Mansion party, on August 23, 1856. (This room was originally the Houston bedroom but was restored as the Pease room during the 1979–82 renovation of the Mansion.)

The bill for a "Superior Bed Stead, mahogany" still exists. The bed was delivered to the Mansion just before Christmas in 1859, and it remains the centerpiece of the Houston bedroom and the most symbolically significant Mansion artifact: a twentieth-century first lady gave birth to a son in this bed and named him Sam Houston Allred. Today the bed displays a hand-stitched Lone Star quilt. Also in the bedroom are love seats and a chair from the French legation to the Republic of Texas.

The upstairs family quarters begin across the central hallway from the Pease and Houston bedrooms and encompass the remainder of the second floor.

The Texas state capitol is visible from the Mansion grounds.

The two-acre Mansion grounds have evolved over the years. Governor Pease built a stable, later used by occupying Union troops after the Civil War. A carriage house constructed in 1900 is now staff offices, and there is a replica of a gazebo first installed in the 1870s. One governor kept a small menagerie, including a pet parrot that greeted him with "Papa!" when he walked home from the capitol each evening. Another doted on tame deer that roamed the spacious Mansion grounds. Governor Jim Ferguson and First Lady Miriam ("Ma") Ferguson added a greenhouse, which Ma Ferguson also enjoyed when she served two terms as the state's first woman chief executive. Today the grounds feature formal planting areas defined by brick walks that lead to a spacious fountain plaza, the scene of frequent outdoor events. To the north of the Mansion is a kitchen garden and the first designated Texas Wildscape Backyard Wildlife Habitat, featuring native Texas shrubs and flowers.

Texans will tell you their state is a place of legend, and they have a Governor's Mansion that surely proves it.

IOWA

TERRACE HILL
DES MOINES

PHOTOGRAPHS BY DAMON BULLOCK
AND SCOTT LITTLE

Terrace Hill.

he richest man in Iowa knew he deserved the best. Young Benjamin Franklin Allen came to remote Fort Des Moines in 1848, and within twenty years he owned thirty-five thousand acres of land and pieces of five prospering railroads, three insurance companies, a cluster of banks, even a meat-packing plant. The hill overlooking Des Moines where he decided to build his house was a symbol of his financial eminence, and the house itself, with its ninety-foot tower and plush interior, was hailed as "the finest residence west of the Hudson River" when it was completed in 1869. Mr. Allen held a reception on a chilly January evening soon after he moved in. He claimed to have spent eight thousand dollars on food and flowers alone, and few doubted that lavish estimate as they approached the house called Terrace Hill.

The architect, William Boyington of Chicago, had been urged on to grandeur by Allen's ambition. Terrace Hill was a soaring monument, built for an astounding quarter of a million dollars in an Italianate Second Empire style. The ceilings reached fifteen feet above woodwork and floors of cherry, walnut, maple, oak, butternut, rosewood, and pine. The heavy furnishings, designed by the New York firm of Jacob Ziegler, shouted wealth. The four downstairs marble mantelpieces were said to have cost twenty-five hundred dollars apiece; they were actually placed on public display in Chicago before being shipped by mule team to Des Moines, and the public there called them "exquisite." From the outside, Terrace Hill's three grand stories stretched skyward in an eclectic design topped by a front tower and turrets that proclaimed the structure a castle, an effect enhanced by the twenty-nine-acre grounds, carefully landscaped to frame the house. The guests who dined on oysters and dipped into an ice-cream sculpture shaped in the form of George Washington thought the Allen empire would go on forever.

It didn't. Within three years, Allen was scrambling to preserve his financial holdings in the wake of a disastrous railroad deal that forced him to mortgage everything he owned, including Terrace Hill. By 1875 he was in bankruptcy and living in Chicago. The castle on the hill sat empty, and even when Allen sought refuge there his creditors continued to hound him. In 1883 he emerged from bankruptcy, stripped of most of his wealth. A year later he sold Terrace Hill to Frederick M. Hubbell, who had been among his guests on that memorable night in 1869.

Hubbell had also invested wisely in railroads, real estate, and banking. As a lawyer and the founder of Iowa's first large life-insurance company, he had escaped the kind of speculative collapse that befell Allen. The new master of Terrace Hill prospered for the rest of the nineteenth century, hosting many public events at the hilltop mansion, which he redecorated in lavish style. When his daughter married a Swedish nobleman in 1899,

The drawing room. The furniture is a Belter parlor suite and the seventeenth-century Flemish tapestry was acquired during the Hubbell era.

Hubbell invited seven hundred guests, liberally sprinkled with European nobility, and draped the grand staircase in smilax and carnations.

Hubbell lived to the age of ninety-one. His son Grover occupied Terrace Hill, but his stewardship of the stately home irked some of his relatives. "A lot of men are tearing the house to pieces," one wrote as Grover Hubbell sought to modernize it during the 1920s. "They claim to be improving it. I don't like it." Still, Grover's daughter Mary Belle was enchanted with the house. At first, she said, it "seemed enormous, cavernous, mysterious—even a little frightening. But I had the freedom to explore and to play as I wished, and so my fears were gone quickly." She said her bedroom "seemed like a princess's." When Grover died in 1955, Terrace Hill was approaching its centennial, but it was again threatened by excessive upkeep costs. Grover's widow, Anna, soon moved to an apartment. For the next fifteen years, only a caretaker lived at Terrace Hill, lodging in the carriage house and guarding the old mansion. A 1971 magazine article described it as "a house of dark shadows and private memories. It sits there, alone and aloft, in silent dignity, awaiting an uncertain fate."

That fate suddenly became enmeshed with the condition of a much smaller Des Moines residence, the home of Iowa's governors. From statehood in 1846 until 1947, Iowa first families had found their own accommodations in Des Moines, with the exception of Governor William L. Harding (served 1917–21), who had lived in a house adjacent to the capitol that was later used as a state office building. In 1947 the state purchased a Colonial-style house built in 1903, but by the 1970s it was worn and inadequate. There was talk of building a new mansion, perhaps even on the Terrace Hill grounds, but the persistence of local preservationists and the Hubbell family finally paid off in 1971. The family offered the house to the state and even volunteered to underwrite some of the costs involved in the transfer. Four generations of Hubbells took part in a ceremony in which the keys to Terrace Hill were formally handed to Governor Robert Ray.

The V.I.P. suite. Overnight guests at Terrace Hill use this spacious suite, which has a floral-pattern chintz fabric and Louis XVI furnishings.

Although state officials at first thought to convert the historic mansion into a museum, a consensus emerged in favor of making it Iowa's executive residence. The third floor would be converted into the first family's living quarters, the second floor arranged to accommodate guests, and the massive first-floor rooms would be restored for entertaining and public events. Workers remodeling the venerable home soon found unexpected relics: a bricked steam tunnel that led from the Terrace Hill kitchen to the nearby carriage house, and an original boiler room and coal storage well. Scaffolding enfolded Terrace Hill as the work progressed for several years under the direction of the architect William Wagner, who called Terrace Hill his "dream project."

The Ray family moved in on October 17, 1976. The modified third floor held their master bedroom, two other family bedrooms, living and sitting rooms, and the original tower room, ninety feet above the city. (In the 1980s, Governor and Mrs. Terry Branstad remodeled the third floor once again, restoring much of its original Victorian design.) Downstairs, the remodelers had preserved the main-floor living and dining rooms, library, entry vestibule, and the reception and drawing rooms, but they removed the garage in order to restore the original entrance. Amid controversy over rising costs, Governor Ray appointed the Terrace Hill Authority to oversee the continuing preservation and restoration efforts. By 1978, Terrace Hill was ready for its first open house.

Today Terrace Hill draws more than thirty thousand visitors per year. The carriage house has been converted to a visitors' center, the stables now hold an exhibit room, and the icehouse was made into the gift shop. Books detailing the needlepoint designs and heritage of Terrace Hill are for sale there, along with a cookbook that presents recipes and chronicles memories from Terrace Hill. There is a Terrace Hill Society and Foundation working to preserve the home, with its unique design and enduring magic.

The lower entry hall affords visitors their first view of the ascending grand staircase, with tall bronze lamps rising from the downstairs newels, the immense dark wood handrails, and a majestic stained glass window overlooking the landing. The window was added during the Hubbell years. At the landing, the staircase branches to the left and right to form a twin staircase leading to the second-floor upper hall with its elaborately stenciled ceiling, covered by Grover Hubbell in the 1920s but since restored. In the lower entry hall are two Elizabethan Revival chairs, also Hubbell acquisitions, an antique gilt candelabra, and a marble-top Federal pier table. The east hall also has an Oriental chair from the Hubbell era and a Chinese garden bench said to have been given to a Des Moines family by the Empress of China after the family was briefly imprisoned there during the Boxer Rebellion.

In the reception room, which Allen originally used as a library, are furnishings that once belonged to prominent Iowans. On the mantel is a statuette titled *Rebecca at the Well,* and the mirror behind it reflects light from the brass chandelier. The room includes one of the original Chicago fireplaces, of pink Spanish marble, and the fireplace screen is also made of brass. The room also contains two Renaissance Revival chairs and a small kneeling bench in front of the fireplace, as well as a gilt sofa covered in French tapestry fabric. In the 1890s under Hubbell's ownership, the room was adorned with a tiger-skin rug. Arched doorways lead from the reception room to adjoining hallways.

The drawing room is Terrace Hill's most formal and impressive section. Allen installed an overmantel mirror and a large pier mirror here, and the Hubbells later added a seven-foot Czechoslovakian silver-and-crystal chandelier and a seventeenth-century Flemish tapestry, which hangs on the raspberry-colored wall above two chairs designed by the nineteenth-century New York craftsman John Henry Belter. The Italian marble fireplace is white, and wool damask draperies and upholstery match the wall coverings. Research is under way to restore the original stenciling from the late 1890s, both here and in the music room.

Each of the large first-floor rooms has a twelve-foot walnut and butter-

The designers of Terrace Hill planned fifteen-foot ceilings. They used cherry, walnut, maple, oak, butternut, rosewood, and pine for the floors, woodwork, and moldings.

The grand staircase.
The Wilton carpet was
English-milled.

nut pocket door that can be closed on heavy iron rollers; the doors weigh four hundred pounds each.

In the music room, guests can sit on a unique tête-à-tête or play the antique Steinway parlor grand piano, which was acquired for Terrace Hill in 1986. The glass-and-brass chandelier is from the 1880s.

The library was used as a billiard room during the Allen years, but Frederick Hubbell converted it to its present use. As the room was being restored in the modern era, workers uncovered as many as three layers of stenciling; today the room bears a pattern dating to 1910. An 1880 walnut armchair belonged to Mr. Hubbell.

In the dining room, a silver-and-brass chandelier hangs above the Chippendale table and chairs. Green and gold damask draperies add lightness to the room. The dining room is decorated in oak, Iowa's state tree, and the chair seats display needlepoint oak-leaf patterns. These were among the few items brought to Terrace Hill from the previous executive residence. The dining room has been restored to its original state using the 1913 stencil pattern. A pair of restoration painters took two years to complete the painstaking job.

The sitting room is the only main-floor room with a measure of privacy. It contains one of the few remaining Civil War–era sewing stands and a Turkish pierced brass chandelier. On the second floor are a V.I.P. bedroom suite with a brass bed that once belonged to the Hubbell family, other guest bedrooms, offices now used by the incumbent governor and first lady, and a tower room that is part of Terrace Hill's noted tower. The room has been used as a playroom, office, and conference area.

Meticulously renovated, Terrace Hill is once again "the finest."

A detail of the window atop the grand staircase.

WISCONSIN

THE EXECUTIVE RESIDENCE
MADISON

PHOTOGRAPHS BY STANLEY SOLHEIM
AND CRAIG WILSON

The Wisconsin Executive Residence.

From the "White House" to the house by the lake . . .

When Wisconsin's first territorial governor, Henry Dodge, called the legislature into session at Belmont, there was something missing: a capitol building. James Doty, who would succeed Dodge as governor of the new territory, convinced the legislature to journey to Madison, and by 1837, when the first settlers arrived, work was already under way on a capitol. Wisconsin joined the Union in 1848, but it would be another thirty-six years before the chief executive would have a home he could call the state's.

Doty's brother-in-law, General Julius T. White, had constructed a fine two-story stone home in Madison in 1854. It had the first central-heating system in town, and local residents often gathered there for music recitals and discussions. In 1857, General White moved to Chicago and sold his home to a local developer who had once served as secretary to the governor. It later passed into the hands of a state legislator, and in 1884, Governor Jeremiah Rusk convinced the state to acquire the "White House" as Wisconsin's first executive residence. Through the years it was host to visitors from presidential candidate Wendell Willkie to the poet James Russell Lowell. It would serve eighteen first families for sixty-five years.

After World War II, Governor Oscar Rennebohm noted that whenever famous guests stayed at the mansion they had to share a bathroom with the first family. The house was "cramped, drafty, and cold" in winter. It was time to move. In 1949, Wisconsin acquired a new mansion and sold the "White House," which today is used as a student dormitory.

The new home had been built in 1927 by Carl A. Johnson, a Madison businessman. He sold it to banker Thomas R. Hefty, and Hefty willingly sold it to the state in 1949, at a price only one-fourth of its assessed value. Officials searching for a new executive residence wanted a roomier, more elegant home for the state's first families. Once they saw the Johnson-Hefty home, the search was ended.

The modern Wisconsin Executive Residence was built in the Classical Revival style, with ample space inside and with four acres of grounds overlooking Lake Mendota. Although it underwent extensive renovations in the 1960s, the Residence today is much as Johnson originally planned it, with thirty-four rooms and sixteen thousand square feet of living space. Its tall, six-column portico, white exterior, and foyer chandelier, a replica of one that hangs in the White House in Washington, D.C., give it a resemblance to the presidential residence.

The foyer is one of the broadest and most impressive of any state executive residence's. The chandelier, a replica of a 1900 candle lantern, weighs five hundred pounds and is supported by a steel beam. It hangs above the foyer floor, two steps down from the compact entryway and flanked by the

Above:
The reception room. The room is furnished in eighteenth-century antiques, including a French Kittinger sofa.

Left:
The dining room. The hand-painted wallpaper depicts native Wisconsin flowers and birds. The rug bears the state flower, the wood violet.

ascending double staircase. Through the foyer and across the reception room, large windows afford a view of Lake Mendota; this walk-through with a view was the only major architectural change made by the state during the 1960s renovation. The present reception room was originally a garden room, separated from the foyer by French doors.

The foyer walls were re-covered in 1991 with a damask string fiber in white on white. The carpet on the double staircase is handmade, while foyer furnishings include a "fainting sofa" from about 1820 in French Empire style, an antique mahogany English armchair from about 1750, two Hepplewhite console tables, and an 1800s secretary, which was moved from the old residence and refurbished in the 1990s. The double staircase, with its ornate banisters, neatly frames the foyer; the foyer opens into the adjoining small powder room, with its French wallpaper, designed in the late 1800s in an Indian motif to appeal to the American trade. The powder room is also decorated with an Italian bronze chandelier and sconces framing amethyst grape clusters originally installed in the reception room, as well as Louis XVI armchairs and a nineteenth-century pier mirror, which was in the house when the state acquired it in 1949.

Guests are drawn to the reception room, which was also redecorated in the 1990s with the string fiber wall coverings used in the foyer. The reception room holds a fine collection of eighteenth-century antiques: a satinwood English game table, a French Kittinger sofa, an English Hepplewhite love seat with fabric by Scalamandré, and a mahogany plate bucket,

The ladies' powder room. The high pier mirror was among the home's original furnishings. The small powder room is adjacent to the foyer.

to which a copper lining was added later to allow storage and transport of wood. This unique artifact has a side opening, which allowed English servants to inventory the warmed plates before carrying them from the detached kitchen to the main house. The reception room also contains a

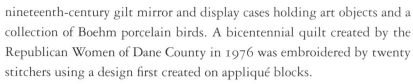

nineteenth-century gilt mirror and display cases holding art objects and a collection of Boehm porcelain birds. A bicentennial quilt created by the Republican Women of Dane County in 1976 was embroidered by twenty stitchers using a design first created on appliqué blocks.

The second major public room in the Residence is the drawing room, which serves as a center for entertainment and large functions, as well as for the first family's use. The drawing room is furnished in a combination of antiques and more modern traditional pieces, which range from the Chippendale camelback sofa with scroll arms from about 1765, to the hand-carved pine mantel, a modern copy of an eighteenth-century English design. The drawing room features a twenty-nine-foot rug designed for the Residence, the original oak floor, and draperies created from an eighteenth-century print. On one wall is a gilt carved-wood mirror in Chippendale design, which is a twin of one hanging in the Victoria and Albert Museum in London; it bears the image of the phoenix, symbol of eternal life. The drawing room also contains a Georgian-style commode, a 1765 Chippendale wine cooler, and an eighteenth-century walnut traveling case. In the hallway outside the drawing room is a bronze bust of Abraham Lincoln, along with Queen Anne walnut chairs that once belonged to the British royal family.

The ground-floor kitchen was remodeled in 1988. It serves the dining room, where hand-painted wallpaper created by Charles Grace & Co. depicts native Wisconsin flowers and birds. The dining-room rug is of woven and sculptured wool, with the state flower, the wood violet, in each corner. The draperies were designed to hang inside the framework to display the Roman-arch window design used throughout the Residence. The dining room's mahogany table and chairs are Kittinger Chippendale, with different needlepoint designs on each of the twenty-four chair seats; the

Left:
The foyer. The double staircase rises past walls decorated with damask string fiber.

Above:
The library. The walnut paneling was attached entirely with wooden pegs. The chandelier and sconces were originally used in the dining room.

artists were asked to weave their initials into the leaf design. Overhead hangs a Waterford reproduction chandelier, and on the walls are matching crystal sconces. Dining-room furnishings include a Georgian-style serving table, a late Georgian server and Sheraton buffet, both brought from the old mansion, and a nineteenth-century Georgian butler's service tray and stand.

A Sheraton settee from about 1795 once belonged to Lord Lonsdale, earl of Lowther Castle. It is one of many additions acquired by the Wisconsin Executive Residence Foundation, created in 1966 to preserve and improve the Residence. The china bears the state seal.

The library features pegged walnut paneling, a leather Chesterfield sofa, solid cherry table and chairs, and a silver-plated chandelier and sconces once used in the dining room. The library is cozy and inviting, with its collection of books by Wisconsin writers and personal memorabilia kept here by the incumbent first family.

The garden room. The chandelier is a French reproduction with a rose design. Beyond the arched windows is a gazebo.

Upstairs are family living quarters and guest bedrooms. The Residence also has a first-floor breakfast room, where the table is surrounded by windows affording a view of Lake Mendota. The chandelier here is an old gas fixture. The garden room, which was redecorated in the late 1980s in soft pastel colors, overlooks the Residence grounds; it holds a game table, rattan furnishings, and a reproduction French chandelier with a rose and gondola design. A beautiful walled garden, including a gazebo, is visible through the arched windows. The grounds have three hundred forty-four feet of frontage on Lake Mendota, and the dome of the Wisconsin state capitol building is visible through the trees.

MINNESOTA

THE GOVERNOR'S RESIDENCE
ST. PAUL

PHOTOGRAPHS BY FRANK MIKACEVICH
AND PATRICK O'LEARY

The Minnesota Governor's Residence.

Every city has a street like St. Paul's Summit Avenue, where malls and expressways and the whir of urban life seem reassuringly distant. The Summit Avenues of America preserve time as it was, when couples strolled the sidewalks under leafy elms and the rare passage of a chugging motor car was occasion for comment. Today, tourists cruise slower there and local residents know the houses by the names of their original owners. There are holiday tours and preservation boards. So treasured is Summit Avenue that in 1954 a future chief justice of the United States, Warren Burger, went to court to maintain its historical zoning status. Burger won, and Summit has been called "the best preserved American example of the Victorian monumental residential boulevard."

The Minnesota Governor's Residence, at 1006 Summit Avenue in St. Paul, was not constructed with its present use in mind. Horace Hills Irvine was the heir to his father's lumber company and a member of all the "right" boards, from railroads to banks and insurance companies. Three years after he married Clotilde McCullough of Memphis in 1907, Irvine bought land for his house on Summit Avenue, which was even then the address of distinction in St. Paul. The architect William Channing Whitney designed a fifty-thousand-dollar red-brick and white-stone mansion in a Beaux-Arts Tudor style. The home had twenty rooms, nine fireplaces, and eight bathrooms. The first floor housed the foyer, solarium, drawing room, dining room, library, and kitchen. Upstairs were six second-floor bedrooms, three more on the third floor, and a top-story ballroom, in keeping with the Irvines' social standing and entertainment needs.

The growing Irvine family moved in in 1912, and they were delighted with Whitney's meticulous craftsmanship. The main floor exhibited some of Summit Avenue's most original paneling—African mahogany in the drawing room, Circassian walnut in the dining room, and natural oak in the library and foyer. The grounds were arranged in formal Tudor-style gardens, and there was a carriage house connected to the main house by a tunnel. Over the years, the Irvines added archways and enlarged the solarium, but their home was always one of Summit Avenue's showplaces. It was featured in a national magazine in 1930, and Mrs. Irvine told the writer that her house was "as satisfactory to us today as it was the day it was built." And so it remained until long after Horace Irvine's death in 1947. Mrs. Irvine would remain in the home for another seventeen years, until she died in 1964.

In 1965, her daughters, Clotilde Irvine Moles and Olivia Irvine Dodge, offered to donate the house at 1006 Summit Avenue to the state of Minnesota as its executive residence. From statehood in 1858, Minnesota's first

The drawing room.

families had been responsible for their own lodging. In the early 1950s, state leaders had balked at an opportunity to acquire a free governor's mansion when the state seized a 1915 St. Paul estate for back taxes. Legislators refused to accept it, and the house was demolished. Though acceptance of the Irvine house did not come easily to the legislature, it finally agreed to convert the home into the Minnesota Governor's Residence.

The state also acquired a neighboring lot for parking and appropriated funds for initial renovations that included wiring and plumbing repairs, new carpet, fences, and furnishings. The Irvine family had left a number of treasures to the state, including a selection of Jacobean and Chippendale furnishings, but when Governor Karl Rolvaag (served 1963–67) and his family moved in, the house was mostly bare. This presented a serious problem because the first official function, a visit from Crown Prince Harald of Norway, was only weeks away. Governor Rolvaag called upon citizens of the state to donate or lend furnishings to the house for the event, and as he expected, Minnesotans responded generously.

Since that time the Residence has undergone many changes in decor, but through them all, each first lady has sought to preserve the history of 1006 Summit Avenue and make the decor truly representative of Minnesota and the historical period in which the house was built. The Governor's Residence Council helps the first lady in that endeavor. The council is charged with development and implementation of an overall restoration plan for the Residence. The members oversee all maintenance and improvement of the public areas of the home and screen all gifts to the Governor's Residence.

A sense of history surrounds visitors to the Minnesota Governor's Residence. In 1970, the sculpture *Man-Nam* by artist Paul Granlund, a memorial to Minnesotans who died in the Vietnam War, was installed at

Below:
The dining room. The Circassian walnut paneling is original to the house. The portrait over the mantel is of Henry Sibley, the first governor of Minnesota.

the Residence. In 1976, the Needlework Guild of Minnesota was commissioned to make needlepoint covers for the sixteen dining-room chairs with the state motto, "L'Etoile du Nord" (Star of the North), as the centerpiece. Portraits of former first ladies have been collected at the Residence, and in 1993, First Lady Susan Carlson dedicated a children's garden on the grounds, complete with plaques remembering the children who have lived at the home. Historical photos of the house during the Irvine years as well as displays of memorabilia of previous administrations also help to preserve the history of the Residence.

The Residence's first floor is its public area, while the second and third floors are considered private quarters. Visitors approach the Residence from the sidewalk on Summit Avenue, pass beneath a wrought-iron arch bearing the house number, and walk up five steps to the arched front doorway. Inside, past a smaller foyer and interior doors with frosted glass panels, a grand foyer opens into several of the ground-floor rooms and affords access to the staircase. Overhead hangs a crystal and silver chandelier, and a grandfather clock rests on the stairway landing. The wall paneling here is golden oak, making the foyer warm and inviting.

The dining room is still paneled in its original Circassian walnut. Like most of the public rooms, its high, vaulted, molded plaster ceiling gives an impression of space and grandeur. The dining room seats eighteen on Chippendale dining chairs and contains a Hepplewhite sideboard and table. The dining room is also home to the state's official Lenox china, bearing the Minnesota state seal. The fireplace here is of white stone.

The drawing room also reflects the Residence's 1912 splendor in its dark African mahogany paneling, with a broad dark-green-marble fireplace and hand-carved mantel. At one end of the room, a bay window looks out on the front grounds. The spacious, rectangular drawing room—largest in the house—easily holds a substantial antique mahogany breakfront.

In the library, paneled in oak, sits a rent table with eight drawers. (Such tables were used by landlords, who kept different accounts in separate drawers and turned the table to the proper drawer while remaining seated.)

The solarium was doubled in size by the Irvine family. It remains one of the most inviting rooms in the Residence, with its floor a highly polished gray marble, walls of white stone ashlar, and many windows and French doors. The ceiling is painted green. Outside is a patio leading to the Minnesota Garden, planted in native trees and flowers.

Upstairs, the Sibley room is reserved for important guests. It is named for the first governor of Minnesota, Henry Sibley, and contains artifacts from the historic Sibley house. Even before the house was the Governor's Residence, First Lady Eleanor Roosevelt stayed here as a guest of the Irvine family, and the room has also hosted First Lady Hillary Rodham Clinton, members of Norwegian and British royalty, Charles Lindbergh, movie stars,

The foyer. The chandeliers are of crystal and silver, and the paneling is golden oak.

and Chief Justice Warren Burger, who had fought for Summit Avenue's preservation as a young Minnesota attorney. The upstairs bedrooms include a master bedroom, child's room, guest rooms, and a den.

The third floor has been modified a number of times to fit the needs of resident first families. One first lady created a private office there, and another family added a small kitchen and dining area for private use. On the lower level is a family room, where today's first families spend time together as the Irvines did nearly a century ago. Olivia Irvine Dodge recalls

listening to the radio in the library as Bing Crosby sang. Her father, so right about how to build a house and a business, said, "He'll never last six weeks." Much later, Crosby was one of those who sang the classic "On the Street Where You Live" from *My Fair Lady.* He might have been singing of Summit Avenue, where a treasured past has been preserved and restored as home to Minnesota's first families.

The solarium is often used for breakfast meetings and family dinners.

OREGON

MAHONIA HALL
SALEM

PHOTOGRAPHS BY EVAN G. SCHNEIDER

Mahonia Hall.

An English flower of a home . . .

Opening page:
The coat of arms
that visitors see at
Mahonia Hall.

n the spring of 1803, as President Thomas Jefferson prepared his instructions for what was to become the legendary journey of Meriwether Lewis and William Clark to Oregon, the president urged the leaders of the expedition to pay particular attention to the plants they found growing west of the Mississippi. "The great object," he wrote, "is to ascertain whether from its extent and fertility the . . . country is susceptible of a large population." Lewis and Clark followed those instructions diligently; when they returned, in 1806, they had discovered one hundred seventy-eight new plant species, and the seeds they collected were carefully tended by the Philadelphia botanist Bernard McMahon. One bundle of seeds blossomed as the Oregon grape, scientifically labeled *Mahonia aquifolium.* It would later become Oregon's state flower, and in 1988, when state officials asked for suggestions in naming the newly designated executive residence, a thirteen-year-old schoolboy turned to his Oregon history for the perfect solution: Mahonia Hall. In this unexpected way, the seeds gathered by America's most famous explorers had taken root, one hundred eighty-five years later, giving a name to the governor's mansion of the state they discovered and opened to immigration.

For most of the century following the Lewis and Clark Expedition, Oregon was an adolescent America's great destination. Settlers hung "Gone to Oregon" signs on their shuttered East Coast shop windows and scrawled "Oregon or Bust" on the Conestoga wagons that lumbered west. Oregon's lush valleys and scenic coast drew farmers and merchants who prospered as the new territory became a new state.

Oregon's governors had no official residence for most of the state's history. Chief executives lived in private homes or rented one of several state-owned houses, but by the 1980s, sentiment was growing to select and acquire an official governor's mansion. Ultimately, the state chose a two-and-a-half-story English Tudor house near the state capitol building in Salem, and it was purchased and renovated in 1987–88, largely with private funds.

The house, with nearly ten thousand square feet of living space, was built in 1924. It was designed by a young architect, Ellis F. Lawrence, who had headed west for California but liked Oregon enough to stay, and who eventually founded the School of Architecture at the University of Oregon. The first owner was Thomas Livesley, a onetime mayor of Salem and the state's leading grower of hops. Livesley died in 1947, and subsequent owners included a realtor, a radio-station owner, an orthodontist, and an industrialist; at least two of them claimed that the home had an uninvited tenant, the "ghost" of Thomas Livesley.

In 1987, owner Iral D. Barrett agreed to sell the home to a group of private donors, who in turn deeded it to the state of Oregon as its new governor's mansion. Supporters of the mansion immediately launched an extensive renovation of the interior, and by Christmas the home was ready for its initial first family, that of Governor Neil Goldschmidt.

The original English Tudor style has been preserved at Mahonia Hall, as have the circular driveway and the stands of mature oak and fir trees that dot the grounds. Inside, arches and oak woodwork and floors continue the theme of an English country house. The 1988 renovation established the color schemes, using taupe, blue, and peach, seen throughout the spacious rooms and corridors. Furnishings gathered from a variety of modern and historic sources, but primarily from the Oregon Historical Society, add to the homey feel.

The entry hall reflects the overall Tudor theme and leads visitors to a broad stairway with banisters of Honduran mahogany. Visitors are guided into the reception room, which was originally designed as a drawing or music room, with a grand piano in a small alcove. Even the radiator grills here are made of oak; Lawrence also designed window seats and other devices throughout the house to further conceal the home's original hot-water heating system. In the reception room is a stone fireplace, and to the left, French doors lead onto a side porch. The reception room's furnishings include a Chippendale-style camelback sofa from the 1920s, as well as items acquired during the 1987–88 decoration of Mahonia Hall.

The first floor combines public and semiprivate rooms in a way that leaves no doubt that this is both an official state residence and the home of a family. In the family living room, more modern furnishings have joined a bronze chandelier and matching wall sconces that bear the lion and unicorn from the Livesley family crest. The sunroom is equally inviting, but in the dining room the family atmosphere yields to more formal matters of state.

The built-in corner china cabinets in the dining room are original to the house. The hand-built dining table is actually three four-by-four-foot tables that can be separated for less formal occasions. The chairs were drawn from two sources, including the estate of an early Oregon railroad tycoon, Ben Holladay. Along the walls are sideboards that hold formal dinnerware bearing the Oregon state seal. The dining room seats up to twenty-four guests in a variety of possible arrangements.

At the bottom of the stairway is a breakfast room that forms a part of Mahonia Hall's most delightful architectural feature, a central Tudor tower reminiscent of those at many English castles and country homes. The tower divides the second floor into two wings connected by a long hallway, with the original bronze ceiling lights and a nineteenth-century Aurora Colony bench constructed of maple with a fir seat. The floor is oak, but in the second floor's bedrooms the flooring changes to maple. At one end of the second-floor hallway are three family bedrooms and a study and office used by the incumbent chief executive; at the other, visitors enter

The dining room. The mahogany and Oregon chestnut table can be divided into three smaller tables.

the second wing, which contains an office for the first lady and two additional bedrooms, each with its own history.

The first bedroom has a sleigh bed purchased at the Lewis and Clark Exposition in 1905, celebrating the centennial of the arrival in Oregon of the famed explorers. The second bedroom is the Carter suite. Originally a pair of connecting bedrooms for servants when Mahonia Hall was a private home, the two were joined after the state acquired the residence. The bedroom is named for its first distinguished overnight guest, former President Jimmy Carter. It contains one of Mahonia Hall's historic artifacts, a hinged tobacco chest once used for drying raw tobacco leaves.

From the hallway outside the two bedrooms in this wing, a stairway descends to the first-floor kitchen and service area. Upstairs, the third floor is almost entirely taken up by the ballroom, a maple-floored expanse that in turn opens into a smaller card room, a vestige of the era when gentlemen retired for cards and brandy after an evening of entertainment.

Atop the tower, at the third-floor level, is yet another small office used by past governors. The antique desk was once that of the editor of an early twentieth-century Oregon newspaper.

Mahonia Hall also had an expansive basement, which originally included a number of smaller rooms—including an area containing the blower for an organ that was once in the reception room—but which has

The reception room. The Rococo fireplace was installed in the 1960s. The windows, like many others in Mahonia Hall, are of leaded glass.

Below:
The dining room. The table was specially built by Oregon craftsman Eric Shumate.

Right:
Stairway banisters in Mahonia Hall are of Honduran mahogany.

Light from the grounds filters into every room of Mahonia Hall.

been remodeled as a living and recreation area. The basement also contains a bathroom, an exercise room, and laundry and storage areas.

At the rear of the house, the basement opens into a ground-level area that includes the billiard room, complete with fireplace, and a small wine cellar. Doors open into the backyard. Mahonia Hall's grounds are bordered by oak and fir trees, and there is a lavish rose garden at the rear of the grounds, where a terrace permits outdoor entertaining.

As he neared the Oregon country as leader and scribe of the historic expedition of 1803–6, Meriwether Lewis walked to the top of a hill and scribbled this notation: "I had a most pleasing view of the country particularly of the wide and fertile valleys." Later, when they reached their destination, his coleader William Clark wrote, "Ocean in view! O! the joy!" Oregon was brand-new then, a place of dreams and limitless potential on a young nation's western flank. Today it is more mature, but the tower of Mahonia Hall and the vaulted angles and wide rooms of Oregon's official state residence continue to symbolize the vistas Lewis and Clark revealed to the rest of America.

KANSAS

CEDAR CREST
TOPEKA

PHOTOGRAPHS BY NATHAN HAM

Cedar Crest.

A mansion on the prairie . . .

Opening page:
*The front doorway
of Cedar Crest.*

he old cowboy tune sings of "land, lots of land, under starry skies above." It could have been written about Kansas. From the moment in 1541 when Francisco Vásquez de Coronado first entered what would become Kansas in search of the mythical Seven Cities of Cibola, he and his men were amazed at the immensity of its open spaces; its endless prairies would one day grow one-fifth of America's wheat crop. Kansas has been many things—terminus for the great cattle drives, symbol and focal point of the battle over the westward extension of slavery, home to historical figures from Carrie Nation to Dwight Eisenhower. But it has always been about land, and it is no surprise that the modern Kansas executive residence, Cedar Crest, sits at the center of a two-hundred-forty-four-acre park where deer graze and the land rolls on past ponds and groves of trees.

Like most western lands carved out of the huge Louisiana Purchase in the early 1800s, Kansas was a destination for settlers before it truly had an organized government. Its early territorial and state governors usually lived in hotels or leased a home. Kansas spent only seven years as a territory, from 1854 until the opening year of the Civil War, and those years were a period of intense turmoil as pro- and antislavery forces battled over whether Kansas—and by extension, every new territory west of the Mississippi—would be slave or free. Ten territorial governors came and went in those years, living on military posts or in hotels. After four tries at writing a state constitution that would satisfy conflicting factions in Congress, Kansas finally entered the Union in 1861, as a free state, and Governor Charles Robinson took up residence at the Tefft House Hotel in Topeka.

Later chief executives lived there or at the larger Copeland Hotel. In 1901, the state finally acquired its first executive residence, the grand home built in Topeka by Erasmus Bennett in 1886. A newspaper later sought to describe the house: "[It] defies classification. There is perhaps a hint of Tudor from the tall towers and turrets . . . an Italian influence. . . . The high tower on the northeast corner could have been borrowed from India. Ample 'gingerbread' ideas are thrown in for good measure." Bennett, who had emigrated from the dairy country of New York, apparently borrowed architectural inspiration from a variety of sources. Inside, the house was all dark and heavy wood, with a fireplace in each room, a billiard room, even a ballroom with an orchestra platform. Bennett kept his imported Clydesdale horses in a stable at the rear of his property, but it was all an illusion; he soon went broke in the financial panic that struck the nation in the 1890s.

The state bought the house at a bargain price, and twenty first families would live there during the next six decades, including Governor Alfred M. Landon, the 1936 Republican nominee for president. Some, however, were unhappy with the house. At least two governors lived elsewhere, and a later news article called it "a hovel . . . leaky, ramshackle, rat-infested house." By the time the south portico collapsed under the weight of a heavy snowfall in 1960, Kansans were ready to install their first families in better quarters.

Those quarters had been built in the Roaring Twenties. Frank P. MacLennan had come to Kansas as a boy and made his fortune in the publishing business. As owner of the *Topeka State Journal,* MacLennan wanted a large home on a spacious plot of ground. The result, forever known as Cedar Crest, rose in 1928 on bluffs overlooking the Kansas River valley. MacLennan mixed the style of the French Loire Valley with his Scottish heritage. Cedar Crest could have been a suitable setting for F. Scott Fitzgerald's *The Great Gatsby.* Its spired central roof and stone-framed windows speak of the opulence of an age when America was entering the world arena as a brash upstart determined to go old Europe one better. Inside, MacLennan decorated rooms with the Scottish thistle, reflecting his heritage, and ancient printer's marks, in keeping with his profession.

In Cedar Crest's reception hall, dark wood floors lead to a staircase, and a grandfather clock chimes in the corner. The library fireplace is made of chiseled Kansas stone, and the house has a solarium, a garden room, and spacious living areas, done in heavy wood. In summer, residents can remove the garden room's glass windows to let in the prairie breeze; in winter, a fire warms guests in the wood-paneled library.

MacLennan lived in his house for just three years. After his death, his widow, Madge, stayed at Cedar Crest for twenty-two years. When she died, in 1955, her will gave the house and its extensive grounds to the state of Kansas for use as an executive residence, but state officials were far from unanimous about how they should utilize it.

At less than six thousand square feet, Cedar Crest was smaller than the old mansion. It was not ideally designed for entertaining or for state functions, and one chief executive called it a "white elephant." But the home had its undeniable charms, and five years after Madge MacLennan bequeathed the house to Kansas, the legislature in 1961 appropriated funds to renovate and furnish it as the state's new executive residence.

In 1983, the Friends of Cedar Crest Association was formed to restore and preserve the residence, which had been added to the National Register of Historic Places the year before. One goal of the nonprofit group was to assemble a collection of furnishings and artworks that would reflect the character of Cedar Crest and its role as an executive residence. Changes came quickly: heavy velvet draperies were replaced with lighter material; worn carpet was removed from the first-floor rooms, where the rich wood floors were carefully restored; and the twelve dining-room chairs were redone in needlepoint, with depictions of native Kansas wildflowers.

The redecoration effort paid special attention to colors. The sunroom walls are peach, the library is carpeted in light navy, and a small first-floor powder room combines white and blue. It has become a tradition at Cedar

The dining room. The sunflowers adorning the centerpiece and the chairs recall Kansas's nickname, the Sunflower State.

Above:
The sitting room on the second floor is a private retreat for the first family.

Right:
The master bedroom includes the works of Kansas artists Margaret Whittimore and Birger Sandzén.

Crest that the upper two floors, with bedrooms and living quarters, be decorated at the discretion of the incumbent first family.

The association also added cherished furnishings to the Cedar Crest collection. Artifacts that reflect past administrations include a Victorian marble-top sideboard from about 1885 and a Simon Willard lighthouse clock.

The Cedar Crest restoration has proceeded at a gradual pace, with each first family working with the Friends of Cedar Crest Association to contribute its own touches. One first family added watercolors by Pauline Shirer of the old and new mansions. Another restored MacLennan's rare book collection in the library and added a portrait and plaque honoring Madge MacLennan. The 1970s saw extensive repainting, and a Kansas family donated a 1700 handwoven French tapestry, which now hangs on the stairway wall. Cedar Crest's future appears to be assured; there are plans for even more extensive renovation and restoration efforts in the final years of the twentieth century.

A Duncan Phyfe table, moved from the original governor's mansion many years before, is the centerpiece of the solarium adjacent to the dining room.

But nowhere at Cedar Crest is Kansas's heritage more apparent than on the spacious grounds, which were designated a backyard habitat by the National Wildlife Federation in the late 1980s. Of all America's governors' mansions, Cedar Crest is perhaps the closest to nature. It is not unusual for terrace guests to see deer grazing on the meadow at dusk, and the expansive grounds are an endless delight. There are three fishing ponds, a skating pond, and miles of wooded hiking and nature trails.

The family of Governor John Anderson (served 1961–65) was the first to live at Cedar Crest and immediately sensed the charm of the grounds. The family brought Shetland ponies to roam the meadows, and visitors often lined the fences to feed and pet the horses. Easter egg hunts, begun in the 1960s, can draw seven thousand visitors. There are bird feeders at every turn, and sugar maples, sweet gums, sycamores, and oaks line the front lane. One first lady enjoyed cross-country skiing on the snowy

The library. The fireplace is of native stone.

lawns. There are footbridges and benches along the hiking trails, marshy areas hospitable to wildlife, and beds of native Kansas flowers and grasses. There has been an effort to introduce a number of small wildlife species to the grounds, including squirrels, chipmunks, wild turkeys, and Canada geese. Groups of children come to Cedar Crest each summer to learn about fishing at the ponds stocked with bass and catfish. In these and many other ways, Cedar Crest is rooted in the land that gave it birth, the broad undulating fields and hills at the center of America.

WEST
VIRGINIA

THE GOVERNOR'S MANSION
CHARLESTON

PHOTOGRAPHS BY STEVE ROTSCH

The West Virginia Governor's Mansion.

Out in the mountains and wooded hills of what were once the western counties of Virginia, they take the state motto seriously: *Montani semper liberi* ("Mountaineers Are Always Free"). As early as 1776, when residents petitioned the Continental Congress for separation, western Virginians were already contemplating the creation of an independent state. On the eve of the Civil War, the fiery abolitionist John Brown was hanged in Charles Town for his role in the brief occupation of the federal armory at Harpers Ferry. There was sympathy for Brown's sentiments, if not for his actions, in the western counties, where slavery had never been economically viable. When Virginia voted to secede in 1861, western Virginians stood defiantly aloof. Thirty-two of the forty-seven delegates to the state secession convention from the western counties voted with the minority, to stay with the Union.

That left what was to become West Virginia in a brief but agonizing limbo as the war began. In two quick protest conventions held at Wheeling, Unionists accused the Virginia convention of bad faith and established their own, alternative government for Virginia, loyal to the national government. They ultimately declared themselves a new and distinct state, originally to be called Kanawha. Interestingly, no decision was made at that time to abolish slavery, but by the spring of 1863, what was now called West Virginia finally took that important step. On June 20 of that year, West Virginia became the thirty-fifth state, the only one to be carved out of an existing state in wartime. West Virginians remained steadfast in their attachment to the Union; Baily Thornsberry Brown of the Second West Virginia Volunteers had been the first Union soldier to be killed by Confederate fire in 1861. Tens of thousands of mountaineers served in President Lincoln's army throughout the war.

In 1869, Charleston was named the new state capital, but until 1893, West Virginia governors provided their own lodging. In the latter year, Governor A. B. Fleming told the legislature that, because of a law requiring him to live in Charleston, and his slim salary, "the state should provide a suitable house." The lawmakers agreed and soon purchased a house across the street from the state capitol building. It had been built around 1890 by the Jelenko brothers, leading local dry-goods merchants, and in the next thirty-two years, eight first families occupied the Jelenko house. It was a comfortable, rambling, two-story frame house with a roofed porch and inviting front steps, set just back from the street on a large but hardly imposing residential lot. In the 1920s, local authorities were planning a street extension near the capitol to accommodate the needs of that novelty the automobile, but the original mansion stood in the way, and to complicate matters, the old state capitol building burned in 1921. The West Virginia legislature saw an unusual opportunity to erect a new statehouse and

Left:
*The foyer. The marble floor incorporates
materials from Belgium and Tennessee.*

Above:
*The drawing room. The mantel is
a replica of one in the President's
Cottage at the Greenbrier Hotel,
located in White Sulphur Springs,
West Virginia.*

The library. The paneling is native butternut wood; the rug is a Turkish Oushak.

a new executive residence at the same time. It enacted a special sales tax to cover both projects.

The residence site came first. The state acquired several adjoining parcels in Charleston, including three with existing houses. It also commissioned a mansion design from the architect Walter F. Martens, which he modeled to conform to plans for the next-door state capitol building. Cass Gilbert, who was designing the statehouse, showed Martens his plans, and together they focused on a Georgian Colonial style. Mansion construction began in 1924, and on March 4, 1925, the family of Governor Ephraim Morgan moved in—one week before his term expired. Morgan had provided the leadership necessary to fund and build both the new state capitol building and residence, and his wife had been active in decorating the residence, but they were destined to spend just seven nights there.

The wide and spacious three-story Governor's Mansion was faced in Harvard Colonial brick. Inside were ten bedrooms, along with ample first-floor public rooms designed for entertaining. Downstairs, visitors could wander through the reception hall, library, living room, ballroom, sunroom, and state dining room. Martens had planned the public areas well. Before sketching the reception hall and double stairway, he visited the White House in Washington, and his design copied that of the presidential residence. The double stairway was to be easily accessible from any of the large public rooms, an effect that makes West Virginia's Mansion especially welcoming. The first floor also contained a kitchen and smaller family dining room. Family living quarters and guest bedrooms occupied the second floor. Martens planned a third floor, but it was not added until 1946. Today it contains office space, storage, and a playroom for children of the first family. Shortly after the Mansion was completed, the state added landscaping, a garage, and servants' quarters. From the street, the Mansion is one of the most inviting in America. There is a tall, columned portico facing south, with a smaller portico on the east side.

The Mansion was extensively renovated in 1965, during the term of Governor Hulett C. Smith, and underwent extensive interior redecoration in 1977 by Mrs. John D. Rockefeller IV during her husband's term as governor, but it remains remarkably faithful to Martens's original design.

Today the Mansion bears the marks of the first families who have lived here. West Virginia's first ladies have been consistent in their efforts to preserve and continually restore the Mansion, and its decor reflects many hands. First Lady Shelley Moore, whose husband, Arch, served two terms as governor, 1969–77, and another in the mid-1980s, enjoyed the unique chance to oversee the Mansion during two different eras. She organized the West Virginia Mansion Preservation Foundation, with a focus on interior restoration and on adding to the Mansion's collection. The results were

The state dining room. The chair cushions bear the initials of West Virginia.

impressive. The Foundation acquired furnishings, rugs, and other artifacts that have formed the core of a collection in keeping with the Georgian exterior of the house.

The Foundation acquired an 1830 English Regency table for the reception hall and a Turkish Oushak rug for the library, along with an antique settee and companion chairs from a company that was remodeling its corporate offices. In the ballroom, the chandeliers are historic relics of old Charleston; they once hung in a downtown drugstore. The mantel is from an Irish castle.

The twenty-two-seat table in the state dining room dates from the 1820s. The drawing-room chandeliers have much in common with those in the ballroom; they came from an old Charleston hotel lobby. The mantel is a replica of one in the President's Cottage at the Greenbrier Hotel in White Sulphur Springs. The Mansion's library is paneled in West Virginia hardwood.

During successive restoration efforts, and especially since the second Moore administration in the 1980s, the Mansion collection has increasingly come to reflect native West Virginia materials, colors, and sources, all within the Georgian Colonial theme. As it approaches its ninth decade, the West Virginia Governor's Mansion continues to reinvent itself.

The sunroom. Formerly a screened porch, the sunroom retains the outdoor feel of wicker furniture.

NEVADA

THE GOVERNOR'S MANSION
CARSON CITY

PHOTOGRAPHS BY SCOTT KLETTE

The Nevada Governor's Mansion.

Opening page:
Outdoor Mansion events are held in the gazebo.

The house that silver built . . .

Orion Clemens, appointed secretary of the fledgling Nevada Territory in 1861, needed help. He asked his brother Samuel, a sometime printer and riverboat pilot, to join him on the trek west, and when they arrived in what seemed to the boys from Missouri to be a vast, desolate wasteland, they found that the only place for a new government official to live was in what Sam derisively called a "state palace . . . a white framed one story house" in the town of Carson City. Samuel, of course, went on to write a humorous tale about a frog, changed his name to Mark Twain, and became the most famous American ever to be disappointed by an executive residence. Nevada still has a white frame house for its chief executives, but it and the state are all grown up.

For a while, it seemed that Nevada was not meant to be. Originally a neglected part of Mexico, it was ceded to the United States after the Mexican War, along with California, Utah, and portions of what would become four other Western and Southwestern states. There was no Nevada at first; it was part of Utah Territory, and when early residents there chafed under the administration of Mormons headquartered in Salt Lake City, Congress ignored them—until the discovery of the Comstock Lode. Nothing talks like acres of silver. Nevada was designated an official territory in 1861, and just three years later—President Lincoln needed the help of every potential state in prosecuting the Civil War—Nevada became the thirty-sixth state, despite a sparse population.

After the war, the silver boom gave way to periods of bust, but new silver discoveries in 1900 rejuvenated the economy. The railroads came, and the state launched an extensive program of dam and river projects designed to bring water to the arid land. Nevada also discovered gambling, in 1931, and with it came tourism—a different kind of silver mine, but a more dependable one.

The first effort to erect a permanent home for Nevada's governors failed, in 1879, when an opponent said that the whole idea was "founded upon a tendency toward aristocratic distinctions." By the early 1900s, with the state enjoying a second mining boom, a mansion looked far less aristocratic. A committee was chosen to find a site in Carson City. After some squabbling over bids, designs, and locations, George Ferris of Reno submitted the winning set of plans for a mansion. A newspaper report described Ferris's artistry: "The style of the building is classic Colonial. Foundations of concrete below ground and of concrete blocks to capstone. Brick rampart . . . outside color yellow trimmed in white . . . roof dark green. . . . There are three rooms on the first floor and nine on the second . . . seven bedrooms and a roof garden over the morning room." It sounded ideal, and construction was under way by mid-September 1908.

Left:
The grand stairway. Light from the chandelier is reflected from the foyer's marble floor.

Above:
The grand stairway. The crystal chandelier is reflected from a wide smoke mirror at the top of the unusual split landing.

Governor Denver Dickerson and his family moved in before all the furniture was delivered. Within a few months Mrs. Dickerson scored a first, and last, for the Governor's Mansion: her daughter June was born there.

Dickerson's successor, Tasker L. Oddie, had lost his silver fortune in the latest bust. On the night that he won election as Nevada's new chief executive, he pulled a postcard from his pocket, displayed the inviting photo of the columned and porticoed Mansion, and said, "There's my new home . . . it was either that or a tent."

Governors came and went—none in such straits as Oddie—and by the 1960s it was apparent that the Mansion required major repairs. The wiring was original, and unsafe. The legislature did its part, and so did private citizens, who raised funds and collected items at "Mansion showers" held around the state. The ensuing remodeling relocated and expanded the kitchen, added a fireplace to the family room, and extended the upstairs and downstairs porches. The basement was also remodeled to include a laundry room, wine cellar, and game room. Outside, the Mansion gained a four-car garage and a broad, curved driveway. Later, in the 1980s, the Mansion was repainted inside and out, and an Italian marble floor was added to the entryway.

The grounds also feature a gazebo for outdoor entertaining (guests can look past its ornate columns to the distant mountains), a mature stand of shade trees, and manicured flower gardens. The rear of the Mansion has a roofed sun deck that spans the length of the building.

The Nevada Governor's Mansion brings a sense of the Old South to the mountain and desert West. It has nineteen rooms, and a steady effort has been made to coordinate the furnishings in the Williamsburg style. First Lady Bette Sawyer began a second Mansion tradition in 1967 when she established an ever-growing portrait gallery of the state's first ladies.

From the front, the Mansion is decidedly symmetrical in appearance. Visitors ascend a brick and concrete walkway to the wide front steps, flanked by two pairs of Greek columns. The second-story balcony extends across the front of the building beneath the central pediment, while downstairs

The salon. The portrait of Abraham Lincoln is one of the few depicting him without a beard.

The dining room. Corinthian columns connect the reception room and entry hall.

an equally wide covered porch is supported by slimmer, matching columns. Guests enter through tall double doors, only to discover a vestibule and a second set of double doors inside, replicas of the entry doors to the Governor's Palace in Williamsburg, Virginia. Past those doors, the entryway widens across the white-marble floor, where still more columns flank the broad doorways into the first-floor rooms.

The grand stairway dominates the entryway, sweeping up to the second-floor landing beneath a crystal chandelier. At the top of the stairway, a wide smoke mirror reflects light from the chandelier. The landing is divided around the central stairway well; visitors climb a second, brief flight on either side to reach the second-floor hallway.

Downstairs, the reception room and salon, facing each other across the marbled entryway, are furnished in Williamsburg antiques and reproductions. There are heavy red draperies on the wide windows. The family room, with its dark wooden ceiling beams, is furnished in more contemporary red leather. The fireplace and paneled walls give the impression of a hunting lodge.

The Mansion has two dining rooms: the formal dining room, decorated in blue and green, and a smaller, less formal room at the rear for family dining. The latter overlooks the gazebo and grounds and is furnished with a 1782 Duncan Phyfe set.

The second floor contains family and guest bedrooms, while the basement boasts a billiard and family rumpus room, with a ground-level exterior doorway.

If Samuel and Orion Clemens returned to Carson City today, they would never recognize the place.

NEBRASKA

THE GOVERNOR'S MANSION
LINCOLN

PHOTOGRAPHS BY RANDY BARGER

The Nebraska Governor's Mansion, with holiday decorations.

A house on the way west . . .

ebraska was on the route to everywhere. Lewis and Clark trekked through what is now Nebraska in 1803. Trappers navigated the Platte River on the way to the beaver streams of the Rockies. The Oregon Trail cut through Nebraska, taking farmers to the Pacific Northwest and gold prospectors to California. Mormons fleeing persecution in the East carved their own trail, and Pony Express riders traversed the Platte Valley for a few brief days of glory. But it was not until 1854, with the passage of the Kansas-Nebraska Act during America's decade-long struggle with the issue of slavery, that Nebraska was opened to permanent settlement. Settlers came in a hurry, driven by the Homestead Act's offer of free land and by the rapid westward expansion of the railroads. Nebraska swiftly became part of America's great midland breadbasket, and in 1867 it joined the Union.

The nation was still mourning Abraham Lincoln, and the commissioners selected to pick a capital for the new state chose his name for their planned city. The plans for Lincoln did not, at first, include an official executive residence. An 1854 newspaper said the first territorial governor, who came from South Carolina, expected to "dwell in nomadic style, that is tents, until [he] can knock-up log houses in the wilderness." Until 1899, his successors did much the same; if their houses were not made of logs, they were all private dwellings, ill-suited for entertaining or for matters of state. One territorial governor hosted church services in his home. When an especially large congregation showed up one Sunday morning, an onlooker, surprised by the crowd, ran to the governor's office to tell him his house was on fire. Later in the nineteenth century, another governor had to use a room at the state capitol building for his inaugural reception. Among the guests was Buffalo Bill Cody.

Nebraska legislators discussed a possible governor's mansion as early as 1873. Later, legislators allowed the executive a thousand dollars per year for "rent money," but it was not until the turn of the century that Nebraska had an official mansion. The state spent twenty-five thousand dollars to buy a two-and-a-half-story neoclassical frame home just east of the site of the present executive residence. Built in 1899 by Lincoln businessman D. E. Thompson, the original mansion was heavily done in oak and dark wood inside. Its first floor contained an oak stairway, a sun porch, a parlor and sitting room, a dining room, and a smaller lunchroom. Upstairs were four bedrooms, a smoking room, servants' quarters, a third-floor ballroom, and a second-story wraparound balcony that matched the wide downstairs porch. Thompson, who later served as American ambassador to Brazil and to Mexico, had designed it as a private home, but it served well as Nebraska's first executive residence when Governor William

H. Poynter moved in. Thompson had included many furnishings and other items with the house, which was home to Nebraska's governors for the next fifty-seven years.

William Howard Taft stayed there in 1908 while he was running for president. During World War I, the first family raised a lamb for auction to benefit the Red Cross. Years later, a dog owned by Governor Dwight Griswold bit former Governor Charles Bryan while he was visiting the mansion. "Must have known I was a Democrat," Bryan joked to his Republican successor. By the end of World War II, the old mansion was showing its age. All six fireplaces were out of order, windows rattled and admitted winter drafts, and the only way to reach the second-story veranda was to climb through a window. In 1955, the legislature appropriated funds for a new mansion, but there was a great deal of lingering affection for the old house, which was to be demolished. Wood paneling, a fireplace, kitchen fixtures, furnishings, even some bathroom fixtures were carefully salvaged for transfer to the new residence, rising on a next-door lot. Nebraskans were allowed to purchase other artifacts from the old house at auction.

The architect Selmer Solheim designed a modified Georgian Colonial home with twenty-seven rooms, eleven bathrooms, and a three-car garage. Its exterior of pink sandstone brick enclosed an interior decorated in five distinct styles: French Provincial, Georgian, Louis XVI, Empire, and Regency. Furnishings in the public rooms are largely reproductions from those eras, with some items transported from the old mansion. When Governor and Mrs. Victor Anderson moved in in 1958, the public dropped by for a large open house. Some eighteen thousand Nebraskans toured the Governor's Mansion over two days in March, forming lines that wound around the block. By 1965, two presidents had added their names to the guest book (John Kennedy and Lyndon Johnson), and the Mansion was a comfortable fifteen-thousand-square-foot home for the state's first families, and a roomy place for entertainment and official events.

Mansion visitors today enter a delicate foyer paved in white Pennsylvania marble. The walls are papered in a light forest green, and a curved stairway leads to the second floor, which houses the family living quarters. On each step is carved a pineapple symbol, a traditional token of welcome and hospitality. According to legend, leaving part of such artwork unfinished banishes evil spirits, and on the eighth step the pineapple was left unscored. The foyer also contains marble-top petticoat tables with concealed mirrors underneath.

The expansive state drawing room is the Mansion's center for greeting guests and hosting receptions. Keats Lorenz, a Nebraska craftsman who also carved the Indian-motif senate chamber doors in the state capitol building in 1929, created the room's white-pine fireplace. The state drawing room's walls are covered in gold silk above an emerald green carpet. The Lorenz fireplace is flanked by curio cabinets holding gifts to the first families, and the chandeliers are hand-cut crystal from Czechoslovakia.

Above:
The state drawing room, an expansive center for Mansion entertainment.

Left:
The foyer, with the stairway to the second floor.

The state dining room. The U.S.S. Nebraska *silver service dates to* 1908.

Both the Empire sofa and the piano are antiques from the old mansion, the piano dating to 1941. The honeybee is Nebraska's state insect, and its likeness adorns chairs and benches in the room.

The first ladies' and gentlemen's hall displays portraits of past first ladies and governors, a collection launched in 1932 during the Charles Bryan administration. Most of the portraits of first ladies depict them in their inaugural gown, but one subject—Mrs. Julia Savage (first lady in 1901–3)—was superstitious and rarely allowed herself to be photographed or painted. The Mansion finally acquired a photo of her in 1972, taken years earlier at the launching of the battleship *Nebraska*.

The first floor also contains a small office for the governor, with a marble fireplace and antique Spanish oak paneling carefully removed from the old mansion, restored, and installed in the Governor's Mansion. French doors in the office open to the sun porch, a favorite gathering place for first families and visitors.

In the state dining room, the table can seat twenty-four on chairs created in the 1980s. The needlepoint chair cushions depict historic Nebraska buildings, including an 1888 opera house in Fremont and an Omaha Indian earth lodge. The stitchers were chosen in a statewide competition. Also displayed in the state dining room's alcoves is the silver service from the U.S.S. *Nebraska,* created in 1908. The ship was decommissioned in 1920. The silver bears engravings of the first Nebraska territorial capitol building, railroads, boats on the Missouri River, and other scenes from the state's early years. The state dining room's buffet has two candelabras, gifts from the Anderson family, the first to occupy the Mansion, in 1958. The candelabras and the silver gleam in light from the wide windows that make the state dining room one of the Mansion's brightest.

The smaller family dining room is decorated in French Provincial furniture and contains Blue Danube china, a copy of the china used in the old mansion. The kitchen is a modern facility that still uses some appliances acquired during a kitchen upgrade at the old mansion.

The Mansion has a meeting room on the lower level, which includes the first ladies' doll collection, inspired by local artisans. The dolls are likenesses of past first ladies in miniature reproductions of their inaugural gowns. (Rose Higgins Sheldon, first lady in 1907–9, insisted that her doll use her real hair.) The room also contains delicate artifacts, among them a Fabergé egg created to honor the seventy-fifth birthday of Boys Town, and twenty-four place settings of hand-painted Lenox china presented to the state by the Nebraska Chapter of the World Organization of China Painters. The pieces depict native Nebraska flowers and grasses, and each is unique. There is also a model of the submarine *Nebraska* and a collection of books by Nebraska authors, including autographed works by Mari Sandoz and Willa Cather. On the walls hang changing exhibitions of works by Nebraska artists. The lower level also includes staff offices and a small kitchen.

On the second floor are three family bedrooms, three guest bedrooms, a family living room, and a kitchenette. The Mansion grounds feature a lighted fountain in the south garden, which is planted in roses and Nebraska wildflowers. Across the street from the Governor's Mansion stands the capitol dome, which overlooks the plains and prairies surrounding Lincoln—the pathway west for so many Americans in the nineteenth century.

The meeting room, with its unique first ladies' doll collection.

COLORADO

THE GOVERNOR'S MANSION
DENVER

PHOTOGRAPHS BY VIC MOSS

The Colorado Governor's Mansion.

Opening
page:
*A small stone
garden temple
decorates the
east lawn.*

Rocky Mountain high . . .

The soaring peaks of the Rocky Mountains, the high rooftop of America, have lured visitors to the states that straddle the Continental Divide. Nowhere are the mountains more immediate than in Colorado, where the state capital of Denver lies just below them. The Rockies have ever demanded of those who live there an upward-reaching spirit, and it is fitting that Colorado's Governor's Mansion sits atop a hill.

It was built there as a private home by one of the state's leading pioneer families. Walter Scott Cheesman rode an oxcart from Chicago to Denver in 1861, where he joined his brother in the drugstore business. He became an enthusiastic and effective booster of his new city, helping to bring it railroad service, developing the town's fledgling real-estate industry, and rising to local and regional prominence. But in 1907, just as he was planning to erect a landmark mansion on Denver's Logan Hill, Cheesman died. His wife and daughter proceeded with the plans, and the result was an elegant, soaring home of three stories that soon became the envy of Denver high society.

From outside the wrought-iron fence, citizens gazed at the mansion's west portico with its two-story Roman Ionic colonnade. They marveled at the widow's walk and the first-floor arched windows. And those who were lucky enough to visit the mansion gaped at the main entry hall, stretching eighty-six feet from the double entry doors to the rear garden door.

Cheesman's daughter Gladys married John Evans in 1908. They added further features to the house over the years: a fountain-centered rose garden, a lily pool and pergola, and a solarium, constructed in 1915 over what had become known as the palm room.

In 1923, the mansion was sold to Claude K. Boettcher, a leading Western businessman. Where the Cheesman-Evans era had focused on expanding the mansion and its grounds, the Boettcher family toured the world acquiring furnishings and artifacts, many of which remain part of the modern residence's collection. Among their finest additions was a Waterford cut-crystal chandelier that hung in the White House ballroom in 1876, when President Grant presided over America's centennial celebration (and Colorado's admission to the Union). The Boettchers also expanded the palm room to enclose the former porch into a broad bay, with floor-to-ceiling windows overlooking the fountain and gardens; the view extended to Pikes Peak, seventy miles to the south. They also remodeled the upstairs bedroom suites, eliminating the solarium. Among their many guests in the years they occupied the mansion were Charles Lindbergh, a close friend of the Boettchers' son; and a future president, Dwight D. Eisenhower.

Claude Boettcher died in 1957, and his wife, Edna, followed a year later. She left the mansion to a private family foundation, with the hope

COLORADO   283

that Denver's most storied home would become the executive residence of Colorado's governors. Ironically, several state agencies initially rejected the gift, but in the closing days of 1959, Governor Stephen McNichols gratefully accepted the foundation's offer. It was not the first time McNichols had seen the inside of the home. He had lived in the neighborhood as a boy, and when Charles Boettcher II, son of Claude and Edna, was kidnapped and held for ransom in 1933, young Steve McNichols was among those who peeked in the windows during the sensational case. Charles Boettcher returned home unharmed, and twenty-six years later, he handed over the deed to his family's home to his former neighbor.

Visitors to the Colorado Governor's Mansion today are surrounded by artworks and artifacts with connections to the pioneer Cheesman, Evans, and Boettcher families. In the wings added to the palm room, hand-crafted leaded glass windows that overlook the grounds bear the Boettcher family initials. The palm room and its wings have floors of white Colorado Yule marble with Italian Carrara marble statuary throughout—a nymph figure in the central fountain, scrolled pedestal tables, benches, and urns. The white leather furniture and ample greenery make the room ideal for entertaining.

The Grant chandelier hangs in the ground-floor drawing room, which also displays a pair of four-foot Chinese cloisonné urns, remarkable for their size and distinctive azure. The Tiffany garniture on the mantel—a clock and candelabra of ormolu and alabaster—was a gift from Mrs. Cheesman's granddaughter, the only items in the house from the Cheesman era. The room also boasts two eighteenth-century Venetian chairs, antique French crystal wall brackets, a Gobelin tapestry, Chinese carved-jade vases mounted as table lamps, and a Chinese carved-amber elephant. The drawing room's mixture of European and Oriental carries through the Mansion's public rooms—the heritage of the eclectic tastes of its private owners.

It is the grand entry hall that still commands a visitor's immediate attention. The broad, columned corridor features ornate chandeliers stretching the one hundred feet from the foyer to the bay window view of Pikes Peak in the distance. Artworks from France, Italy, and China line the walls above furnishings that include an Italian ebonized table with silver metal mountings and a hand-carved Italian Baroque credenza dating from the sixteenth century. Also on display in the hallway is a 1740 Beauvais tapestry, one of several rare tapestries that decorate the Mansion.

The ground-floor public rooms open off the central hallway. In the state dining room, the table and thronelike chairs are from Italy, where they were hand-carved in walnut. The massive table features lion and shield supports. Flanking the fireplace are antique French Rococo-style mirrors atop console tables, and on the mantel is a loving cup made in 1824 by the English silversmith Paul Storr. Over the table hangs an eighteenth-century French chandelier with fruit-shaped pendants in amethyst. The Mansion is

Above:
The drawing room. The Waterford crystal chandelier was hanging in the White House ballroom in 1876, when Colorado joined the Union.

Opposite:
The master bedroom.

Above:
The library. A portrait of Louis XV hangs above the desk, which is from the Louis XIV era. The paneling is of crosscut inlaid oak.

Left:
The state dining room. The hand-carved walnut table and chairs are from Italy. Antique French mirrors flank the fireplace.

also home to the silver service from the U.S.S. *Colorado,* which saw service in World War II.

The library was remodeled in 1927, when the Boettcher family added uncommon architectural detailing. Crosscut inlaid oak paneling covers the walls, and Romantic landscape paintings are hung in lunar-shaped arches above the doorways. The centerpiece of the library, and of the Mansion, is the Louis XIV French cylinder desk made of rare and delicate tulipwood with massive ormolu mounts. Created by André Boulle, the most celebrated of Louis XIV furniture makers and designers, the desk is said to be one of only three still in existence. The library also boasts four 1690 armchairs, one of Aubusson tapestry; a glass display case that holds unique jade sculptures from the sixteenth and seventeenth centuries; and four Tang mortuary horses.

The second and third floors of the residence are the private quarters of

The small dining room provides a setting for more intimate meals.

the first family. The second floor includes the elegant guest suite that is a showpiece of the Mansion. After a 1987 remodeling, the three-room suite was outfitted with a set of unusual painted-finish Venetian furniture stored since the 1920s. The pieces include twin sleigh beds, an armoire, a desk, and the chandelier. This was the room known as "Charlie's room" after its most famous early guest, Charles Lindbergh.

The Mansion's grounds are in keeping with the classical decor of the marble palm room. The grounds include a small, columned, stone garden temple with a wrought-iron dome and a wide Italianate balustrade around the upper terrace. There is an alcove below the balustrade with stone benches, a lion's-head lavabo in the center fed by the overflow from the fountain above. In the years since the home was constructed, trees have reached full height around the grounds, and the original wrought-iron fences now have mantles of clinging greenery.

The palm room looks out on the Mansion's grounds.

The Colorado Governor's Mansion began as a landmark private home, was transformed into a display of old-world elegance, and remains one of the West's treasure houses as it approaches its second century. Part executive residence, part repository of museum-quality furnishings and objets d'art, it is in keeping with the magnificence of the state's lofty peaks.

NORTH DAKOTA

THE GOVERNOR'S RESIDENCE
BISMARCK

PHOTOGRAPHS BY D. J. ARNOLD

The North Dakota Governor's Residence.

"Expressive of her native materials and her sturdy people . . ."

The Missouri River enters North Dakota in the northwest, winds southeast across the plains past the modern state capital of Bismarck, and flows south to its ultimate junction with the great Mississippi. It was along this route that the first French trappers paddled in the eighteenth century, and in 1804, when the Lewis and Clark Expedition established winter quarters on the Missouri near the present-day town of Washburn, they hired the trader Toussaint Charbonneau and his wife, the Shoshone Indian Sacajawea, to show them the way into the unknown. Sacajawea proved the better guide; settlers, commerce, and railroads were all destined to follow her trail for the next century. The Homestead Act, the landmark law that gave free Western land to any man with the will to work, drew a steady flood into the Great Plains, which had long seen only the buffalo and the Indian tribes who hunted them. By the time North Dakota joined the Union in 1889, much of the land had already been claimed, surveyed, and planted in the great rush west that followed the Civil War.

Yankton, in modern South Dakota, was the original territorial capital, but in 1883 the legislature had shifted it to Bismarck, which then had about five thousand people and, thanks to its central location and proximity to the Missouri River, a brighter future. In the next month, two million dollars' worth of Bismarck real estate changed hands. One lot fell to Asa Fisher, a liquor dealer and banker who had opened his first store in the new territory in a tent. In 1884 he built one of the growing town's most impressive residences. The Fisher house was a fine two-story frame dwelling surrounded by an iron fence. Inside, the woodwork was of black walnut and the stairs of white oak. There were two open downstairs parlors, a spacious dining room, a kitchen with attached shed, and, upstairs, three large bedrooms and quarters for the servants. The house was one of the first in Bismarck with indoor plumbing and steam heating. Out front were a wooden sidewalk and a hitching post.

North Dakota's first territorial governors had roomed in hotels or rented private homes. But soon after statehood, legislators began pushing for a permanent executive residence. They bought the Fisher house for just under six thousand dollars, and Governor Eli C. D. Shortridge moved in in 1893. The streets were still unpaved, and in 1903 legislators added funds for "one closed carriage, one open carriage, harness, and other necessary equipment for the governor"—but no horse. There were also improvements to the new mansion: paint and wallpaper, the removal of a noxious cesspool, screens for the porches, and, by 1913, a new electric stove. In 1919 the mansion got a new roof, and the original porches were removed. During the 1930s the attic was remodeled as a recreation room, and as motor travel replaced the horse, the carriage house was converted into a garage.

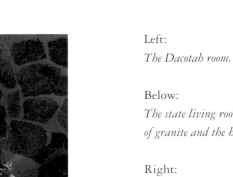

Left:

The Dacotah room.

Below:

*The state living room. The fireplace is
of granite and the hearth of slate.*

Right:

*The dining-room chairs were decorated
in needlepoint in the 1970s.*

By the turn of the century the Fisher house was increasingly viewed as too small and too antiquated for a governor's mansion. North Dakota pursued several funding sources, but it was not until 1953 that the legislature fully addressed the problem, dramatized when Governor C. Norman Brunsdale moved his family to a hotel because the mansion was too cold. First Lady Carrie Brunsdale said the old house was "somewhat like a refrigerator. . . . To prevent frostbite we were inclined to wear overshoes in the kitchen, and citrus fruits often froze overnight." In 1955, the state set aside two hundred thousand dollars to construct a new mansion on the state capitol's grounds. A local architectural firm was hired to design a home. The architects were urged to create "a house expressive of North Dakota's future, her native materials, and her sturdy people . . . a truly Dakotan prairie architecture completely new in idea." Their first design was rejected as "too grandiose," and new architects were hired. Ritterbush Brothers completed the Mansion in 1960; the old mansion, after twenty-one first families and sixty-seven years, became for a time offices for the state's health department and was later retired in the custody of the North Dakota Historical Society. It has been extensively restored and now serves as a museum and historical site.

Above:
Rear view of the Governor's Residence.

Opposite:
The kitchen. Centrally located in the Residence, it was remodeled in 1992 with whitewashed oak cabinetry.

The present Governor's Residence is a sprawling, modern ranch-style home at the southwest corner of the state capitol mall. Faced with tan brick, it incorporates as many North Dakota materials as possible in ten thousand square feet. On the lower floor are the large Dacotah room for meetings and large events, two family bedrooms, and laundry and service areas. The main floor includes the state living and dining rooms, a state guest bedroom, offices for the Residence manager and the first lady, family dining and living rooms, an additional family bedroom, and a master suite. The spacious kitchen is also on this floor, centrally located between the two dining areas.

The foyer floor is paved in New England slate, which is also used to surround the living-room hearth. The foyer walls are of granite. In the living room, the walls are sheathed in walnut, with large windows that overlook the rear grounds.

In the state dining room, the custom-built table seats eighteen. Appropriately, the state china bears a wheat pattern by Lenox, and the sterling-silver flatware has a matching wheat-stalk design. Republican women's groups donated Swedish Orrefors crystal. In 1977, the state sponsored a contest to decorate the state dining room's chairs. Eight needlepoint patterns were selected as representative of North Dakota's heritage and culture, with motifs including the sunflower, the wild prairie rose, wheat, and a meadowlark. Fourteen stitchers created the seat covers; their initials and those of the creators of the designs adorn the chairs today.

The Residence also includes a state guest bedroom adjacent to the foyer. In the past it has accommodated such visitors as Nelson Rockefeller, Robert Kennedy, and Lawrence Welk, the North Dakota–born bandleader. In 1986 the room was redecorated with a desk and four-poster bed in dark walnut, manufactured in North Dakota. A wheat design was hand-carved in the head- and footboards, and a hand-stitched quilt covers the bed.

The kitchen was remodeled in 1992; it has a large bay window that overlooks the state capitol building. There are four family bedrooms, two on the main floor and two downstairs.

The Dacotah room downstairs was completed in 1972 and remodeled in 1989. Staff and cabinet meetings are held here, and with its copper-hooded stone fireplace, the room also serves as a comfortable family living area.

The Residence has been slightly modified since its completion in 1960. The east balcony was opened to make the grounds visible from the state living room, and the house was reroofed in 1988. These and other projects are carried out under the auspices of Friends of the North Dakota Governor's Residence, a private nonprofit foundation dedicated to the Residence and its preservation.

SOUTH DAKOTA

THE GOVERNOR'S RESIDENCE
PIERRE

Holiday lights and freshly fallen snow decorate the South Dakota Governor's Residence.

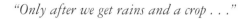

"Only after we get rains and a crop . . ."

he same Missouri River that carried the Lewis and Clark expedition through present-day South Dakota in the first years of the nineteenth century also brought to the area, in 1832, a daring young French fur trader. He was Pierre Chouteau, Jr., and he would give his name to both Fort Pierre and its sister city of Pierre (pronounced "peer"), which grew along the opposite shores of the historic river.

South Dakota entered the Union in 1889, igniting a fifteen-year controversy over where the state capital would be located. In 1889, 1890, and again in 1904, Pierre won raucous statewide elections characterized by political chicanery and a picnic atmosphere. With the issue finally settled, the ever-frugal South Dakotans made some small changes in the blueprints that Montana had used to build its state capitol in Helena. The architect C. E. Bell called the new South Dakota capitol a "modified Ionic" structure, and it was completed in 1910 in Pierre.

The "capital wars" were resolved long before South Dakota addressed the issue of permanent housing for its governors and their families. Beginning in 1889, the legislature had given each chief executive a housing allowance of seventy-five dollars per month, and he was responsible for finding his own living quarters. Some lived in various houses around Pierre; others rented apartments at the Wells House, the Locke Hotel, or the St. Charles Hotel.

In 1920 the legislature purchased a block of land and a five-room yellow cottage east of Capitol Lake for the purpose of housing the first family. The cottage served as the governor's residence from 1925 until 1936. It was far from palatial; Governor William Bulow once said he awoke many times in his unfinished attic bedroom to find a snowbank on his bed. In 1936, Governor Tom Berry decided that better quarters were definitely needed.

Like other states heavily dependent on agriculture, South Dakota had suffered terribly during the Depression. There was no legislative enthusiasm for buying or building a new executive residence, and Berry turned to the federal W.P.A., which was then completing public works projects all across America in an effort to keep people at work. Would they be interested in building a new official residence? They would. Later that year, W.P.A. crews erected a modified two-story Colonial home in Pierre. The old cottage was sold for twelve hundred seventy dollars and moved to another lot. Governor Berry lost the election that fall; he would never live in the house he had fought so hard to build.

The new Governor's Residence measured fifty-seven by ninety-seven feet and stood on a four-and-a-half-acre lot. It had eighteen rooms, but few furnishings. In 1937 the legislature set aside funds to furnish the Residence, but Governor Leslie Jensen vowed to spend the money "only after we get rains and a crop." It rained, and the Residence was soon furnished.

Family living quarters occupy much of the Residence, with a living room, dining room, a first lady's office, and kitchen downstairs and six bedrooms, including a master bedroom, on the second floor. The Residence's exterior was finished in native South Dakota materials—wood and brick— with a garage on one side of the two-story central wing.

Over the years, the Residence has changed with the times. In the 1950s, the shaft of an elevator originally designed for a visit by President Franklin D. Roosevelt was converted into closets. (Roosevelt visited Pierre in 1936, but his tour did not include the house, which was still under construction.) In the 1960s the state added a fallout shelter, and in the 1980s Governor Bill Janklow used convict labor to build a patio. A local politician had criticized Janklow for his plans to assign inmates to public improvement projects. "If these inmates are such good workers, you should put them to work in your own backyard," the politico complained. Janklow recruited four prisoners, who built a spacious patio of thirteen thousand antique railroad-siding bricks on the west side of the Residence. He then mailed a picture of the finished project, and of the convicts who built it, to the politician with a note that said, simply, "I did."

The Residence's exterior and grounds are among its most notable features. Flowers and shrubs line the curved front driveway, and the Residence is surrounded by native trees. The back lawn slopes down to the ten-acre Capitol Lake, which is fed by an artesian spring that produces warm water laced with natural gas. The spring bursts forth in an eternal flame. The Flaming Fountain, burning in blue and yellow, has been designated a memorial to South Dakota residents who have served the nation in time of war. The ninety-two-degree lake water attracts ducks and geese throughout the year, and the birds commonly approach visitors begging food.

Above:
The state dining room. The painting over the mantel is Harvey Dunn's Something for Supper *(The South Dakota Art Museum Collection), also shown at the left.*

The state capitol looms across Capitol Lake, which borders the rear of the residence. The lake is fed and warmed by an artesian spring and attracts waterfowl year-round.

Across the lake from the west patio, the state capitol looms above the surrounding hackberry trees.

Because it is the daily living quarters for the first family, the Residence is not open for public tours, although the grounds and house frequently host receptions and other public events. Pierre is the second smallest state capital in America—next to Montpelier, Vermont—and its thirteen thousand residents live and work in a relaxed, neighborly atmosphere; the governor's name and home telephone number are still listed in the phone book. The Governor's Residence lies within a short stroll of two libraries, Riggs High School, Hyde Stadium, Hollister Field, the State Cultural Heritage Center, and the forty-acre Hilgers Gulch Park. Almost two centuries after Lewis and Clark passed this way, visitors to Pierre and the Capitol Complex continue to discover a place where history is not just a thing of the past.

MONTANA

THE GOVERNOR'S MANSION
HELENA

PHOTOGRAPHS BY J. K. LAWRENCE

The Montana Governor's Mansion.

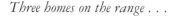

Out here, you can drive forever across broad expanses of the most open country you ever saw. That's why they call Montana "Big Sky Country." It is our fourth-largest state—only Alaska, Texas, and California have more land area—and assuredly one of the most visually striking. The majestic Glacier National Park straddles Montana's northern border with Canada; to the south, the state shares Yellowstone country with neighboring Wyoming. To the west, the peaks of the Continental Divide wrinkle the map and spill over into Idaho. The headwaters of the great Missouri River spring from Montana, and there are place names here redolent of a distant, boundless frontier: towns called Two Dot, Roundup, and Wolf Point, mountain ranges named Big Belt and Crazy, even a Hungry Horse Reservoir. Lewis and Clark trekked across Montana in 1805, outbound for Oregon. So did thousands of settlers who followed them, and those who sank roots in these broad plains and rocky foothills were a durable lot indeed; when they selected an official state flower, it was the aptly named bitterroot. A year after Montana joined the Union in 1889, the census takers tallied fewer than 150,000 inhabitants scattered about its vast territory.

Montana had an official executive residence before it was a state. The first mansion was a log cabin, and it cost four hundred dollars. The cabin, built in 1864, was located in the settlement of Bannack, near Grasshopper Creek. It had plank floors, a stone fireplace, a sod roof (they had to wear hats indoors when it rained), and four large rooms. The territorial first family cooked on a sheet-iron camp stove. Their children sat on kegs, because there were few chairs. This was frontier country, at a time when the Army was busy back east with the Civil War, and the territorial governors were custodians of a small howitzer, which they kept under a bunk in the "mansion."

Montana's capital moved to Virginia City and then on to its modern site, Helena, in 1875. In that same year, a self-made man named William A. Chessman bought property in the new capital, on a ridge that formed the edge of an area local placer miners called Last Chance Gulch. Chessman had sailed around Cape Horn from Massachusetts in 1849, bound for the California gold fields. He later tried Montana, during that territory's gold fever of the 1860s, and if Chessman had less than perfect luck in his hunt for gold, he found something equally valuable—water. He made his fortune in water rights, and in 1884 he hired the architect Cass Gilbert to construct a "proper" family home on his lot in Helena. It would have the best: brick hauled from Ohio, wood from the East and from South America, and heavy, traditional furnishings shipped by steamboat and mule train all the way from his native Massachusetts.

The Chessman home had three stories and a basement, twenty rooms, seven fireplaces, and a grand ballroom. The Queen Anne–style mansion

The living room. The vaulted windows give guests a view of the Big Sky country in the distance.

was the talk of Helena—until Chessman went broke. In 1900, he sold his home to a local bank, and the bank soon passed it on to Peter Larson, a Danish railroad engineer. After Larson's death in 1907, the home went to a third owner, the banker George Conrad, and in 1913 the state of Montana acquired it for thirty thousand dollars as the first official executive residence since territorial officials abandoned the Bannack cabin. From 1913 until 1959, nine Montana first families would live there, hosting such celebrity guests as Dinah Shore and Montana native Gary Cooper.

As the years passed the Chessman mansion showed an increasing number of disadvantages in its role as governor's residence. The original ballroom had been subdivided into smaller rooms, and there was nowhere to hold a large public gathering. The dining room seated at most sixteen guests. An earthquake in 1935 damaged the fireplaces, and by the late 1950s the historic home was in need of major repairs. Its life as Montana's official executive residence ended in 1959, but it has been lovingly restored by local and state agencies. Today it is a state-owned house museum and a main Helena tourist attraction.

Once the decision was made to abandon the second Montana mansion, Governor Hugo J. Aronson urged swift action to construct a new one. The architect Chandler Cohagen designed the Governor's Mansion as a modern "ship of state," a two-level concrete-and-steel residence constructed on a gently sloping suburban corner lot two blocks from the more traditional, domed Montana state capitol building. From the front, it seems to be a single-story ranch-style house; from the rear, its two levels are more apparent. It is a spacious home of fifty-seven hundred square feet, with a large

The painting is by the famous Western artist Charles M. Russell.

reception room, dining room, ample living quarters, and a three-car garage. There is little about it to suggest an official residence; recent first families have made it a gathering place for friends of their teenage children, and the Mansion is on the neighborhood Halloween route for trick-or-treaters.

At its completion, the Mansion was the butt of considerable public and media scorn. One story of the period called it a "symbol of ridicule" and "that monstrosity." But when the Aronson family moved from the old mansion to the new one in September 1959, the first lady said she was "delighted." In the years that followed, the Mansion won gradual acceptance, thanks in large measure to its space and convenience.

The Mansion's rooms are broad, many with high, vaulted ceilings that resemble the cutting prow of this "ship of state." At one end of the main living room, a peaked wall of picture windows affords a true Big Sky view of the Helena Valley and the mountains beyond. The original decorator selected colors like those of Montana itself, with its blue sky, green forests, amber prairies. A balcony opens off the master bedroom. There is a broad vestibule and—a surprise to visitors who first encounter the Mansion as a seemingly single-story home—a staircase leading down to the lower level, at the rear of the house.

The main floor has eleven rooms and a number of bathrooms. The reception and living rooms are designed for public entertainment, and the huge reception room can hold several hundred visitors for large public functions. In the reception room the walls are paneled in mahogany and the floor is of flagstone, continuing a theme first encountered in the welcoming vestibule. The reception room is one of two centers to the Mansion; it opens into two cloak and powder rooms, the same-floor state room, a smaller family living room, and a hallway that leads to main-floor bedrooms. The staircase descends from the reception room as well.

The dining room is the second center of the main floor. It is smaller and rather cozy, and here visitors find some rare remnants of the splendor of the old Chessman mansion. Silver place settings and Lenox china gleam in the light from Swedish crystal chandeliers. There is an intimate oval

Opposite:
The reception room. The Montana state seal decorates the carpet.

Above:
The painting, Heavy Shield, Blackfoot, *is by Harley Brown. Robert Scriver created the bronze sculpture and the pottery is by Mary Hasson, whose works decorate several Mansion rooms.*

mahogany table with matching chairs. Adjacent to the dining room are a smaller breakfast room and a sun porch, as well as a small office or den for the chief executive's use.

The Mansion's kitchen is thoroughly modern, with a wide central island and a good deal of cabinet space. Like most of the rest of the Mansion, it has few of the touches usually associated with an executive residence. A family lives here, clearly the designer's first priority.

The Mansion's second or rear level is largely devoted to family living areas, including a huge recreation room with a fireplace. It originally had a tile floor, and it still has easy access to the backyard and the three-car garage through a trio of doorways. Also on the lower level are an entrance lobby, two additional bedrooms, and storage and utility areas. Throughout the Mansion there is much space; even the storage rooms are large.

Is the modern Montana Governor's Mansion an ornate, striking, or historically significant home? No. Montana preserves that aspect of its heritage in the form of the Chessman property, officially designated as "The Original Governor's Mansion." There is a sense that these buildings are two members of the same extended family—one the venerable patriarch, all tweed and leather suspenders, the other a bright upstart with ambition and a firm focus on tomorrow. In their different ways, both recall their earliest antecedent—a log cabin with a cannon under the bed to ward off marauders. Three homes from three distinct eras, but all under the same Big Sky.

WASHINGTON

THE GOVERNOR'S MANSION
OLYMPIA

PHOTOGRAPHS BY DICK BUSHER

The Washington Governor's Mansion.

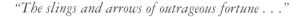

"The slings and arrows of outrageous fortune . . ."

One of the first British explorers to venture into the Pacific Northwest was searching for the fabled Northwest Passage, a hoped-for transcontinental water route that would link Europe and India. It didn't exist. The first missionaries sent to the future state of Washington had little luck, and some did not survive. For a time in the 1840s, Britain and the United States disputed the territory's fate, and the gold fever that intermittently gripped the Pacific and Mountain states from 1840 through the 1880s seemed to result in big strikes and economic booms everywhere but in Washington. When the territorial government first applied for statehood in 1876, Congress virtually ignored it. Like many Western states, it was not until the last half of the twentieth century, in the postwar industrial boom, that Washington seemed to reach its full potential. By 1990, the state was rated as one of America's most desirable places to live and work.

The fortunes of the Washington Governor's Mansion have paralleled those of the state. As it approaches its centennial, the residence has endured a major earthquake, a fire, periods of neglect and decay, threats of replacement—even bats in the attic. But like the state it symbolizes, the Mansion is now more splendid than ever, a Pacific Northwest treasure.

Washington became a state in 1889, and for two decades, the first families were responsible for their own lodging in Olympia. As the twentieth century dawned and Washington's hopes for the future crystallized, state leaders allocated funds for a three-story Georgian mansion on a crest of land overlooking Puget Sound and the distant Olympic Mountains, in what was becoming known as the state capitol campus. The nineteen-room frame and brick-veneer home was completed in time for the inauguration of Governor Samuel Cosgrove on January 27, 1909, but Governor Cosgrove was unable to attend the Mansion open house and ball the next day due to illness. He died two months later, and Lieutenant Governor Marion E. Hay was the first chief executive to occupy the new official state residence. His wife, Lizzie Muir Hay, acquired many of the original furnishings that still grace the home's public rooms. Lizzie Hay also holds the title of "first mother"; her youngest daughter, Margaret, was the only child ever born in the Mansion.

The Governor's Mansion did not enjoy a smooth first century of life. In 1915, a disgruntled first family moved out, complaining that it was too cold and drafty. There were leaks in the roof and plumbing problems, and as the Mansion aged it revealed a number of structural flaws. As recently as the 1960s, another first family found itself swatting at invading bats that had occupied the attic. On at least two occasions, in the 1920s and again in the 1960s, state legislators sought to raze and replace the Mansion. So did nature. On April 13, 1949, a major earthquake that struck the Puget

Sound area toppled one of the Mansion's chimneys, ruptured water pipes, and cracked the brick facing. Chimney fragments crashed through a skylight, narrowly missing the incumbent first lady. By the 1970s, critics of the Mansion were calling it "not architecturally wonderful and not historically ancient," to which Governor Daniel Evans replied, "It's a lot more ancient than a new one would be."

That statement launched a historic effort to save and refurbish the Mansion. Through a private foundation, Mansion backers set out to repair the structure and restore the soul of the historic home. They chose English and American antique furnishings from the period 1780 to 1830 for the decor and launched a massive structural rebuilding effort that virtually gutted the original interior. The 1974 reconstruction effort also added four thousand square feet to the south side of the Mansion, including a new family living area downstairs and new guest bedrooms upstairs. When the foundation's efforts were complete, the Washington Governor's Mansion was, for the first time since 1909, a home for comfortable family living and public entertaining.

One of the most notable gifts to the Mansion during the 1974 refurbishing effort was a marble mosaic state seal in the floor of the vestibule; Washington's seal includes a reproduction of a portrait of the first American president, and George Washington is always the first to greet Mansion visitors today. The vestibule opens into a lateral great hall, which is flanked by a pair of Empire pier tables from 1810. A set of eight chairs from the same period graces the hall and the drawing room, to the right. These unique chairs are upholstered in gold silk and feature the claw feet and reeded legs said to be by Joseph Barry of Philadelphia. The great hall also features a mahogany and bird's-eye maple demilune server from 1800, attributed to John Seymour.

In the drawing room, four Duncan Phyfe pieces—two Pembroke tables, a Federal worktable, and a mahogany and bird's-eye maple piano—can be seen by visitors as they inspect the room's historic collection, which also includes an 1810 mahogany sewing stand, a 1795 Sheraton sofa, and an 1800 Constitution mirror topped by an American eagle, hallmark of the Federal period. A portrait of George Washington hangs over the drawing-room mantel, above a French Empire gold and bronze clock.

At the opposite end of the great hall is the Mansion's ballroom, the largest room on the first floor. The crystal chandeliers are original to the room. The ballroom also features part of the Mansion's historic silver, from the U.S.S. *Olympia,* Admiral George Dewey's flagship during the Spanish-American War. The twenty-seven-piece silver service was executed in honor of the Navy's victory at the Battle of Manila Bay and manufactured by Shreve & Company of San Francisco from silver and gold mined in Washington. After the *Olympia* was decommissioned, the silver was given

Below:
The sterling-silver tea set was designed in the George II style.

Opposite:
The vestibule. State and national flags flank the Washington state seal, embedded in the floor in a mosaic design.

to the city of Olympia, and the city presented it to the state for use at the Mansion.

Other pieces from the *Olympia*'s silver set are displayed and used in the state dining room, where murals depict historic Washington scenes including sailing ships on Puget Sound. The wall coverings were painted by the artist Edwin Chapman in the style of the early nineteenth-century French artist Jean Zuber. The state dining room's eighteen chairs have needlepoint covers with a unique leaf design.

The library features a Federal convex mirror and other period furnishings, as well as an assortment of books with an emphasis on Washington

Below:
The ballroom. The chandeliers were designed when the house was built.

Opposite:
The drawing room. The Queen Anne chair was once owned by Oliver Wolcott, a signer of the Declaration of Independence.

authors. Also in the library is a Mansion guest book with the signatures of distinguished visitors over the years. President Harry Truman, his wife, Bess, and their daughter, Margaret, all signed on June 10, 1948, and other guests have included presidents Coolidge, Franklin D. Roosevelt, and Nixon, the last two kings of Norway, and the prime minister of Japan.

All of the public rooms are maintained by the Governor's Mansion Foundation at no public expense. The Foundation is also active in acquiring works of art and other items for the Mansion collection.

The 1974 addition at the rear of the Mansion included a modern kitchen and spacious family living and dining rooms. The upper floors, reached by a split staircase rising from the great hall, contain both original and new bedrooms and other family areas.

The Mansion's grounds merge seamlessly with those of the adjacent buildings of the Washington state capitol; in fact, the capitol dome, next

door to the Mansion, is clearly visible from many of the windows. Broad, columned porches on two sides of the Mansion overlook flower gardens and shaded walkways lined with native shrubs.

Its life has not always been blessed, but the Washington Governor's Mansion, like the state itself, has enjoyed a great flowering in the final quarter of the twentieth century.

The library. The guest book on the foreground table has been signed by presidents, movie stars, and visiting royalty.

WYOMING

THE GOVERNOR'S RESIDENCE
CHEYENNE

PHOTOGRAPHS BY RICHARD COLLIER

The Wyoming Governor's Residence.

yoming is a state of mountains and high plains. The Tetons, the Wind River Range, and the Big Horn Mountains rise in the west like sentinels. Wyoming encompasses most of Yellowstone National Park, the majestic Devils Tower, and places whose names speak of its rugged frontier heritage—Cody, Jackson Hole, Shoshoni. Jim Bridger trekked across Wyoming, and it was the land of the Sioux, Crow, Cheyenne, and Arapaho warriors who were among the last to yield to the white settlers' westward incursions. Wyoming became a territory in 1868, and in 1890 our forty-fourth state, but as late as 1909 it was still the scene of bitter frontier range wars. Today it is ninth in land area but fiftieth in population, a vast, open realm.

Just one year after becoming a territory, Wyoming became the first government in America to grant women the right to vote. In 1924, the state of Wyoming scored another first by electing Nellie Tayloe Ross as the first woman governor in the United States.

By that time the state's chief executives had been living in an official residence for two decades. In 1901, the legislature had set aside thirty-seven thousand dollars and hired Charles W. Murdock of Omaha to design a home for Wyoming's first families. It was a two-and-a-half-story red-brick Colonial Revival home with a separate carriage house. The original mansion also had a full basement and was well designed for family living. In 1910, the first family gathered in an upstairs bedroom to gaze at Halley's Comet through a dormer window. The children of another governor kept their pet pony in the carriage house.

When Governor John B. Kendrick moved into the ten-year-old mansion in 1915, he immediately set out to improve it. He added an oak-paneled mantel in the drawing room and installed all-electric fixtures to replace the original dual-purpose fixtures, which used either gas or electricity. William Jennings Bryan, "the great commoner" from Nebraska who had run for president three times, visited the mansion in 1917, as did President Warren G. Harding in 1923. Harding was traveling west to San Francisco; he died there a few days later, making the old Wyoming mansion one of his last official stops. Coincidentally, the Wyoming governor he visited there also had little time to live: William B. Ross died of appendicitis in 1924, and the secretary of state, Frank Lucas, who officially succeeded him until a special election could be held, graciously allowed the governor's widow to remain in the mansion. Mrs. Ross defeated her opponent in the election, and it was then that she took office as America's first elected woman governor.

During the Depression two governors declined to live in the mansion, citing the need to cut costs. It served for a time as the state headquarters of the W.P.A. and E.R.A. relief agencies, but by 1937 the incumbent governor had moved back in. In that year the legislature underwrote a major remodeling project. The mansion got a new breakfast room, and the second floor was extensively altered, cutting the number of bedrooms from six to four and adding three bathrooms and several closets.

After World War II, the mansion received the silver service from the decommissioned battleship *Wyoming*. President Truman visited in 1948, and Governor Lester Hunt added a photo gallery of past Wyoming first ladies. In the 1950s Governor Milward Simpson furnished the den with pieces created by Thomas Molesworth, made from native Wyoming pine and cedar and upholstered with fabric in patterns that included the state flower, the Indian paintbrush. The den is today called the Wyoming room and retains the Simpson furnishings. Subsequent first families added, and later enclosed, the sun porch, redecorated the drawing room, and remodeled the third floor, which had been originally used as maids' quarters. They entertained an eclectic range of guests, from presidential candidate Richard Nixon to the author James Michener, who was in Wyoming to do research for a historical novel. The mansion's carriage house was also the neighborhood polling place on election days; from 1906 until 1958, area residents gathered there to cast their ballots, often for the governor who lived in the adjacent house. The original mansion was a place for family life and state functions, and today it is a state museum, restored in part to its original condition while maintaining improvements by the first families who called it home. A number of its early 1900s furnishings have been tracked down and repurchased to preserve their role in Wyoming history.

Governor Ed Herschler was the last chief executive to live in the old mansion. In 1976 he became the first to occupy the new one. The state decided to invest in a new executive residence to provide more room for public functions and first family privacy. The site of the new mansion was the former American Legion Park in Cheyenne, a nine-acre section of the city. There rose the new mansion, a nearly eight-thousand-square-foot, one-story ranch-style home with a basement, constructed with wood siding and moss rock from Iron Mountain in the Horse Creek region of the state.

The present Governor's Residence is notable for its openness. Its front glass doors and tall windows admit ample light, and visitors approach along a wide sidewalk canopied by trees carefully preserved by the builder from the days when the area served as a municipal park. In the foyer, a large area rug bears the Wyoming state seal. The rug was trimmed from the foyer carpeting at the historic mansion, one of several artifacts to make the move from old to new.

The state living room is the center of the Residence's public rooms. At one end of the room, a tall stone fireplace reaches to the high ceiling, which is supported by dark-wood beams. Bookcases hold a collection of volumes by Wyoming authors dating to the last century. A 1905 grand piano and a 1937 grandfather clock are among the treasures moved from the historic

The open dining area features needlework chair designs created for Wyoming's 1990 centennial.

Opposite:
The state living room. The two Philadelphia Chippendale chairs have been re-covered in cowhide.

Above:
The dining-room chandelier features bronze figures and an elk-hide shade.

mansion. The Philadelphia Chippendale chairs here have been re-covered in cowhide to add a Western flavor. The Governor's Residence is decorated throughout with outstanding examples of contemporary and historical Western art.

The state dining area is adjacent and open to the state living room. Here, the artist Tina Close created needlework designs for the dining-table chairs featuring Wyoming wildflowers. Representatives from each county in the state completed the chairs, which are done in thirty-seven colors depicting seven flowers. The chairs bear the initials of each stitcher and the names of their home counties. The central attraction of the dining area is a striking chandelier. It is conical in shape with an elk-hide shade ringed at the base with bronze figures of Western riders, including Indians, cowboys, and, fittingly for "The Equality State," cowgirls. The bronze base on which they stand is shaped as a rope and decorated with a variety of Western symbols. The dining area also contains the sculpture *Hope of a Nation* and a display of historical china and silver.

The Residence has two guest bedrooms, one decorated in 1930s French Provincial furnishings brought from the old mansion. The second guest bedroom is decorated in traditional Western style and displays items that represent Wyoming industries—wool, minerals, and native artwork. The public portion of the Residence also has offices for the incumbent governor and first lady and her assistant.

The family wing of the Residence, by simply closing two doors, becomes a private five-bedroom home with a large kitchen and dining, living, and family rooms. Outside is a flagstone terrace, with fossils embedded in the stones. The terrace overlooks grounds that resemble a mountain setting, with ancient pines, granite boulders, and spacious meadows, as well as a newly designed Children's Discovery Park for young visitors.

Cheyenne, with a population of fifty thousand, is the largest city in this state of fewer than half a million people. They are close neighbors to a historic mansion and the modern Governor's Residence—symbols of the new and the old in a city on the high plains.

Utah

The Governor's Mansion
Salt Lake City

PHOTOGRAPHS BY SCOTT ZIMMERMAN

The Utah Governor's Mansion.

Opening page:
The dome over the
central stairwell of
the Mansion.

When James Bridger first came upon the Great Salt Lake, he tasted it and assumed it was an inland extension of the Pacific Ocean. Later, when Utah's wide deserts and snowy mountains had been mapped and explored, fur trappers held their annual raucous rendezvous at Bear Lake. It was the Church of Jesus Christ of Latter-day Saints that launched modern Utah; persecuted in Illinois, they staged one of the great mass migrations in American history, in 1845 and 1846, arriving in the Great Basin after a twelve-month journey. Fortune did seem to smile on Utah, even when federal authorities did not. When locusts threatened the Mormons' first crops, seagulls arrived to save them. In 1850 Utah was designated a territory, but the federal government remained less than tolerant of the Mormon doctrine of polygamy. The U.S. Army invaded in 1857, and there were bitter battles and court actions for several years, until the territory abolished polygamy in 1890. After seven unsuccessful applications, Utah became our forty-fifth state in 1896.

Utah shared much untapped mineral wealth with its neighboring Mountain States, and it eventually drew immigrants like Thomas Kearns. Born in Canada, young Kearns moved with his family to Nebraska and later left home at seventeen, drawn to the West by its frequent silver and gold strikes and the lure of immeasurable fortune. He arrived in Park City, Utah Territory, in 1883, began work as a mine laborer, and wound up owning the mine. By the turn of the century, Kearns was a millionaire. He was part owner of the daily newspaper in Salt Lake City; married his partner's beautiful niece, Jennie Judge; and was ultimately elected to the United States Senate.

In 1902 Kearns's lavish three-story home was completed. Designed by Carl M. Neuhausen in the French Châteauesque style, it was built to last. The home was constructed of limestone and elaborately crafted and furnished inside. The Kearns mansion had thirty-two rooms, four baths, ten fireplaces, a bowling alley, a billiard room, and three secure vaults—one each for silver, jewelry, and wine. The reception hall was done in French oak woodwork. Within a year, Kearns hosted a good friend at the home, President Theodore Roosevelt.

In 1918, Senator Kearns was struck by a car and killed. Jennie Kearns and their three children continued to live in the mansion, which was soon regarded as one of Salt Lake City's most lavish landmarks. Mrs. Kearns remodeled the original French and Turkish parlors, creating a single large drawing room. She proved an able custodian of the house, and in 1937 she executed a simple transfer deed donating it to the state on the condition that it would be used as the official residence of the governor. The state was delighted; there had been no state executive residence prior to the unexpected bequest, and officials moved swiftly to prepare the historic Kearns home for the first family. The decorator Florence Ware and her father, the architect Walter Ware, installed new appliances and drapes and upgraded the electrical system. Mrs. Kearns was a generous benefactor, donating rugs, the dining-room table and chairs, and other furnishings to the state; the Wares selected furnishings to replace those that she decided not to leave behind. The Ware team worked for months preparing the new Governor's Mansion, and Florence Ware, who was teaching a class in interior decorating at the Utah Extension Division, kept her students posted on their progress. A member of that 1938 class later transcribed these notes: "The state has a priceless possession in the Governor's Mansion . . . lovely things in it. . . . It is an interesting house with a personality and a bit of romance and history . . . beautiful wood all solid: solid oak, solid walnut, solid bird's eye maple with gold-plated door knobs, costly chandeliers. Staircase beautifully carved from main floor clear up to third floor. In perfect condition. No scratches or mars."

The Mansion, she added, was "perfect for entertaining." In addition to the large state dining room, it had private dining and living quarters for the first families. The third floor contained a spacious ballroom, and the changes made by Mrs. Kearns had assured that guests could mingle in large numbers in the expanded drawing room—a "large room with quite a lot of windows."

The Mansion served well for two decades, but by the 1950s it needed extensive repairs. The legislature ultimately handed it over to the Utah State Historical Society, and Governor J. Bracken Lee and his family moved out to a newly constructed home in the Federal Heights neighborhood of Salt Lake City. For a time the basement bowling alley at the abandoned Mansion was used for book storage. The Historical Society could not afford the necessary maintenance and upkeep, and by 1977 the Mansion was badly in need of an advocate.

Help came from Governor Scott Matheson and First Lady Norma Matheson. They believed the old Kearns home could and should be restored as Utah's Governor's Mansion. Matheson convinced leaders to devise a master plan for restoration and preservation of the historic property, and most of the work was accomplished using donated private funds. Governor and Mrs. Matheson moved in in 1980, and the Mansion was once again home to the state's first families. Soon after the move, a woman who had worked there under a previous governor joined the daily tour. She peeked into the kitchen, saw a woman pulling a tray of cookies from the oven, and asked, "Do they treat you good here, dearie?" First Lady Norma Matheson turned around and said they certainly did.

On December 15, 1993, the Christmas tree in the Mansion's grand hall was ignited by faulty wiring. The ensuing fire was devastating, roaring up the main stairway and charring the dome at the top, which collapsed and fell to the ground floor. Smoke damage throughout the Mansion was

On the following spread

Left page, top:
*The state dining room. The table
and chairs were originally owned
by the Kearns family.*

Left page, bottom:
The grand hall.

Right page:
The central stairwell.

extensive, although quick action by firefighters, including the building of makeshift dams to prevent water from entering several rooms, prevented further losses. No one was hurt in the fire, but the Mansion was once again in jeopardy.

A three-year restoration effort sought to preserve what could be saved of the original Kearns home and to replicate as closely as possible what had been lost. The original plasterwork was carefully cleaned and restored or, when necessary, replaced. Most of the interior walls were removed and rebuilt, using the same metal lathe and plaster construction Kearns had employed in 1902. The white-oak wood carvings that adorned many of the Mansion rooms had been crafted in Europe at the turn of the century, but Agrell & Thorpe, Ltd., of California, was able to duplicate most of the

original work, calling it "the largest wood-carving project undertaken any-where in the world in the past ten years." Interior paint was copied from Victorian-era examples. The Mansion craftsmen paid special attention to the historic dome over the central stairwell, where the worst of the fire damage was concentrated. Hayles & Howe of Baltimore constructed a replica, and today the restored dome is virtually identical to the original.

The restored Utah Governor's Mansion reopened in July 1996, and the first visitors were made aware of the quality of the home's 1902 construction and of the equal care that had gone into its restoration. The grand hall, where the fire had been centered, has been restored with paint and rugs modeled on the 1902 originals. The table in the center of the grand hall was salvaged from the fire, and an antique chair, reputedly once owned by William Gladstone, the British prime minister, also graces the hall. On the grand hall's mantel is a carving of Neptune. (When the Kearns children were small, Jennie Kearns hid Easter eggs in Neptune's mouth.) A new etched glass skylight has been added to the first floor; the entire stairwell had originally been open to the third floor.

In the library the walls have been restored, and the room has an original Kearns-era Saruk Persian rug.

In the state dining room, the Kearns table and chairs have been repaired and refurbished, as has the mahogany wainscoting. A French tapestry wall covering has been replaced by a mural, painted by Bruce Robertson, depicting Utah harvest scenes.

The two original parlors, adapted by Mrs. Kearns as one drawing room, remain a single parlor. The inlaid hardwood floor was restored, and new drapes and rugs were added. The parlor also contains a nineteenth-century Italian Rococo-style gilt-wood and porcelain table and a portrait of Jennie Kearns.

The informal dining room, kitchen, and pantry all underwent extensive restoration. In the dining room, fragments of wall served as a guide to replicating the original colors. The dining room also has a built-in breakfront and original plaster relief on the ceiling in the Wedgwood style.

The second-floor bedrooms have also been refurbished, with an eclectic combination of furnishings: an original Kearns carpet, items from the state historical collection, and furnishings added in the 1930s and the 1970s. The third-floor ballroom was one of the most heavily damaged portions of the Mansion; it has now been adorned with new period stenciling.

The library.

The Mansion's grand reopening in 1996 drew large crowds. The event was timed to coincide with Utah's centennial year, a century after the state beside the Great Salt Lake had joined the Union. "This," Governor Michael Leavitt said, "is one of the most outstanding historic restorations in the country. We pay tribute to the fine craftsmen who have restored the Mansion to its original splendor."

OKLAHOMA

THE GOVERNOR'S MANSION
OKLAHOMA CITY

PHOTOGRAPHS BY SHANE CULPEPPER

The Oklahoma Governor's Mansion.

Oklahoma is a state of right angles, with sweeping horizons interrupted by the vertical towers of bustling urban centers and by rural windmills and oil derricks. The Governor's Mansion captures those contrasts. Jutting from broad green grounds two blocks east of the state capitol building in Oklahoma City, the modified Dutch Colonial Mansion rises three stories in Indiana Carthage limestone, its twin chimneys and steeply pitched red-tile roof reaching into the sky.

This is the house that Oklahoma built, and because Oklahoma grew out of a rich interchange between Indian and settler cultures, it is also a home that reflects astonishing diversity. No two rooms are alike; each floor is distinct, and the one common thread visitors quickly sense as they enter the Oklahoma Governor's Mansion is the uncommon tribute it pays to that diversity.

Oklahoma became a state in 1907, when the former Oklahoma and Indian Territories merged, and for more than two decades its governors lived in private residences or hotels. By 1914, as work moved ahead on the state capitol building, Governor Lee Cruce designated a site for the state executive residence, but it remained a grassy field until 1927. That year brought a roaring oil boom to the state (there was even a producing well on the south lawn of the capitol), and there was little debate as the legislature decided it was time to build a permanent home for Oklahoma's governors.

Architects Layton, Hicks, & Forsyth, who had designed the state capitol building, chose to use the same Indiana limestone as in the Mansion's large neighbor to the west. The three-story Mansion (with basement) would face toward the capitol. Construction began in the summer of 1927,

Right:
The Mansion's swimming pool is in the shape of the state of Oklahoma.

and Governor Henry Johnston and his family dedicated the nineteen-room Mansion in the fall of 1928. A two-story matching garage and maid's quarters, added one year later, is just east of the main structure.

During the Depression, one colorful chief executive brought a team of mules to the Mansion and personally plowed the broad lawn, converting the grounds into a vegetable garden. He invited poor neighbors to plant potatoes. Later, drillers found oil beneath the Mansion and added a producing well to the grounds. Other chief executives have added their own distinctive touches. In the 1960s, a hastily constructed helipad at the southeast corner of the Mansion grounds allowed President Lyndon Johnson to land conveniently during a visit to Oklahoma City; after he left, the concrete surface was adapted as a tennis court. A sculpture of playing children that overlooks a small pond and fountain on the south Mansion grounds recalls the youngsters who have lived in the Mansion. Private donors constructed a swimming pool in the shape of the state of Oklahoma in the 1970s. Twenty years later, a first family expanded the second-floor family room and reduced the original number of bedrooms from five to four. Other first families have added furnishings, changed interior paint or wallpaper, or upgraded portions of the grounds, each leaving its personal mark on Oklahoma's house. But unlike the committee-designed horse that becomes a camel, in this case the absence of a constraining master plan during these decades of change has actually allowed for a more spontaneous kind of unity. Oklahoma's house simply reflects Oklahoma.

Friends of the Mansion, Inc., a privately funded foundation, was created in 1995 to establish a permanent, historically representative collection of furnishings and to sponsor major restoration projects. At a statewide open house in 1995, Oklahomans were invited to bring gifts that would become permanent parts of the Mansion collection. Thousands visited the Mansion on a cool late-winter day to add their contributions to the restoration effort, and many of those gifts are on display throughout the residence today. They include china and crystal, Persian rugs, furnishings, even family heirlooms with symbolic connections to Oklahoma's land-run heritage and its frontier and Indian spirit. The modern Mansion was furnished not by any single designer, but by thousands of Oklahomans who imbued it with their collective taste.

The Mansion's fourteen thousand square feet encompass twelve rooms that have been fully restored to their original grandeur. The dark-wood elegance of the intimate interior makes a strong contrast to the clean, smooth lines of the modified Dutch Colonial exterior. From the outside, there is a sense of simplicity, but as guests move through the entryway into the library, the focus of the first floor, they encounter elaborate molding, leaded glass cabinet doors, a broad winding central staircase—a hundred small indications of the care first families have lavished on this home over the decades.

To enter Oklahoma's Governor's Mansion is to open the family cedar chest and find it packed with the collected treasures of four generations, from the ornate and precious to the everyday. Artifacts range from a crystal eagle, donated by the widow of the state's first oil millionaire, to an antique Montgolfier chandelier contributed by an entire community. In room after room, rich wood paneling and stout, comfortable furnishings combine with distinctively Oklahoma items to give the impression of an elegant English drawing room transplanted to the open prairies. The Mansion is a home that has evolved over time within the flexible boundaries of the original architectural design.

Below:
The dining room. The chair cushions bear the state seal and the emblems of the Five Civilized Tribes.

Opposite, above:
The library. Shelves and woodwork were restored to their original stained darkness in the 1995 restoration. The sculpture on the mantel is of Will Rogers.

Opposite, below:
The foyer. The rug bears the names of Oklahoma's thirty-six federally recognized Native American tribes and the three tribal towns. Above the piano is a painting by Thomas Moran.

There are two modern dens or family rooms, one in the basement and one in the second-floor living quarters. The first-floor main kitchen has been completely remodeled to accommodate modern entertainment needs. These areas are not unlike any fine suburban home of recent vintage.

The public rooms are different, and each is unique. Doors have the original brass doorknobs and etched-glass windows marked by the state seal. The ground-floor surfaces, as well as those on the second-story landing, are the original oak, restored plank by plank. At the foot of the broad, winding central staircase, where holiday decorations often denote the season and a grand piano suggests entertainment, there is a sense of being at the center of the house's life. The entry-hall floor is adorned by a handmade rug bearing the names of Oklahoma's thirty-nine Indian tribes, a tribute to the state's extensive Native American heritage and to its original status as the Indian Territory. The staircase that leads to the upper floors is covered by a runner bearing, on each step and in chronological order, the names of every governor who has lived here; in the Oklahoma room, the formal parlor opposite the library, a brilliant white rug bears the state seal, precisely rendered in dark blue.

The central library's dark-wood shelves and cabinets, with leaded glass doors, reflect the house as it was in 1928. In the main dining room, a long table seats ten on chairs bearing the seals of the state of Oklahoma and of the Five Civilized Tribes—the Chickasaw, Choctaw, Cherokee, Creek, and

Seminole. Fireplaces in the Oklahoma room and the library, lit during cold weather, extend their warmth into the small office or study often used by governors to conduct state business or greet official visitors. Each of these public rooms is intended to be welcoming to visitors, and even at crowded public receptions, guests wander into the library to scan the titles on the shelves or sit in an inviting chair. A 1995–96 refurbishing of the Mansion transformed the original sunroom adjacent to the dining area into a fully enclosed rose room for informal dining and entertainment. Originally designed as a screen-enclosed sun porch, the rose room now has arched Palladian windows and a chandelier selected to recall the Mansion's 1928 decor. It is a bright and airy throwback to an era when diners sought a connection with the outdoors, when dinner was incomplete without a glimpse of fireflies dotting the lawn at dusk.

In the second-floor living quarters, there are three bedrooms, plus the master bedroom. In one of the rooms guests can sleep on the Maximilian bed, an ornate mahogany piece that once belonged to the emperor of Mexico. The second-floor family room also includes a fireplace and counter and

The ballroom. With its attached kitchen and dressing room, the ballroom occupies the entire third floor. This room was almost completely redone during the 1995 restoration.

shelf areas that serve as a home office, and there is a door leading visitors onto a wide second-floor balcony that overlooks the south Mansion grounds.

The ballroom covers most of the third floor and seats up to sixty guests for formal dinners and special events. Its original maple floor, covered with a Persian Dorokshe area rug, contrasts with the darker oak flooring on the first and second floors. An antique Victorian piano and arched windows, chandeliers, and elaborate moldings re-create much of the aura that graced this room in 1928. The third floor also includes a small dressing room, with two half-baths for guests, and a midsized kitchen.

Throughout the public areas of the Mansion are works of art on loan from the Gilcrease Museum in Tulsa and the National Cowboy Hall of Fame in Oklahoma City, two of the nation's finest collections of Western art. Artists represented in oil and bronze include N. C. Wyeth, Charles Russell, Thomas Moran, and Albert Bierstadt.

The Mansion sits near the center of a five-acre tract, with a grassy mall and a sidewalk extending west to the capitol. The grounds, which also include the tennis court, helipad, pool, and carriage-house complex, are surrounded by an ornate iron fence with limestone pillars and dotted with a variety of native trees and shrubs.

Like the state seal that adorns the rug in the Oklahoma room, the Mansion is a symbol of Oklahoma's diversity. On the seal, the emblems of the Five Civilized Tribes surround the Oklahoma Territory's original seal depicting a tribal chief and a settler clasping hands as the robed figure of Justice holds her scales aloft. It is an eclectic emblem of the state.

NEW MEXICO

THE GOVERNOR'S MANSION
SANTA FE

PHOTOGRAPHS BY JERRY RABINOWITZ

The New Mexico Governor's Mansion.

In search of Cibola . . .

The saga of Alvar Núñez Cabeza de Vaca and his Moorish slave, Estevan, is one of the great tales of American history. Shipwrecked on the Gulf Coast in 1527, they wandered for nearly nine years through what would become the American Southwest. They were captured by Indians, made slaves, escaped. When they returned to the Spanish colonies, they told the viceroy of their travels—and they apparently embellished them a bit. There were seven glorious cities somewhere up there, Cabeza de Vaca and Estevan claimed: the Seven Cities of Cibola. The Spanish government dispatched Francisco Vásquez de Coronado to the region in 1540, and his expedition is rivaled only by Lewis and Clark's in the annals of frontier-opening exploration. Coronado never found the fabled Seven Cities of Cibola, but a colony was subsequently established at Santa Fe by Juan de Oñate, and in 1610 the Spanish governor, Pedro de Peralta, ordered that a palace should be erected there to house himself and his successors. The Palace of the Governors sits there today, on the historic Plaza in Santa Fe, the first and most enduring of America's official executive residences.

The Palace was constructed of adobe, and it was designed as a residence, a seat of colonial government, and a fortress. It was the capitol building for New Spain's northernmost colony. It was also vulnerable; in 1680, a revolt by Pueblo Indians drove the Spaniards from Santa Fe, and tribal leaders occupied the Palace. The Spanish returned in 1692, and even after the American victory in the Mexican War of the 1840s, it was the seat of government and official executive residence of New Mexico.

The region was ceded to the United States in the treaty ending that small but significant conflict. On August 18, 1846, American soldiers raised the Stars and Stripes over the low, one-story Palace of the Governors. It was soon home to American territorial governors and their families, who enjoyed the cool of its adobe walls, the central courtyard, and the sprawling network of rooms. In March 1862, the Civil War spilled into New Mexico Territory. In an unheralded yet dramatic wartime sidelight, a small Confederate force from Texas battled its way across New Mexico and occupied Santa Fe and the Palace of the Governors, driving an inadequate Union garrison into frantic retreat. The Union troops soon returned, and defeated the Confederates in the three-day Battle of Glorieta Pass, fought east of Santa Fe.

New Mexico remained a territory well into the twentieth century. Charles Goodnight opened the cattle trail that bore his name, trekking through eastern New Mexico to Denver. Billy the Kid fought, and died, in the Lincoln County land wars. Phil Sheridan struggled with the Comanche, forced west from Texas into one of the lower forty-eight's last open frontiers. Geronimo led the final Indian uprising in 1885. By 1912, when

New Mexico became the forty-seventh state, it had had twenty-four territorial governors, including Lew Wallace, the Civil War general who wrote *Ben Hur*. Until 1889, territorial governors lived in the Palace. In later years they occupied private homes but continued to use the Palace for ceremonial occasions and public receptions. In 1907, the territorial legislature authorized the construction of a second executive residence on the new capitol grounds. It was a fine Colonial home in the Victorian gingerbread style, with a white-pillared entrance. One room was furnished in Louis XV style. The mansion could have been transplanted from New England or old Virginia.

After statehood, first families lived in the mansion for three decades. There were steady grumblings about its style and suitability. Many local residents wondered why the governor was living in a house incongruous to the rest of the city. In 1945, the Museum of New Mexico (which also operated the Palace of the Governors as the state's major historic landmark) designated a thirty-acre tract of hilly land a mile north of the Palace for a new official state residence. In 1951, the legislature set aside funds for its construction, and the architect W. C. Kruger was hired to design a true New Mexico executive mansion.

Kruger chose the modified territorial style, one that is unique to the Southwest. The Governor's Mansion combines elements from the large adobe communal houses developed by the Pueblo Indians with aspects of the sprawling one-story haciendas built by Spanish and Mexican ranchers. Kruger then added some touches of his own—brick cornices, hard plaster exteriors, and wooden window frames. The eighteen-room Mansion is of brick and block construction with a flat roof. Like its architectural ancestor, the Palace of the Governors, it has multiple wings and seems to spread over the ground, leading residents and guests from room to room and wing to wing in an inviting manner. Visitors reach the central part of the Mansion through a sheltering portal that leads to the front door. In the east wing are four bedrooms, a study for the governor, and a spacious family room. In the remainder of the house, the public areas flow from a foyer to the large formal living room to the formal dining room to the petroglyph room. Perhaps no other executive residence so graphically captures the essence of its state.

The Mansion has been modified several times during its first half century of service. In 1957–58, a new formal dining room was constructed by glassing in a covered terrace on the west end. The west wing was remodeled again in 1965, with the addition of a breakfast room and extensive modifications to the kitchen. A large family room was also carved out of the open L shape between the master bedroom and the bedroom wing on the east. In 1991, the state launched

Opposite:

The Mansion walkways and patios are much like those at the Palace of the Governors.

Above:

The dining room. The hand-stenciled beams bear grapevine and crest designs adapted from a Spanish
palace. The dining room also contains a sideboard on loan from the Palace of the Governors.

another extensive redecoration effort, which also included renovation of one bedroom into a handicapped-accessible rest room and improvements to the front portal.

The Mansion's landscaped grounds overlook the Sangre de Cristo Mountains. Among the plants are native piñon shrubs, and the outdoor facilities include a tennis court and a grassed terrace for entertaining. The grounds are enclosed by a masonry and wrought-iron wall with gates displaying the state symbol.

The Mansion's public rooms carry a Southwestern theme throughout. The foyer's brick floor is covered with a rug bearing the state seal, combining the American and Mexican eagles. The walls were brushed, sponged, and ragged in a careful nine-step process to create a slatelike appearance. Foyer furnishings include a nineteenth-century Italian chair and a Spanish bench and table of the same vintage. Artworks on display include depictions

The foyer. New Mexico's state seal appears on the rug. The walls were created in a nine-step process to create the look of slate.

The petroglyph room. The wall decorations reproduce ancient paintings from Indian caves. The rug is based on a Navajo chief's blanket. The center table is made of cottonwood drums created in Indian style.

of Indians and mountain scenes. Adjacent to the foyer are two smaller rooms: the anteroom, which contains a nineteenth-century Spanish trestle table, Italian chairs, and a 1920s table by New Mexico artist William Penhallow Henderson; and the petroglyph room, an informal entertaining area displaying painted replicas of historical petroglyphs. These replicas depict Spanish soldiers entering New Mexico in the early 1600s and are modeled on rock paintings at Canyon de Chelley. The petroglyph room also contains a massive Taos drum, on loan from the Museum of New Mexico. There are leather chairs for relaxing and end tables adapted from the design of a nineteenth-century New Mexico chest. The rug is based on an 1870 Navajo chief's blanket.

In the living room, where wide windows overlook the grounds and the mountains beyond, rugs employ the Colcha Spanish Colonial embroidery technique in the room's dominant colors—greens, blues, maroons, and ivories. Furniture is mostly contemporary and comfortable, with fabrics chosen to continue the earth-tone design of the room. The living room contains as well a pair of nineteenth-century Italian armchairs and a chest carved in sixteenth- and seventeenth-century Spanish style. Two end tables also carry a Spanish flavor.

The dining room is perhaps the Mansion's most meticulously decorated area. The artist E. C. Shaeffer designed hand-stenciling for the ceiling beams in a motif that incorporates grapevines, adapted from the San Lorenzo del Escorial Palace near Madrid. The beams were stenciled in bright colors, then glazed to create an aged effect. Shaeffer had fallen from a horse before she began the work, and she was in a half-body cast throughout the project; volunteer artists came to her aid to complete the project. The dining-room furnishings, which rest on cooling brick floors, are also of Spanish design. The table by Gene Law combines aspects of two similar pieces in the National Museum of Decorative Arts in Madrid. Law's chairs reflect sixteenth- and seventeenth-century Spanish styles, and one of the two buffets shows the influence of a sixteenth-century chest in Ruidabel Castle. The antique Guatemalan sideboard is on loan from the original Palace of the Governors. The chandelier is of tin and typical of Spanish Colonial work; when the Santa Fe Trail opened, provisions were often packaged in tin containers, and local artisans used the empties to fashion a wide variety of objects. Throughout the dining room, as in other public areas of the Mansion, there are examples of New Mexico pottery, basketry, and painting—a rich blend of Indian, Spanish, and Anglo styles that reflect natural landscape colors and the state's diverse heritage.

The Palace of the Governors is just one mile—and almost four hundred years—away from New Mexico's Governor's Mansion, but they are clearly kin. In spirit, there is little real distance between the oldest surviving executive residence in the Western Hemisphere and one of the newest.

ALASKA

THE GOVERNOR'S HOUSE
JUNEAU

PHOTOGRAPHS BY RONALD KLEIN

The Alaska Governor's House decorated for the holiday season.

The community that was to become Alaska's capital city was founded on gold—and for some time even its name was a matter of doubt. When an Auke Indian tipped Richard Harris and Joe Juneau that gold might be found in the hills overlooking Gastineau Channel, the two staked out an initial township named Harrisburg. Harrisburg was soon renamed Rockwell, in honor of the U.S. Navy officer who oversaw law and order in the new community. But when Harris and Rockwell left town, Joe Juneau finally felt free to name the town as he saw fit. What better name than his own?

Alaska attracted the boldest of pioneers, most of whom settled in the coastal areas. As the unofficial territory grew more organized, its capital shifted from Sitka to Juneau, which by 1900 had a burgeoning population of 1,864. In 1912, the United States formally designated Alaska as its newest territory, and Walter Eli Clark was named governor. Clark had little government machinery and no official government buildings. A 1910 act of Congress had authorized the construction of a residence for the appointed district (later territorial) chief executive, but work did not begin on the house until 1912. Despite the delay, Alaska's executive residence was destined to be finished before any other government building in the new territory.

The architect James Knox Taylor faced few local building precedents. Most early Juneau buildings were constructed of wood; there were no native quarrying or brick-making industries, and it was too expensive to ship heavy construction materials from the lower forty-eight states. Early Juneau homes were functional, like gold-rush houses in California and Idaho. The idea was simple: stake your claim, start digging for gold, and build a house when time permitted. Taylor was determined to avoid that error. He designed a two-and-a-half-story frame house with a touch of the Greek Revival style borrowed from the Federal period. If Alaska was to have one official building, it was going to be as elegant as Taylor's efforts would allow.

The Alaska Governor's House was completed in time for a reception on New Year's Day, 1913. Guests marveled at its nearly thirteen thousand square feet, its many fireplaces and spacious rooms. The first floor, over a full cellar, included a reception hall, a drawing room, a library, the main dining room, office space, the kitchen, and a conservatory. Upstairs were four ample bedrooms, three baths, and a sewing room. The attic structure was originally designed to house servants and a planned territorial museum, which never materialized. In the 1960s, that area was redesigned as two guest suites and a large extra bedroom.

Taylor situated the Governor's House on a hill—Juneau is full of hills—with views of the city below, the southern end of the Gastineau Channel, and the communities of Douglas and Treadwell across the channel. Before

the House could be built, workers had to remove a schoolhouse and other small buildings that had grown, in the haphazard manner of all mining towns, atop the hill. The rising structure's entrance was on the east, but the columned front of the House faced south. The steep gabled roof soared over three irregular gable dormers, and there were two first-floor bay windows flanking the two-story central portico. During a 1936 renovation, the portico was enlarged with the addition of six Corinthian columns, which were again changed to the Doric style in 1963. The gable dormers were also modified as segmental arch dormers, and the east entrance, at the side of the House, was enhanced with the addition of a porte cochère and a driveway. The House today is painted white with green shutters, but its original design has not been altered dramatically, despite the many refinements. One observer has called it a "twentieth-century version of a New England Colonial house."

Above:
The drawing room. The carved fireplace mantel bears the District of Alaska seal from 1912.

On the following spread

Left page:
*The dining room. The high-ceilinged dining
area opens through a wide door to the entry
hall.*

Right page:
*The bed and dresser in the guest bedroom are
the original furnishings used by the first
territorial governor to occupy the residence.*

*A portrait reputedly of Czar Peter
the Great of Russia looms over the
main stairway.*

Inside, Taylor and the designers who followed him painted the wood-work in old ivory; there were beam ceilings in the library and reception hall. The drawing room was planned to serve as a music room or ballroom, with a carved fireplace mantel bearing the original seal of the District of Alaska, while the adjoining library provided a living room. In the dining room, a window seat was constructed around the west wall to take full advantage of the room's generous dimensions of eighteen by twenty-six feet. A main stairway afforded access to the second-floor bedrooms and sewing room, which were arranged off a wide hallway. One chronicler wrote, "There is perhaps not a costlier home in Alaska." In fact, initial appropriations failed to fully furnish the second floor, and the third floor was left largely uncompleted, pending the design of a museum.

There was a change of administration in Washington in 1913, and Governor Clark was soon replaced with a new appointee, the second of nine governors who would serve Alaska during its territorial years between 1913 and 1959. One was Scott A. Bone (served 1921–25), whose daughter would later write nostalgically of her years growing up in the House overlooking Gastineau Channel. The retiring territorial governor had advised the Bone family that the House was "comfortably but sparsely furnished" and urged them to bring silver, china, linen, and blankets. Young Marguerite Bone's friends worried about her moving so far from the lower forty-eight states, but she found the mansion "beautiful . . . I could hardly wait to write my friends in New York, where I had been a pupil at a girl's school, that our new home was not an igloo." There were Friday "musical evenings" at the House. Marguerite often had her friends over to dance, play the ukelele, and make fudge. Marguerite's older sister had her first child there, the only baby ever born at the mansion. President Warren G. Harding visited in 1923. The young lady who thought she was moving far from home to a rugged frontier found herself living an exciting, and civilized, life.

There was an upstairs fire at the mansion in 1922. By 1936, the House needed renovation, and the federal government financed the exterior modifications already mentioned, along with a thorough plastering job that created the brilliant white facade that endures today. Alaska became the forty-ninth state in 1959 and took official possession of the Governor's House from the federal government. In 1967, the third floor was completely remodeled: interior walls were removed and the current guest suites and large bedroom were created. In the early 1980s the state launched an extensive interior renovation of the first and second floors, aimed at restoring the original decor. Wooden moldings and floors were uncovered and refinished, and mahogany bookcases were installed in the library using the design from Taylor's original blueprints. Major structural improvements were made in the wiring and plumbing, and a fire-suppression system was added. All eight fireplaces were restored to working order. Antique furnishings were acquired to recapture the history of the House. Additional improvements have been made in the 1990s to accommodate the public and private uses of the House.

Inside and outside the House are artworks and artifacts that exemplify the diverse history of Alaska. The state's native residents were Inuits,

Indians, and Aleuts. Numerous artifacts represent this rich heritage—baskets made of birch, grass, baleen, willow, and spruce root; wood carvings of figures and wildlife; paintings depicting Inuit legends. Above the library fireplace is a portrait of Secretary of State William H. Seward, whose purchase of Alaska was called "Seward's Folly" until gold, and much later, vast petroleum reserves, were discovered in the new territory. At the head of the staircase is an oil portrait said to be of Czar Peter the Great. The life-size painting dates from the era when Russia owned Alaska; it was acquired by district governor John G. Brady in 1905 from a Russian who claimed he had been allowed to remove it from the residence of the Russian governor in Sitka just prior to Alaska's transfer to American ownership in 1867. A notable mansion artifact is the Harriman punch bowl, a unique silver bowl with ends shaped like walrus heads. The bowl was created to honor the participants in an 1899 expedition to Alaska under the sponsorship of the industrialist E. H. Harriman. Harriman's family presented it to the state in 1967.

The front of the Governor's House is adorned with a three-story totem pole carved from an Alaskan yellow-cedar tree by Tlingit Indians in the late 1930s as a Civilian Conservation Corps project. The pole depicts Alaskan wildlife and figures from Tlingit mythology. The pole's design recounts such legends as the bringing of light to the world, the creation of humanity, of the rising and falling of the tides—even the creation of the mosquito. Both sides of the totem pole are decorated with carved and painted eyes, signifying the good spirit (yek) in which the pole was carved and presented to the state's first family.

The Alaska Governor's House is used extensively for public functions. Juneau has grown up around it over the years, but it remains the House on the hill with the totem pole, overlooking Gastineau Channel, where Joe Juneau once thought he might find gold.

HAWAII

WASHINGTON PLACE
HONOLULU

PHOTOGRAPHS BY BILL HAGSTOTZ
AND THOMAS H. WOOLSEY

Washington Place.

A home for a captain and a queen . . .

I n the 1830s, ships outbound from the great ports of America's Atlantic coast had to laboriously round Cape Horn before they could venture into the vast Pacific. Some hunted whales, others cultivated the growing China trade. They all stopped at a chain of volcanic islands twenty degrees north of the equator, a strand of tropical jewels with the ancient Polynesian name of Hawaii. In 1837 one of those adventurous sailors, Captain John Dominis, master of the *Bark Jones,* decided that the growing island town of Honolulu would be a good place to make his home. He brought his wife, Mary, and son John Owen Dominis out from Boston, and was soon building a house he hoped would reflect Mount Vernon, the residence of George Washington. It took four years; every nail, brick, and plank had to be carried thousands of miles from California or the East Coast in the holds of sailing ships. The lovely two-story house with its wide verandas was completed in 1846, and later that year Captain Dominis sailed for China, hoping to acquire furnishings for his new home. He never returned, and may have fallen victim, with his ship and crew, to a Pacific typhoon.

Mrs. Dominis was soon renting rooms in the large house to such boarders as American commissioner Anthony Ten Eyck. It was Ten Eyck who noted the home's resemblance to Mount Vernon and suggested that it be officially named for President Washington on the one hundred fifteenth anniversary of his birth. King Kamehameha III agreed. "It has pleased His Majesty the King to approve the name of Washington Place," he wrote, "and to command that they retain that name in all time coming."

Mary Dominis died in 1889. Hawaii had already claimed her son John Owen Dominis as one of its own, and in 1862 he married Lydia Kamakaeha Paki, a member of the Hawaiian royal family. In 1891, when her brother, King Kalakaua, died unexpectedly during a visit to San Francisco, Mrs. John Owen Dominis ascended the throne as Queen Liliuokalani. She was a remarkable woman, a gifted musician who composed "Aloha Oe," Hawaii's beloved song, and surrounded herself with flowers.

Soon after Liliuokalani became queen, John Dominis, who had been named prince consort, died of pneumonia at the age of sixty. In her time of grief over the loss of her husband—a companion and a trusted adviser on matters of state—she moved from their upstairs bedroom at Washington Place to a downstairs room that is still preserved as the queen's bedroom. On January 17, 1893, a group of American residents of the islands staged a brief coup that displaced the monarchy and sought closer commercial and governmental connections with the United States. To avoid bloodshed, the queen urged her people not to resist. She had faith that the United States government would reverse the coup and restore the monarchy, but that was not to be. After Hawaiians briefly sought to resist the coup, troops dug up

The music room. The koa wood piano once belonged to Queen Liliuokalani. The bench in the foreground was designed with a unique cleft back to symbolize the queen's love of music.

the cellar at Washington Place in search of weapons and imprisoned Queen Liliuokalani at Iolani Palace. A militia company was put in charge of her home. She was finally allowed to return later that year and died there in 1917. Hawaiian nationalists quietly laid her body in state, placing on her head the crown that had been forever stripped from her family.

Washington Place was designated Hawaii's official executive residence five years later. "It would amount almost to sacrilege to allow this fine old place . . . to be used for any ordinary or common purposes," wrote the attorney general. The first territorial governor was already living there, and in 1921 the house officially became public property. Governor Wallace Rider Farrington oversaw a renovation project later that year; workers eliminated termites, added a porte cochère and a state dining room, and built a glassed-in lanai. Later territorial governors added land to the Washington Place grounds. On December 7, 1941, as Japanese aircraft attacked nearby Pearl Harbor, a stray bomb blasted a crater in the Washington Place lawn. After the war, Washington Place celebrated its centennial, and governors added a garage and servants' quarters and an outside reception pavilion. President Harry Truman visited several times, once playing the "Missouri Waltz" on the same piano on which Queen Liliuokalani played "Aloha Oe." It was a cherished symbol of the late queen, made of koa, a native hardwood.

In 1959, Hawaii joined the Union. Each successive first family added improvements, and in the 1960s Governor and Mrs. John A. Burns supervised yet another major renovation and restoration project. Burns was followed by Governor George R. Ariyoshi (served 1974–85), Hawaii's first chief executive of Japanese descent. First Lady Jean Ariyoshi gathered a number of artifacts related to Queen Liliuokalani and returned them to Washington Place, work that brought her the honorary designation "Ka Lei Nani O Ka Aina" from the Sons and Daughters of the Hawaiian Warriors. In 1987 Washington Place came full circle: Governor John D. Waihee became the first elected chief executive of Hawaiian ancestry to live in the house. He added a stairway to the family dining area; his wife, Lynne, launched a docent program and initiated historic tours, titled "A Visit with the Queen," for schoolchildren. A full-length portrait of Queen Liliuokalani in the state dining room was the centerpiece of the Washington Place collection. When the Waihee family left office, they gathered in front of the portrait and said farewell to their official home. In October 1996, Governor Ben Cayetano, Hawaii's first governor of Filipino ancestry, celebrated the one hundred fiftieth anniversary of Washington Place with public events. Over thirty-five hundred people toured the mansion, a single-day record, to see historical displays and rarely seen paintings of Washington Place.

The modern Washington Place remains essentially unchanged from its original appearance, despite the many alterations it has undergone over the years. The portico, with its four thick columns, displays three flags: the American flag in the center, Hawaii's state flag, and a special governor's flag that flies only when the chief executive is in the state.

In the music room is the queen's piano, which she received as a fifty-third-birthday gift. The blue room is decorated in antique furnishings that reflect Hawaii's status as our most vividly multicultural state: Chinese Ching Dynasty carved chairs, a Victorian easy chair, Oriental carpeting over the oak floor, late Georgian crystal chandeliers. The blue room is connected to the state dining room by double French doors, and everywhere in the public rooms are plush draperies and colorful rugs and wall coverings. The queen's bedroom is preserved much as she left it, with a heavy seven-by-seven-foot mahogany bed covered by a Hawaiian quilt bearing the purple crown flower, the queen's favorite. A black and red marble clock that belonged to the queen still ticks on the dresser.

The reception room contains items unlike those in any American executive residence, such as a marquetry round table made from 496 pieces of wood from twelve different island trees. A cabinet holds pieces of the queen's favorite jewelry, including a gold-link bracelet given to her in 1869 by the duke of Edinburgh. It rests beside a second bracelet made from the hair of her adoptive father. Nearby is her most famous musical composition, "Aloha Oe," and a copy of her autobiography.

Below:
The reception room, where visitors waited to see the queen.

Opposite:
The blue room. Through the doorway is the state dining room.

Opposite, below:
The portrait of Queen Liliuokalani dominates the state dining room.

The queen's bedroom. The vast mahogany bed was a gift to Queen Liliuokalani from her relatives. The clock on the dresser was hers.

The queen's portrait hangs in the state dining room, along with a portrait of King Kalakaua and a scenic view of Washington Place painted in 1852. Also here is china used during Hawaii's territorial period and flatware presented to King Kamehameha IV in 1858 by Napoleon III of France.

The Washington Place gardens are rich in color, with graceful tropical plantings of ferns, bamboo, and exotic trees, as visitors might expect on the grounds of a Hawaiian residence. Beside the front gate stands a stone monument erected in 1929. It was meant, a contemporary historian wrote, to acknowledge "friendships and goodwill and the relegation to oblivion of remembrances of differences occasioned by the change of monarchy for a republic." The local newspaper collected one-dollar donations from its readers to add a bronze plaque to the stone. It bears the lyrics to "Aloha Oe," composed long ago by the queen, and ending: "One fond embrace, one kiss farewell, until we meet again."

Six States That Chose
a Different Path

MASSACHUSETTS

No state has a richer heritage. Massachusetts is where the American Revolution began. No state has had more prominent leaders, from Benjamin Franklin, John Hancock, and John and Samuel Adams to Daniel Webster, Calvin Coolidge, and the Kennedys. Massachusetts's roster of governors is a who's who of Americans who have written history: Hancock, first to sign the Declaration of Independence and first of the state's chief executives elected under the Massachusetts Constitution; Elbridge Gerry, for whom the practice of gerrymandering was named; Coolidge, who went on to the White House; Michael Dukakis, who achieved national attention as a presidential candidate. There were also men like Christian Herter and John Volpe, who attained presidential Cabinet rank.

Surprisingly, Massachusetts has never had an official executive residence. Governors have lived in homes that at times may have been temporarily designated "the mansion" or "the governor's house," but today Massachusetts first families still call their own homes home.

There have been efforts to create an executive mansion. John Hancock's house, built in 1737 on Boston's Beacon Street, was the first major site considered. After his second term as governor, Hancock sought to present it to the state as a permanent executive residence. He died before he could sign his will. The Hancock house was demolished in 1863.

Colonial governors had lived in the old Province House, a 1769 Colonial mansion built by trader Peter Sargent. When he died in 1714 the Colonial legislature bought the home. British royal governors lived there for years; it was in the Province House that General Thomas Gage laid his plans to march out to Lexington and Concord on April 19, 1775, and seize the arms that the patriots were rumored to be concealing. After the Revolution, the Province House was home to offices and bureaus of the new Massachusetts government, and Governor Caleb Strong (served 1800–1807 and 1812–16) lived there. Later, the house was sold, becoming first a private residence and later a tavern. It burned in 1864.

During the nineteenth century, Massachusetts first families lived in their own homes or rented Boston lodgings during their tenures. By 1917, Governor Samuel McCall hoped to change that practice. McCall surveyed states that owned governors' mansions and found that, of the twenty-one that did, none was in New England; the idea was shelved once again.

For fifty years, from the 1930s through the 1980s, officials debated converting the old Shirley-Eustis house into an executive residence. This home is one of the oldest Colonial mansions, built in 1747 in the Roxbury district of Boston. The Colonial governor William Shirley was the first to live there; Washington, Franklin, and Lafayette were guests; later, in 1810, William Eustis bought it, and in 1823–25 Eustis also served as governor of Massachusetts. By the 1930s it was a boardinghouse. Governor Christian Herter petitioned the legislature for an executive residence—specifically, a restored Shirley-Eustis house that would symbolize the state's rich heritage. In 1957, Massachusetts established a commission to study the proposal. Although the commission apparently rejected the idea, it did allocate ten thousand dollars per year for first families to rent suitable lodging.

The Shirley-Eustis house briefly came under consideration again in the 1960s as legislators introduced a series of bills suggesting that Massachusetts needed an official executive residence. There was also some thought of the Endicott Estate, a 1905 country home on twenty-five acres in Dedham. Family heirs hoped to leave it to the local town for "educational, civic, and recreational purposes." It wound up in the state's hands, and mansion speculation promptly shifted from the Shirley-Eustis house to this new possibility. But the hopes of mansion boosters faded when restoration estimates soared over seven hundred thousand dollars, and there was additional newspaper criticism of the "outdated mansion [which] would have secluded the state's governors in suburbia indefinitely."

Today, Massachusetts governors continue to live in private homes and use the large reception halls in the statehouse for public functions. One of our oldest and most historic states has never truly had an official executive residence.

RHODE ISLAND

Rhode Island never had a royal governor, escaping the pomp so often associated with the emissaries sent out from Britain to rule the American colonies. Its founders, most notably the stubborn Roger Williams, eschewed ceremony in favor of a stern determination to protect religious liberty, and early Rhode Island became a refuge for the persecuted of many different kinds, from Quakers to Jews. It was here, in 1772, that the Revolution was foreshadowed when defiant Rhode Islanders burned the British revenue ship *Gaspee*. General Nathanael Greene, one of Washington's finest commanders, came from Rhode Island, and his skeptical neighbors were the last to ratify the Constitution in 1790. The most self-governing of the original thirteen colonies, Rhode Island continues something of that tradition today.

You are never far away from the capital in Rhode Island. The state measures a scant thirty-seven by forty-eight miles, with the capital at Providence located in the east-central region, at the head of Narragansett Bay. Modern governors, wherever they may live, are always only a brief commute from work. If you live just down the road, you don't need an executive residence.

Rhode Island further complicated the question of where first families would live with a unique rotating-capital system they created in 1703 and retained, in modified form, until the beginning of the twentieth century. For most of its history, Rhode Island's five counties took turns serving as the state's seat of government. The legislature moved from county seat to county seat, conducting its deliberations as close to the people as possible. It was not until 1854 that the rotation of legislative sessions among the five county seats was abolished, but Rhode Island retained a custom of alternating sessions between Newport and Providence until 1900, when the permanent statehouse was completed in Providence. Where was a governor to live when his government kept moving?

In addition, Rhode Island's early state constitutions severely limited the powers of the chief executive. Historically, the office itself has not been a power center. Governors have traditionally hosted public events in the statehouse or another facility, and there has probably been less discussion of establishing an official executive residence in this, the smallest of our states, than in any other. It has only occasionally been floated as a legislative topic, but like their ancestors, who were the first to declare royal British rule invalid in 1776, Rhode Islanders prefer to keep things simple.

VERMONT

The name Vermont is from the French, *vert mont,* for "green mountain." During the Revolution, Ethan Allen and his Green Mountain Boys—a troop of woodsmen "irregulars" who effectively served the Patriot cause—captured Fort Ticonderoga on Lake Champlain in 1775, giving the rebellious Colonists one of their first key victories. Vermont joined the new Union in 1791. Vermont has often been a restful refuge: the English author Rudyard Kipling lived in Brattleboro for a time, and during his exile the Russian dissident Aleksandr Solzhenitsyn made his home here in the 1970s. With the Green Mountains bisecting Vermont from north to south and the capital conveniently located at Montpelier in the north-central portion of the state, Vermont's governors have never seen the need to acquire or build an official state residence. Like some of their fellow chief executives in other small Northeastern states, Vermont's governors can drive to work from almost anywhere, or they can rent quarters in the capital with a state-appropriated allowance.

The state has occasionally discussed establishing a mansion. In 1953, the legislature formed a committee to study the question, but its report was rejected. In the 1960s a second mansion initiative ended quickly. Vermont officials have rarely raised the issue since.

CALIFORNIA

California is our most populous state—and no one lives in its governor's mansion.

How this rich land of beaches and harbors, mountains and deserts and storied natural beauty came to have an executive residence with no one at home is a tale that says much about its diversity and rapid growth. California had been a Spanish outpost fronting the Pacific. When it became a part of America—first as a territory and later as a growing state developed by gold, railroads, shipping, and agriculture—California spawned more than its share of wealthy families. The scion of one such family, Albert Gallatin, whose prospering hardware firm had a contract to help build the state capitol building, built his palatial home in Sacramento in 1877. It was a soaring Victorian edifice with three stories, twenty-three rooms, and a distinctive two-story cupola that made it unique for its time and place. Writers of the era described it as "a very handsome structure," "elegant," and "one of the most imposing and attractive residences in Sacramento." Gallatin lived there for ten years, and in 1887 he sold the house to Joseph Steffens, whose son Lincoln would become a renowned author. Gallatin and Steffens were friends and fellow patriarchs of wealthy Sacramento families, and the transaction reflected that relationship: Steffens swapped a parcel of land and ten dollars for the house. In 1903, the state of California, realizing that the impressive house sat just eight blocks from the state capitol building, purchased it from the Steffens family for use as the Governor's Mansion. The price was thirty-two thousand five hundred dollars.

Governor George Cooper Pardee was the first to occupy the mansion. One of his successors almost didn't survive his tenure there: in 1917, radicals tried to assassinate Governor William D. Stephens by exploding a bomb in the kitchen. He survived, but the kitchen needed extensive repairs.

Governor Earl Warren (served 1943–53) later became chief justice of the United States, but during his time in the mansion it was falling into a state of disrepair. One newspaper called it "stale," and a critic said it was "poorly arranged for modern living." Soon the epithets grew harsher: the mansion was a "monstrosity," "an eyesore," and a "rat-infested firetrap." The legislature ultimately set aside funds to build a new mansion on land near the capitol, but Warren delayed the project. There was again talk of a replacement mansion in the early 1960s, but it was not until the administration of Governor Ronald Reagan (served 1967–75) that the state acted.

The old mansion had been officially declared a fire hazard as early as 1941. By 1967 a highway ran right in front of the mansion, subjecting first families in residence to noise and exhaust fumes. The Reagans soon moved out and occupied a rented home. In 1973, a group of private donors acquired land and began building a twelve-thousand-square-foot modern mansion in the Sacramento suburb of Carmichael, fourteen miles east of the old mansion. The house was finished and donated to the state in 1975, but the succeeding governor, Jerry Brown, Jr., who followed the Reagans, chose not to live there. In 1983, the state sold it to a private citizen.

The former California Governor's Mansion, Sacramento.

The former mansion is now a permanent historic site in the California State Park System, and it is no longer available as a gubernatorial residence. Every governor since 1975 has chosen to live in private quarters, and since 1967 the mansion has been a museum, open to daily public tours. Its rooms are fully furnished, and the California Department of Parks and Recreation has gathered memorabilia from most of the thirteen first families who have lived there.

IDAHO

The Eastern Seaboard states can take pride in many firsts: the earliest European colonies in what would become the United States, the first stable governments in the New World. But Idaho has a remarkable first of its own: it is probable that the very first humans to enter what would become the lower forty-eight states came initially to this high prairie. They followed the land bridge from Asia tens of thousands of years ago, entered what would eventually become Alaska, made their way gradually down the western slopes of the Continental Divide, and may have reached the land that became Idaho as long as thirteen thousand years ago. Later,

Idaho acquired this residence from its current first family and is considering establishing a permanent executive residence.

long after Europeans "discovered" and settled America, Meriwether Lewis and William Clark led their epochal expedition through Idaho, wintering there with the Nez Percé tribe. But Idaho remained little more than a way station on the Oregon Trail until 1860, when Mormon farmers founded the earliest permanent settlement. Others followed the gold and silver rushes to Idaho, which became our forty-third state in 1890.

Idaho retains much of its frontier, high-country flavor. For more than half of its history as a state, its governors had no official residence. A newspaper account says that one governor even lived in a "remodeled garage." In 1947, the state purchased a modest two-story frame house in Boise and designated it Idaho's official executive residence. The home had been built on the eve of World War I by a Boise resident, W. E. Pierce. It had a wide porticoed front porch and a large sitting or living room, bedrooms upstairs and in the basement, and a dining room. Like most homes built in the era before television, it was a place for family living—and the first families who lived there in the years after World War II found it little more than ordinary. An official history of the house called it "a large bungalow with a porch." The front yard was shallow (most of the lot was out back), and the best face several first families could put on the situation was to call the residence "modestly adequate." There was government talk of a better, more suitable mansion, and in 1967 the Idaho legislature appropriated funds to acquire a site for a new residence. The hopeful backers of the mansion concept even began acquiring donated furnishings and selected china and silver patterns.

The dining room at the Idaho residence.

It was not to be. Committees, legislators, and pundits discussed the concept of an official state residence for Idaho's first families, but no action was ever taken to locate a site or build a home. The old frame house remained home to those governors who chose to live in it—which not all of them did. After some years of neglect, the house was sold, and first families returned to the practice of securing their own lodging.

In the 1990s, when Governor Philip Batt took office, his family moved several times during his first months as chief executive. They finally purchased a three-bedroom suburban residence in Boise, and the state in turn purchased the home from the Batts and designated it as Idaho's official residence, at least during the governor's term of office.

As Idaho entered its second century of statehood there was increasing talk about the desirability of an official, permanent mansion, but at this writing, no action has been taken on the issue, and it has not yet been determined whether the current residence will be returned by the state.

ARIZONA

Arizona's state motto—*Ditat Deus,* or "God Enriches"—perfectly describes one of the great success stories of the second half of the twentieth century. Arizona was the last of the contiguous forty-eight states to be admitted to the Union. From that day in 1912 until the years after World War II, it was viewed by many Americans as a remote outpost, site of the fabulous Grand Canyon, and a great deal of lightly populated open space. But the move toward the Sun Belt that typified the postwar years revealed Arizona as a treasure. During the 1950s, Arizona's population increased by nearly 74 percent. By 1970, Phoenix had passed Denver as the largest metropolis in the Rocky Mountain region.

Arizona has had two officially designated executive residences. In 1864, Territorial Governor John Goodwin asked the government for funds to build a house for him and his staff. It was a four-thousand-square-foot hewed-log building with six rooms, a kitchen, a sleeping loft, and a covered porch, located in Prescott and called Pinal Ranch by local residents. In the fall of that year, Goodwin was elected territorial delegate to Congress, and his secretary, Richard McCormick, succeeded him as governor. In 1867, the territorial capital moved to Tucson, and Governor McCormick —who had married but then become a widower—followed.

The original mansion was sold to a private owner, but the state reacquired it in 1917 as a historic site. In 1927, officials authorized Miss Shallot Hall to live there as she undertook a restoration of the old log structure. Today it is a museum bearing her name.

In the 1970s, a Phoenix business executive, Tom Chauncey, donated his home to the state for use as Arizona's second executive residence, with an unusual stipulation. The home was actually deeded to the state's board of regents, and in the bequest Chauncey insisted that if the state's chief executives decided not to use the home as an official residence, it should be sold and the proceeds used to establish a loan fund for low-income students attending state universities. Governor Raul Castro was the first chief executive to occupy the mansion. The two-story hillside home of fifty-five hundred square feet had a pool and twin balconies.

Castro's successor chose not to live in the home. When he died in office, his attorney general, Bruce Babbitt, became governor. Governor Babbitt was not enamored of the house either, and he proposed that the mansion be sold, to satisfy the Chauncey bequest. In 1980, the mansion was sold for three hundred seventy-five thousand dollars, and those funds have formed an endowment with all interest distributed to universities, based on their enrollment.

Today, Arizona remains without an official executive residence.

FOR FURTHER INFORMATION

Alabama
State of Alabama Bureau of
Tourism and Travel
401 Adams Avenue, Suite 126
P.O. Box 4927
Montgomery, AL 36103-4927

Alaska
Alaska Division of Tourism
P.O. Box 110801
Juneau, AK 99811-0801

Arizona
Arizona Office of Tourism
Suite 4015
2702 North Third Street
Phoenix, AZ 85004

Arkansas
Arkansas Department of Parks
and Tourism
One Capitol Mall
Little Rock, AR 72201

California
Gold Rush Historic Sites District
802 N Street
Sacramento, CA 95814

Colorado
Colorado Travel and Tourism
Authority
P.O. Box 3524
Englewood, CO 80155

Connecticut
Connecticut, Office of Tourism
Division
865 Brook Street
Rocky Hill, CT 06067-3405

Delaware
Delaware Tourism Office
99 Kings Highway
P.O. Box 1401
Dover, DE 19903

Florida
Florida Division of Tourism
107 West Gaines Street
Tallahassee, FL 32399-2000

Georgia
Georgia Department of Industry, Trade and Tourism
Tower 2, Suite 1000

285 Peachtree Center Avenue,
NE
Atlanta, GA 30303

Hawaii
Hawaii Visitors and Convention
Bureau
2270 Kalakaua Avenue, Suite
801
Honolulu, HI 96815

Idaho
Idaho Division of Tourism
Development
700 West State Street
P.O. Box 83720-0093
Boise, ID 83720-0093

Illinois
Illinois Bureau of Tourism
James R. Thompson Center
100 West Randolph
Suite 3-400
Chicago, IL 60601

Indiana
Indiana Department of Commerce
Office of Tourism
One North Capitol, Suite 700
Indianapolis, IN 46204-2288

Iowa
Iowa Department of Economic
Development
Division of Tourism
200 East Grand Avenue
Des Moines, IA 50309

Kansas
Kansas Department of Commerce and Housing
Travel and Tourism Division
700 Southwest Harrison Street
Suite 1300
Topeka, KS 66603-3712

Kentucky
Kentucky Division of Historic
Properties
Berry Hill Mansion
700 Louisville Road
Frankfort, KY 40601

Louisiana
Louisiana Office of Tourism
1051 North Third Street
P.O. Box 94291
Baton Rouge, LA 70804-9291

Maine
Maine Department of Economic
and Community Development
33 Stone Street
59 State House Station
Augusta, ME 04333-0059

Maryland
Maryland Office of Tourism
Development
9th Floor
217 East Redwood Street
Baltimore, MD 21202

Massachusetts
Massachusetts Office of Travel
and Tourism
100 Cambridge Street,
13th Floor
Boston, MA 02202

Michigan
Michigan Travel Bureau
Michigan Jobs Commission
P.O. Box 30226
Lansing, MI 48909

Minnesota
Minnesota Office of Tourism
100 Metro Square
121 East Seventh Place
St. Paul, MN 55101-2112

Mississippi
Mississippi Division of Tourism
Development
P.O. Box 849
Jackson, MS 39205

Missouri
Missouri Division of Tourism
301 West High Street
Truman Office Building,
Room 290
P.O. Box 1055
Jefferson City, MO 65102

Montana
Travel Montana/Department of
Commerce
1424 Ninth Avenue
Helena, MT 59620-0411

Nebraska
Nebraska Travel and Tourism
Division

Department of Economic Development
P.O. Box 94666
Lincoln, NE 68509-4666

Nevada
Nevada Commission on
Tourism
Capitol Complex
5151 South Carson Street
Carson City, NV 89710

New Hampshire
New Hampshire Office of Travel
and Tourism Development
P.O. Box 1856
Concord, NH 03302-1856

New Jersey
Drumthwacket Foundation
354 Stockton Street
Princeton, NJ 08540

New Mexico
New Mexico Department of
Tourism
Lamy Building
491 Old Santa Fe Trail
Santa Fe, NM 87503

New York
New York State Department of
Economic Development
Division of Tourism
One Commerce Plaza
Albany, NY 12245

North Carolina
North Carolina Travel and
Tourism
Department of Commerce
301 North Wilmington Street
Raleigh, NC 27601-2825

North Dakota
North Dakota Tourism Department
Liberty Memorial Building
604 East Boulevard Avenue
Bismarck, ND 58505

Ohio
Ohio Division of Travel and
Tourism
Department of Development
P.O. Box 1001
Columbus, OH 43216-1001

Oklahoma
Oklahoma Tourism and
    Recreational Department
P.O. Box 52002
Oklahoma City, OK 73152-2002

Oregon
Oregon Tourism Commission
775 Summer Street, NE
Salem, OR 97310

Pennsylvania
Pennsylvania Office of Travel,
    Tourism, and Film Promotion
456 Forum Building
Harrisburg, PA 17120

Rhode Island
Rhode Island Economic Develop-
    ment Corporation
One West Exchange Street
Providence, RI 02903

South Carolina
South Carolina Department of
    Parks, Recreation, and Tourism
Suite 248
1205 Pendleton Street
Columbia, SC 29201

South Dakota
South Dakota Department of
    Tourism
711 East Wells Avenue
Pierre, SD 57501-3369

Tennessee
Tennessee Executive Residence
882 South Curtiswood Lane
Nashville, TN 37204

Texas
Texas Department of Commerce
Tourism Division
P.O. Box 12728
Austin, TX 78711-2728

Utah
Utah Travel Council
Council Hall
Salt Lake City, UT 84114

Vermont
Vermont Department of Tourism
    and Marketing
134 State Street
Montpelier, VT 05601-1471

Virginia
Virginia Tourism Corporation
901 East Byrd Street
Richmond, VA 23219

Washington
Governor's Mansion Foundation
P.O. Box 11207
Olympia, WA 98508-1207

West Virginia
West Virginia Division of
    Tourism
2101 Washington Street, East
Charleston, WV 25305

Wisconsin
Wisconsin Department of
    Tourism
123 West Washington
P.O. Box 7970
Madison, WI 53707

Wyoming
Wyoming Division of Tourism
Frank Norris Jr. Travel Center
J-25 and College Drive
Cheyenne, WY 82002-0660

Web Sites and Permanent 1-800 Numbers

Alabama
Web Site: alaweb.asc.edu
1-800 Number: 1-800-ALABAMA

Arizona
Web Site: www.state.az.us/gv
1-800 Number: 1-800-253-0883

Connecticut
Web Site: www2.uconn.edu/ctstate/life.html
1-800 Number: 1-800-406-1527

Georgia
Web Site: www.ganet.org/gov.

Hawaii
Web Site: www.visit.hawaii.org
1-800 Number: 1-800-GO-HAWAII

Kansas
1-800 Number: 1-800-2-KANSAS

Kentucky
Web Site: www.state.ky.us/agencies/
                        gov/govmenu6.htm

Maine
Web Site: www.state.me.us

Massachusetts
Web Site: www.mass-vacation.com
1-800 Number: 1-800-447-MASS

Minnesota
Web Site: www.state.mn.us/mainmenu.html
1-800 Number: 1-800-657-3700

Nevada
Web Site: www.state.nv.us/mansion/

New Mexico
Web Site: www.newmexico.org/
1-800 Number: 1-800-545-2040

Ohio
Web Site: www.state.oh.us
1-800 Number: 1-800-BUCKEYE

Oklahoma
1-800 Number: 1-800-652-6552

Oregon
Web Site: www.governor.state.or.us

Pennsylvania
Web Site: www.state.pa.us

Rhode Island
1-800 Number: 1-800-752-8088

South Carolina
Web Site: www.prt.state.sc.us/sc

Tennessee
Web Site: www.state.tn.us

Texas
Web Site: www.travel.tex.com
1-800 Number: 1-800-8888-TEX, ext. 664

Virginia
Web Site: www.state.va.us
1-800 Number: 1-800-932-5827

Wyoming
1-800 Number: 1-800-225-5996